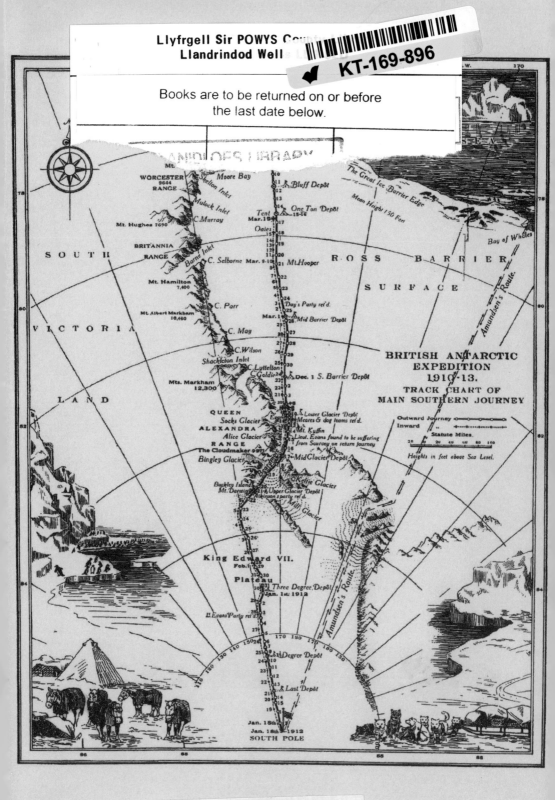

W.   170

SEA

The Great Ice Barrier Edge

Mean Height 150 Feet

Bay of Whales

WORCESTER
9644
RANGE
Skelton Inlet   Moore Bay
Bluff Depôt

Mulock Inlet
C.Murray   One Ton Depôt
Tent
Mar. 19   15-16
Mt. Hughes 7690
Oates
BRITANNIA
RANGE
Barne Inlet
C. Selborne Mar. 9-10   Mt.Hooper
Mt. Hamilton
7,400
C. Parr   Day's Party ret'd.
Mt. Albert Markham   Mar. 11   Mid Barrier Depôt
10,460
C. May

C.Wilson
Shackleton Inlet
C. Lyttelton
Goldie   Dec. 1 S. Barrier Depôt
Mts. Markham
12,300

QUEEN   Lower Glacier Depôt
Socks Glacier   Meares & dog teams ret'd.
ALEXANDRA   Mt. Kyffin
Alice Glacier   Lieut. Evans found to be suffering
RANGE   from Scurvy on return journey
The Cloudmaker 9977
Bingley Glacier   Mid Glacier Depôt

Buckley Island   Keltie Glacier
Mt. Darwin   Upper Glacier Depôt
Atkinson's party ret'd.
Mill Glacier

King Edward VII.
Feb. 1st '12
Plateau
Three Degree Depôt
Jan. 1st 1912

Lt. Evans' Party ret'd.

S O U T H

V I C T O R I A

L A N D

R O S S   B A R R I E R

S U R F A C E

Amundsen's Route

Amundsen's Route

BRITISH ANTARCTIC
EXPEDITION
1910-13.
TRACK CHART OF
MAIN SOUTHERN JOURNEY

Outward Journey
Inward
Statute Miles.

Heights in feet above Sea Level.

Half Degree Depôt

Last Depôt

Jan. 18th
Jan. 18th 1912
SOUTH POLE

86   88   88   88

THE LAST GREAT QUEST

For Sarah

THE
LAST GREAT
QUEST

Captain Scott's Antarctic Sacrifice

MAX JONES

OXFORD
UNIVERSITY PRESS

OXFORD
UNIVERSITY PRESS

Great Clarendon Street, Oxford OX2 6DP

Oxford University Press is a department of the University of Oxford.
It furthers the University's objective of excellence in research, scholarship,
and education by publishing worldwide in

Oxford New York

Auckland Bangkok Buenos Aires Cape Town Chennai
Dar es Salaam Delhi Hong Kong Istanbul Karachi Kolkata
Kuala Lumpur Madrid Melbourne Mexico City Mumbai Nairobi
São Paulo Shanghai Taipei Tokyo Toronto

Oxford is a registered trade mark of Oxford University Press
in the UK and in certain other countries

Published in the United States
by Oxford University Press Inc., New York

British Library Cataloguing in Publication Data
Data available

Library of Congress Cataloging in Publication Data
Data available
ISBN 0–19–280483–9

1 3 5 7 9 10 8 6 4 2

Typeset by RefineCatch Limited, Bungay, Suffolk
Printed in Great Britain by
Clays Ltd., St Ives plc

ACKNOWLEDGEMENTS

I WOULD like to thank the following individuals, institutions, and organizations for giving permission both to quote from their archives, and to reproduce images from their collections: the Alpine Club, the British Library, the British Museum, the Syndics of Cambridge University Library, Christie's, the Fine Art Society, the Hulton Archive, Hugo Frey, Lord Kennet, the David Livingstone Centre, Blantyre, Magdalene College, Cambridge, the National Maritime Museum, the National Portrait Gallery, News International, The Oates Museum, Selborne, the Royal Geographical Society, Matthew Salisbury and the Captain Scott Society, Lady Philippa Scott, the Scott Polar Research Institute, and the Tussauds Group. The quotation from Baden-Powell is reproduced by permission of the Scout Association (licence no. 0303). The author and publishers apologize for any inadvertent omissions, and will be pleased to incorporate acknowledgements in any future editions.

The support of both the Scott Polar Research Institute (SPRI) and the Royal Geographical Society (RGS) has been essential to the completion of this book. The assistance offered by the friendly staff at both institutions proved invaluable, in particular the help of Paula Lucas and Andrew Tatham at the RGS, and Robert Headland and Philippa Smith at SPRI.

I am very grateful to Katharine Reeve and Oxford University Press for their enthusiasm for this book, and for the efforts of the picture editor Sandra Assersohn, Emily Jolliffe, and the copy editor Elizabeth Stratford, in working to a demanding schedule.

This book has been shaped by a number of distinctive institutions. At the University of California at Berkeley, Susannah Barrows, Catherine Gallagher, Martin Jay, and, in particular, David Stoddart and Tom Metcalf, supported my research at an early stage. Jon Parry and the late Mark Kaplanoff made Pembroke College, Cambridge a hospitable place to continue postgraduate study. Scholarships from Berkeley, the Fulbright Commission, the Mellon Foundation, and the British Academy provided essential support at various stages. The informal British history discussion group enriched Cambridge graduate life, especially my friends David Craig and James Thompson.

I am particularly grateful to the Master and Fellows of Peterhouse, Cambridge for electing me to a Junior Research Fellowship, which provided that most precious commodity for a young historian: time. Much of this book was written while I served as Director of Studies in History at Christ's College, Cambridge, and the generosity of the council in allowing me a term of research leave was essential to its completion. Christ's provided an ideal environment in which to study history and I benefited greatly from the encouragement of Susan Bayly, David Reynolds, and Quentin Skinner. I do not have space to list all the Cambridge colleagues whom I pestered about Captain Scott, but Chris Bayly, Martin Daunton, Lucy Delap, Martin Golding, Roger Lovatt, Peter Martland, Kathryn Rix, Jim Second, Brendan Simms, Maria Tippett, and Adam Tooze were all generous with their advice. I am especially grateful to Peter Clarke for his support and encouragement throughout the project. I completed this book after joining one of the most dynamic History Departments in the country at the University of Manchester, and the insights of my new colleagues shaped its final stages.

The convenors of seminars at Berkeley, Cambridge, the

Institute of Historical Research, the National Maritime Museum, Nene College, Northampton, Oxford, York and the University of Virginia provided forums, in which I presented aspects of this book and received valuable feedback. My students, especially Daniel Coetzee, Jessica Meyer, and Scott Worthy, also helped me develop my arguments. Of the many individuals who have helped me at various stages, I would like to thank Ian Agnew, Stephanie Barcszewski, Colin Bishop, Bill Bourland, Clive Bradbury, Justin Butcher, Becky Conekin, John Davis, Felix Driver, Sian Flynn, Martin Gammon, Peter Ghosh, Adrian Gregory, Peter Hansen, Nick Hiley, Ben Hopkins, Rebecca Jones, Paul Kennedy, Luke McKernan, John Nicoll, Ed Norton, Eva Norton, Senia Paseta, Paul Readman, Nigel Rigby, Dominic Riley, Tom Rosenthal, Jan Rueger, Shirley Sawtell, Gary Savage, Ben Schott, Matthew Seligmann, John Shaw, Larysa Smith, and Phillip Ward-Jackson. Klaus Dodds showed great generosity to a student embarking on a Ph.D., while David Cannadine, in particular, offered support and encouragement at some crucial moments. I hope that those whose names I have omitted will forgive me.

I owe the completion of this project to two scholars, who have been consistent sources of friendship and inspiration: Tom Laqueur and Jay Winter. At Berkeley, Tom showed me how exciting the pursuit of history could be. And, both as my Cambridge supervisor and after, Jay has offered guidance, insight, and encouragement, for which I am truly grateful.

Final thanks to my family. The support of my parents, Diana and George, has left me with a debt that can never be repaid. (I'm also fortunate to have a father who operates the finest unofficial press cuttings service in Britain.) My wife Sarah and children Isabelle and Oscar have learned with me that finishing a book, moving house, switching jobs, and changing nappies is a testing combination. Thank you for your patience and for sharing the journey with me.

CONTENTS

CONTENTS

LIST OF PLATES

LIST OF FIGURES

LIST OF MAPS

ABBREVIATIONS

BAAS	British Association for the Advancement of Science
BAE	British Antarctic Expedition, 1910–13
FAS	Fine Art Society
FRGS	Fellow of the Royal Geographical Society
FRS	Fellow of the Royal Society
GJ	*Geographical Journal*
IGC	International Geographical Congress
LCC	London County Council
LMA	London Metropolitan Archives
NAE	National Antarctic Expedition, 1901–4
NMM	National Maritime Museum
PRO	Public Record Office
Proc. RGS	*Proceedings of the Royal Geographical Society*
RGS	Royal Geographical Society
RIM	Royal Indian Marine
RN	Royal Navy
RNR	Royal Naval Reserve
SPRI	Scott Polar Research Institute
WSPU	Women's Social and Political Union

THE LAST GREAT QUEST

Map of British Antarctic Expedition, 1910–1913; track chart of main southern journey.

INTRODUCTION

O N 17 January 1912 five men from the British Antarctic
Expedition commanded by Captain Robert Falcon Scott,
arrived at the spot they calculated to be the South Pole.
To their dismay, they found they had been preceded by a Norwegian
expedition led by Roald Amundsen, which had reached the Pole a
month earlier. 'The wind is blowing hard, T. −21° and there is that
curious damp, cold feeling in the air which chills one to the bone',
Scott wrote in his journal. 'Great God this is an awful place and
terrible enough for us to have laboured to it without the reward of
priority.' The British explorers faced an 850-mile journey, hauling
their sledge across the ice, to reach their base camp at Cape Evans
and safety.

The health of Petty Officer Edgar Evans steadily deteriorated
during the return through hazardous terrain and freezing temperatures on limited rations, and, exactly one month after arriving at the
Pole, he collapsed in the snow. His companions could do nothing
to revive him and he died during the night. On the morning of
17 March, Captain Lawrence Oates, crippled by frostbite, left the
party's tent and walked out into the snow. He did not return.

On 19 March the three surviving men pitched their tent with
only 110 miles to go, as a blizzard came down from the south-west.
With their food and fuel exhausted, they discussed making a final
attempt to reach One Ton Camp. But Captain Scott, Lieutenant
Henry Bowers, and Dr Edward Wilson remained in the tent
and died sometime between 29 and 31 March. They were less than
11 miles from the depot containing fresh supplies.

As Scott lay dying, news of Amundsen's achievement thrilled the world. The thirteen explorers left at Cape Evans waited anxiously for Scott's return, out of reach of all communication and unaware of the Norwegian triumph. But by the time the *Titanic* slipped beneath the icy waters of the North Atlantic on 15 April, all hope had been extinguished: they knew that their comrades were dead.

After spending a grim Antarctic winter confined to Cape Evans, Surgeon Edward Atkinson, who had assumed command of the expedition, led a search party south in the spring, which found a snow-covered tent on 12 November. Inside were the bodies of Scott, Bowers, and Wilson, and the letters and diaries which told the story of their last march. The search party collapsed the tent over the bodies of the dead, and Atkinson read the burial service and a passage from Corinthians. They then built a snow cairn surmounted by a cross of ski-sticks, and left a record of the disaster which concluded 'The Lord gave and the Lord taketh away, blessed be the name of the Lord'.

The search party then retraced Scott's route, in the hope of finding the remains of Captain Oates. They found Oates's sleeping bag, but not his body. The party built a second cairn with the message: 'Hereabouts died a very gallant gentleman, Captain L. E. G. Oates of the Inniskilling Dragoons. In March 1912, returning from the Pole, he walked willingly to his death in a blizzard to try and save his comrades beset by hardship. This note is left by the relief expedition. 1912.'[1]

The ship *Terra Nova* finally broke through the pack ice in McMurdo Sound to pick up the expedition on 18 January 1913. Two days later, eight men left the ship to erect a memorial cross on the summit of Observation Hill overlooking the Great Ice Barrier. It took many hours to haul the cross of Australian jarrah wood, made by the ship's carpenter Francis Davies, across the ice to the bottom of the hill. The inscription on the cross concluded with a line from Tennyson's 'Ulysses', suggested by Apsley Cherry-Garrard: 'To Strive, To Seek, To Find, And Not To Yield'.[2]

The *Terra Nova* docked briefly at Oamaru, New Zealand, around 2.30 a.m. on the morning of Monday, 10 February. The story of Scott of the Antarctic reached London later that day.

A decade ago I set out to try and understand the generation who fought and died in the First World War and found a story, the story of Scott of the Antarctic. The celebration of the death of Captain Scott illuminates the passions and prejudices of Edwardian society on the brink of the greatest massacre in British history.

The second half of the nineteenth century was the age of the explorer hero. Developments in transport and communications opened both new territories for Western explorers, and new opportunities for distributing accounts of their exploits to an ever-expanding readership. The most spectacular expeditions created international heroes, whose endeavours were chronicled in newspapers, lecture theatres, and best-selling books. Dr Livingstone, Henry Morton Stanley, and Fridtjof Nansen became household names. The endeavours of such men achieved the most celebrated goals of nineteenth-century exploration: the North-West Passage, the North-East Passage, the forbidden city of Lhasa, the sources of the Nile, and the North Pole.[3]

Antarctica, however, remained elusive: no recorded landing was made on the continent until 1895. Over the next twenty years expeditions sailed south from Australia, Belgium, Britain, Canada, France, Germany, Italy, Japan, Norway, Scotland, and Sweden, driven by personal ambition, scientific curiosity, and patriotic fervour. The British explorer, Ernest Shackleton, marched within a hundred miles of the South Pole in 1909, but was forced to turn back due to lack of provisions. A few months after Shackleton's return two American explorers, Frederick Cook and Robert Peary, both claimed to have reached the North Pole. The conquest of the South Pole was the 'last great quest'.[4]

Two expeditions set out for Antarctica in 1910, one from Britain under the command of Captain Scott of the Royal Navy, the other from Norway, led by the veteran explorer Roald Amundsen, the first man to navigate the North-West Passage between the Atlantic and Pacific oceans. The Norwegians reached the Pole first, on 15 December 1911. Scott, Henry Bowers, Edgar Evans, Lawrence Oates, and Edward Wilson arrived at the Pole a month later; all perished on the return march.

While many authors have told the story of Scott's life, no one until now has examined the impact of his death, the ways in which the world responded to this tragic story from the south. On the afternoon of Monday, 10 February 1913, news reached London that Scott was dead. 'Nothing in our time, scarcely even the foundering of the *Titanic*,' proclaimed the *Manchester Guardian*, 'has touched the whole nation so instantly and so deeply as the loss of these men'.[5] The announcement caused a sensation, not only in Britain, but throughout the world.

Scott of the Antarctic has proved a durable icon since his canonization in 1913, inspiring six principal biographies based on original research and a steady stream of books about the heroic age of polar exploration. While some authors questioned Scott's methods and delineated his complex personality, all acknowledged his courage in the face of death. But the publication of Roland Huntford's *Scott and Amundsen* in 1979 marked a turning-point in the development of Scott's reputation. Huntford was determined to correct an injustice, to expose Scott as a fraud and retrieve the real hero of the race to the South Pole, Roald Amundsen, from neglect. Huntford's Scott deserves contempt not admiration, pressuring Captain Oates into suicide, and preventing Bowers and Wilson from making a final attempt to reach One Ton Camp. Huntford subsequently entrenched his reappraisal with biographies of Shackleton and the pioneering Norwegian, Fridtjof Nansen.

Debunking Captain Scott has become something of a national pastime since Huntford's intervention. Assaults on the heroes of the past are not a recent phenomenon, of course: Lytton Strachey's classic *Eminent Victorians* is over eighty years old. Yet reassessments of historical icons play a prominent role in popular history today, nourishing both the buoyant biography industry, and two television documentary series: Channel 4's *Secret Lives* and BBC2's *Reputations*. Scott has never lacked defenders, and a number of more balanced accounts have appeared since *Scott and Amundsen*, but new revelations continue to attract national attention. 'Scott's Antarctic myth debunked by deputy', pronounced *The Times*, after critical comments made by the expedition's second-in-command, Teddy Evans, surfaced at Christie's auction house.[6]

The denigration of Scott has been amplified by the recent resurgence of interest in Ernest Shackleton in Britain and America, sparked by an exhibition which drew 150,000 visitors to New York's Natural History Museum in 1999. Attention has focused on Shackleton's *Endurance* expedition, captured on film by Frank Hurley, which set off in 1914 to cross the Antarctic continent for the first time. The *Endurance* was crushed in the polar ice, but Shackleton contrived to save his crew through an astonishing mixture of inspirational leadership, courage, and good fortune. Shackleton's remarkable 800-mile voyage from Elephant Island to South Georgia, one of the greatest boat journeys ever accomplished, followed by his unprecedented trek across the island's mountain range to safety, remains arguably the most compelling tale of adventure in the annals of polar exploration. 'The story of Shackleton has long been overshadowed by the sacrifice of Scott,' claimed Rachel Campbell-Johnson on the eve of the New York exhibition, 'but the time is ripe for revisionism. Those who endure can teach us things we can never learn from the vainglorious.'[7]

Shackleton mania has ignited a polar boom, with special displays in high-street bookshops, a successful exhibition at London's Maritime Museum, a ground-breaking IMAX film, and NBC's Emmy Award-winning mini-series *Shackleton*, which starred Kenneth Branagh in the title role. In part we are simply witnessing the rediscovery of some wonderful stories. But the current fascination with polar explorers, and with figures such as the Everest mountaineer George Leigh Mallory, also expresses a disenchantment with the mundane repetitiveness and moral ambiguity of modern life, a yearning for straightforward tales of heroic endeavour.

Scott's story has continued to resonate, both as an established feature on the British cultural landscape referred to in advertisements and soap operas, and as an inspiration to leading novelists from Beryl Bainbridge to Donna Tartt. But Huntford's incompetent fool is the new orthodoxy, recently endorsed by the doyen of contemporary travel-writing, Paul Theroux.[8] Today the stiff and indecisive Scott lies in Shackleton's towering shadow.

The dramatic journeys and colourful lives of the polar pioneers have received extensive attention, principally through some first-class biographies. But historians have largely left the realms of ice to polar specialists: readers will search in vain for any substantive discussion of the significance of Scott and Shackleton in general surveys of modern British history.[9] The polar pioneers have been cast adrift on a lonely iceberg, marooned from the swirling currents of historical scholarship. This isolation has exacted a price. For while we now know a great deal about Antarctic weather systems, dietary requirements, and the personal animosities which enlivened all expeditions, our understanding of the culture and society which created these explorers and lauded their achievements is strewn with misunderstandings. The legendary figures who first ventured into the unknown remain impenetrable, unless we apprehend the world which made them.

The Last Great Quest revisits the story of Scott of the Antarctic to ask one central question: why did the death of five men in the Antarctic cause such a sensation ninety years ago, not only in Britain but around the world?

In answering this question, the book challenges several entrenched stereotypes about Scott's story: that Scott's scientific aims were a façade, concealing his primary concern with national glory; that Scott chose not to take additional dogs to the Antarctic, because he considered manhauling more noble; that Amundsen's achievement went largely unacknowledged in Britain; that the celebration of Scott's death was primarily motivated by hurt national pride; that the British were unique in their glorification of suffering and failure, revelling in Scott's reliance on men over dogs; and, ultimately, that Scott's heroic reputation grew out of an establishment conspiracy, which suppressed details of his incompetence and created the legend of Scott of the Antarctic through the skilful editing of his sledging journal by his friend J. M. Barrie, author of *Peter Pan*. Each of these claims requires reassessment.[10]

Drawing on a wealth of previously unused papers in the Public Record Office, Royal Geographical Society (RGS), and Scott Polar Research Institute (SPRI), in addition to an exhaustive survey of media coverage of the Antarctic disaster, *The Last Great Quest* approaches heroic icons not as blunt instruments for transmitting a simple ideological message, but as screens onto which a range of meanings could be projected. The dreams and desires of bygone ages flicker across the faces of the heroes of the past, offering a unique insight into a vanished world.

Scott's sledging journal was the cornerstone of his heroic reputation. One of the most remarkable documents in British history, Scott's journal and 'Message to the Public', were the ultimate expression of self-control in the face of death. After reading the edited journal, published in November 1913, former American President Theodore Roosevelt announced that he did 'not know any book of history, of biography, or of romance, of fact, or fiction in which there is set forth a more gallant example of quiet, simple, and utterly disinterested heroism than is contained in the final chapter of Scott's book'.[11] The frenzied response to Scott's 'Message to the Public' exposes an age preoccupied with the endurance of hardship as a test of character, a preoccupation exposed a year earlier after the sinking of the *Titanic*, and a year later at the outbreak of war.

Chapter 1 opens by locating Scott's story within the history of British exploration, investigating the pivotal role of the RGS, the institution which sent Scott to the South Pole. Sir John Franklin and Dr David Livingstone created a model for the explorer hero in the nineteenth century, a template for Captain Scott. But, as opportunities for pioneering journeys steadily diminished after Livingstone's death in 1873, the RGS promoted a vision of exploration as a tripartite process of measurement: explorers measured the world, taking scientific observations; measured manliness, testing their heroic character in the battle against nature; and measured empire, marking the limits of British imperial power.

Chapter 2 reveals the origins of Scott's last expedition and describes its scientific aspirations. It shows how tensions within the

RGS erupted in a dispute over the admission of women as fellows in 1892, a dispute which installed Clements Markham as the Society's President and initiated a campaign for a national Antarctic expedition to reconcile the warring factions. The campaign eventually led to the launch of the ship *Discovery* under Scott's command in 1901. The scientific motives proclaimed by Scott have been treated with suspicion. But to dismiss the scientific aspirations of Scott's expeditions is to misunderstand the nature of exploration in Edwardian Britain. Under the influence of the RGS, Scott's Antarctic expeditions were animated by a spirit of scientific curiosity and sense of wonder at the majesty of the Antarctic, which has been obscured in recent accounts.

Chapters 3 and 4 reconstruct the response to the announcement of the death of Scott, Bowers, Evans, Oates, and Wilson. Far from covering-up, the press speculated widely about the causes of the disaster, acknowledging the superiority of Amundsen's methods. The significance and extent of the censorship of Scott's sledging journals has also been greatly exaggerated. The creation of heroic icons, from Dr Livingstone and Captain Scott, through Lawrence of Arabia to Princess Diana, cannot be explained solely through the actions of censors and spin-doctors. No myth of Scott of the Antarctic was imposed on British society.[12] Different communities told Scott's story in different ways. Indeed, it was the capacity of certain individuals to mobilize an array of sometimes contradictory narratives that gave heroes like Captain Scott their extraordinary power.

Chapters 5, 6, and 7 trace the many forms taken by Scott's heroic figure: naval officer, family man, scientific martyr, imperial scout, national saviour, and icon for pacifists, socialists, and suffragettes. Chapter 5 reveals how members of the expedition and the officers of the RGS, in particular, hailed the dead explorers as martyrs of science. Scott's journals, Teddy Evans's lectures, Edward Wilson's watercolours, and Herbert Ponting's films consistently reinforced the message that the expedition was 'no mere dash to the Pole'. This emphasis on scientific research underwrote the portrayal of the expedition as a selfless quest.

Scott's story resonated in a society beset with anxieties about national decline, loss of religious faith, and the materialism of the modern world. Chapter 6 considers the representation of the dead as national martyrs, who left a triumphant retort to the prophets of decline. The chapter challenges those historians who argue that a potent mixture of militarism and imperialism dominated British popular culture before the First World War. The commemorative pattern suggests that British patriotism was fostered less through the imposition of a particular ideology than by the weakness of central control, which allowed a range of vibrant local, Scottish, and Welsh identities to find expression alongside a loosely defined rhetoric of national and imperial service.

Celebrations of Scott's achievement were united, not by any overarching imperial or military ideology, but through the language of heroism and character which figured so prominently in Victorian and Edwardian intellectual life. Drawing on classical, chivalric, and religious models, the sinking of the *Titanic* mobilized this language ten months before the announcement of the Antarctic disaster. But Scott's 'Message to the Public' offered the ultimate expression of the idea of heroic sacrifice, a unique performance of courage in the face of death. Chapter 7 shows how socialists, suffragettes, and Irish republicans, many deeply suspicious of patriotic bombast, joined in the chorus of celebration.

Finally, Chapter 8 follows the story of Scott of the Antarctic through the First World War and after. Scott's story helps us understand the generation who endured the war, motivated less by simple patriotism than by codes of behaviour which placed com-radeship and the endurance of adversity as the highest expression of manhood. Although Scott's international fame faded, books, films, and radio broadcasts continued to pay homage to Scott and Oates in Britain between the wars, offering a vision of heroism uncontaminated by the futile slaughter of the Western Front.

But the combination of science, empire, and manliness expressed in Scott's Antarctic expeditions collapsed after 1918. Technological developments reduced the need for exposure to risk during the observation of the natural world, and new university departments excluded explorer heroes from academic geography. The nation paid tribute to the bravery of George Leigh Mallory and Andrew Irvine after their deaths on the slopes of Everest in 1924, but the British mountaineers were not widely hailed as martyrs of science. A new breed of aviators like Charles Lindbergh entranced the public after 1918, seekers of sensation, not scientific travellers.

The story of Scott of the Antarctic touches on many aspects of recent British history, involving imperial expansion, class hierarchy, and misogyny. The incompetence, prejudice, and exploitation that is part of this story inspires ridicule, anger, and shame. But if we search behind the stereotypes of our current condescension, we shall find much to pity and even to admire. Perhaps above all, we shall wonder at the strangeness of a world where polar knights rode prototype tanks, a world before the conquest of the South Pole.

· CHAPTER ONE ·

MEASURING THE WORLD

L ONDON, 3.00 p.m., Monday, 10 February 1913. The council of the Royal Geographical Society receives a telephone message informing them that Captain Scott and the southern party have been lost on their way back from the Pole.[1] The announcement of the disaster causes a sensation in Britain and around the world. 'The great tragedy of the Southern White Continent has profoundly moved the heart of the nation', declares the *Daily Chronicle*. 'As on the occasion when the *Titanic* carried its hundreds with it into Atlantic deeps, so it is now.'[2] The RGS council postpones the Society's regular evening meeting, delaying the election of a new group of women fellows. Douglas Freshfield, a senior councillor, pays tribute to 'a band of heroes whose names will shine as an example of that endurance which is the highest form of courage and a noble evidence of the qualities of Englishmen'.[3]

It was ironic that with news of Scott's death the council postponed the election of the first women fellows for twenty years. For if women had not been forbidden from joining the fellowship in 1893, if George Curzon had not returned from his travels in the Far East, if Douglas Freshfield had not resigned as the Society's secretary, if Clements Markham had not been willing to serve as President and launch a campaign for a national Antarctic expedition, then Captain Robert Falcon Scott, RN, might not have died at the South Pole.

If we are to understand why a Royal Naval officer from Devon sailed twice to the Antarctic, and why his death exerted such a profound influence, we must begin our investigation in the corridors of the institution which first sent Scott south, the Royal Geographical Society.

To the Ends of the Earth

The 5.5 million square miles of Antarctica would cover both the United States and Central America.[4] Only small areas of coastline and the peaks of mountains protrude from beneath a permanent covering of 7 million cubic miles of ice, between 1.25 and 2.25 miles thick. In the winter months of August and September mean temperatures range from −20 to −30°C on the coast, and −40 to −70°C inland. The lowest temperature ever recorded, −89°C, was measured on Antarctica in 1983. Gales are a constant hazard, intensifying the cold as every knot of wind speed is the physiological equivalent of a reduction of one degree. The mean height of this frozen landscape lies between 7,000 and 8,000 feet above sea level, making Antarctica not only the coldest but also the highest continent on earth. The tip of the Antarctic Peninsula is 600 miles south of Cape Horn, but New Zealand, South Africa, and Australia are all over 2,000 miles distant.

The Ancient Greeks had first speculated about the existence of an Antarctic continent in the fourth century BC and the revival of classical thought during the fifteenth century renewed interest. European mariners began to chart the southern oceans and in 1642 a Dutchman, Abel Tasman, sailed around Australia demonstrating its separation from any Antarctic continent. A series of voyages through the eighteenth century extended knowledge of the waters around Antarctica, with Captain James Cook, RN, commanding three cruises before his death in 1779. After crossing the Antarctic circle for the first time in January 1773, Cook came within a day's sail of Antarctica twelve months later, before being forced to retreat by the ice which girdles the continent.

Lieutenant Thaddeus von Bellinghausen of Russia led the first expedition to sight the Antarctic continent on 27 January 1820, preceding Lieutenant Edward Bransfield of the Royal Navy by only a few days. A number of expeditions followed, motivated by a combination of scientific curiosity, national competition, and commercial possibility. John Biscoe circumnavigated Antarctica for the first time in 1831–2, while working for the whaling firm Samuel Enderby & Son. Three scientific expeditions, led by the French Captain Dumont D'Urville, the American Lieutenant Charles Wilkes, and the Royal Naval Captain Sir James Clark Ross, mapped sections of the Antarctic coastline. British scientists encouraged the Admiralty to dispatch Ross (who had reached the magnetic North Pole in 1831) to locate the magnetic South Pole on board two specially strengthened ships, *Erebus* and *Terror*. Although he failed in his main objective, Ross's voyages from 1837 to 1843 found that the ice which had thwarted Cook could be navigated to reach open water. Ross named many of the features which would punctuate the story of Captain Scott, including Cape Adare, McMurdo Sound, the volcanoes Erebus and Terror, and the Great Ice Barrier, now known as the Ross Ice Shelf, a vast ice cliff 160 feet high and 500 miles long.

Although the majority of the Antarctic coastline remained uncharted, the disappearance of Sir John Franklin during his search for the elusive North-West Passage diverted attention away from the south. The search for a navigable route between the Atlantic and Pacific oceans had captivated mariners since Martin Frobisher sailed from England in 1576. After the Napoleonic Wars, the domineering Secretary to the British Admiralty, Sir

John Barrow, fixed on polar exploration as the ideal occupation for the Royal Navy in peace-time. John Franklin, William Parry, and John Ross (James's uncle) secured both promotion and acclaim at the head of a series of northern voyages in the 1820s and 1830s.

The final act before retirement of Sir John Barrow, the last Admiralty official to see Nelson before the battle of Trafalgar, was to arrange for the dispatch of a new expedition, and Franklin sailed north with a crew of 133 men on board Ross's old ships *Erebus* and *Terror* in May 1845. In the winter of 1846–7 both ships became trapped in heavy ice in the treacherous channels of the Canadian Arctic Archipelago and Franklin himself died on 11 June 1847. The remaining officers and men eventually left their stricken vessels, and set out in search of a safe haven. The entire crew perished.

Forty expeditions were dispatched in search of Franklin, with, on one occasion, a fleet of no less than fifteen ships simultaneously deployed. Franklin's wife, Lady Jane, campaigned tirelessly to keep the memory of her husband alive, and was raised as an icon of wifely devotion. The mystery surrounding the expedition opened a fertile space for the Victorian imagination. Folk songs, souvenirs, and the names of streets and pubs expressed the intense public interest in Franklin's fate. Finally, in 1858 a search expedition commanded by Captain Leopold McClintock discovered a cairn on King William Island, which contained a record of Franklin's death. Seven of the eighteen gold medals presented by the Royal Geographical Society between 1852 and 1860 honoured participants in the search for Franklin.

The Royal Geographical Society, like Franklin's last voyage, also originated in the mind of Sir John Barrow. At a meeting of the Raleigh Travellers' Club in May 1830, a dining society whose members feasted on foreign delicacies, Barrow had proposed the establishment of a Society to promote 'that most important and entertaining branch of knowledge – geography . . . [which was of] the first importance to mankind in general, and paramount to the welfare of a maritime nation like Great Britain'. The new society would collect geographical information, assemble a library and map room, acquire the latest equipment, advise travellers on areas to visit and research to undertake, and correspond with other learned associations throughout the world.[5]

The mystery surrounding Franklin's fate, the crossing of the Australian deserts, and, in particular, pioneering exploits in Africa, intensified public interest in exploration from the mid-nineteenth century. Dr David Livingstone received a tumultuous welcome when he returned to Britain in December 1856 after fifteen years of missionary work and exploration in southern Africa. His 5,000-mile journey, which included the first authenticated crossing of sub-Saharan Africa by a European, is still regarded as one of the two or three greatest feats of land exploration in history.[6]

Largely ignorant of earlier Portuguese discoveries, south-central Africa was commonly perceived as a dry, infertile area, and Living-stone's descriptions of forests, waterfalls, and grasslands were a revelation. Scientific societies and local councils showered the explorer with honours and his account of the expedition, *Missionary Travels and Researches in South Africa*, sold 70,000 copies, making its author rich. Livingstone proved so popular that he was in danger of being mobbed when he appeared in public. One commentator observed that, if the African explorer was recognized attending church, the service rapidly degenerated as worshippers clambered over pews attempting to shake the hand of their hero.

Livingstone dedicated *Missionary Travels* to the President of the RGS, Sir Roderick Murchison. Such was Livingstone's importance that Murchison interrupted his Christmas holiday with the Prime Minister, Lord Palmerston, to return to England to promote his achievements. A leading geologist who had fought in the Peninsula campaign during the Napoleonic Wars, Murchison served four terms as RGS President for a total of sixteen years, before his death in 1871. Extravagant early expenditure almost brought disaster, but the new society recovered under Murchsion's stewardship, receiving an annual grant of £500 from the Treasury from 1854 for the support of the map room, and a Royal Charter in 1859. Murchison arranged a reception for Livingstone at the Society's headquarters in Whitehall Place, forestalling the London Missionary Society, which, with an overdraft of £13,000, was also anxious to exploit Livingstone's popularity. Murchison cultivated Livingstone's reputation, associating the RGS with his achievements in order to attract subscriptions. It was a mutually beneficial relationship. With substantial connections in Westminster and Whitehall, the RGS President proved to be Livingstone's most influential patron.

Murchison helped secure Livingstone's leadership of a government-sponsored expedition up the River Zambezi in 1858, intended to open a highway into Central Africa. But rapids and waterfalls thwarted plans to reach the Batoka plateau and many of the crew, including Livingstone's wife Mary, died from disease. The expedition was deemed a failure on its return to London in 1864, while Livingstone's earlier achievements had been overshadowed by the exploits of Samuel Baker, Richard Burton, and John Hanning Speke in the search for the sources of the River Nile.

So Livingstone's reputation was in decline when he sailed for Africa two years later, aiming to combine a crusade against slavery in East Africa with a final solution to the Nile question. Although hampered by illness, he mapped Lake Bangweulu in 1868, but no communication from the expedition was received between the autumn of 1869 and the summer of 1871. It was the genius of one of the pioneers of popular journalism, the editor of the *New York Herald*, James Gordon Bennett Jr., to smell a story on the other side of the world. Bennett gambled that the 'discovery' of Livingstone would be headline news and he sent one of the *Herald*'s war correspondents, a former Welsh workhouse-boy, Henry Morton Stanley, to Africa to find him. Stanley made his name by reaching Livingstone at Ujiji in October 1871, coining the famous greeting 'Dr Livingstone, I presume?' Stanley's reports of a man 'as near an angel as the nature of living man will allow' sanctified Livingstone's reputation, while the evidence which he brought back to England contributed to the final closure of the slave market at Zanzibar.

But Livingstone's geographical endeavours proved as unsuccessful as Franklin's and, weakened by dysentery and worn down by fruitless travel, he died on the shores of Lake Bangweulu, 10° S of the Equator where the Nile sources lie. 'It is not all pleasure this exploration,' he wrote two weeks before his death. Livingstone was commemorated with a grand funeral service at Westminster Abbey in April 1874, organized by the RGS. 'With thousands of people, his is the one name that stands for discovery by land,' proclaimed the *Manchester Guardian*, 'as Franklin's stands for discovery by sea, or as Nelson's and as Wellington's stand for victory in war.'[7] The dead explorer's body lay in the RGS map room before the service, a fitting resting place within the Society to which he had contributed so much.

Murchison's investment in Livingstone paid ample dividends. The fellowship increased steadily from 1,000 in 1854 to over 2,000 in 1861 and passed 3,000 for the first time in 1872. On the Society's African nights, one contemporary reported, 'an immense audience thunders at the gate'. When Speke gave a talk on his return after his second expedition up the Nile, so great was the applause that several windows in Whitehall Place were shattered.[8] In 1876 the RGS hired

St James's Hall in an effort to accommodate all those who wished to hear Lieutenant Verney Lovett Cameron's account of his expedition in search of Livingstone, during which he became the first European to make an east–west crossing of Africa. Yet even this venue, with room for 2,000, proved inadequate, and many angry fellows, who regarded attendance at such events as the primary benefit of fellowship, were locked out. In return for his patronage, Murchison would have five geographical features named after him in Africa, including the spectacular Murchison Falls in Uganda, and no less than twenty-three worldwide.[9]

The expansion of the fellowship consolidated the financial position of the RGS. Investments were wisely placed and the Society purchased the freehold of larger premises at Number 1, Savile Row. But the Society was financially dependent on the private subscriptions of fellows and new members were in continual demand to finance the ambitious plans of the Society's officers. The RGS needed popular heroes like Franklin and Livingstone.

The Explorer Hero

How can we explain the Victorian fascination with exploration? Technological advances, commercial possibilities, religious fervour, strategic considerations, scientific curiosity, patriotic sentiment, and personal ambition all drove explorers into the unknown. In part, of course, explorers were simply the leading actors in cracking stories of adventure, set in exotic locations. One of the most famous passages of Livingstone's *Missionary Travels* described his attack by a lion. The publication of such tales in newspapers and books, increasingly accompanied by illustrations, was an integral part of the business of exploration. Marvellous visions of polar wastelands and tropical waterfalls delighted the Victorian public. The support of publishing houses and newspaper proprietors became an essential feature of expedition finance, as Beau Riffenburgh has shown.[10] By sponsoring expeditions, newspaper proprietors like Bennett created news.

Felix Driver's perceptive recent study has mapped the diverse 'cultures of exploration' which circulated through the nineteenth century.[11] Expeditions engaged with a range of mid-Victorian preoccupations: evangelical Christianity, the civilizing effects of commerce, the progress of European science, and Britain's imperial destiny. Explorers proved such compelling popular figures because different communities could express these beliefs by imagining the explorer in different ways. Livingstone, for example, was hailed as a model missionary, pioneering geographer, poor boy made good, prophet of empire, and standard bearer of the spirit of Scotland.

Heroic explorers also exemplified the idea of *character* which figured so prominently in Victorian intellectual life. The most eloquent exponent of the idea of character was the author and social reformer Samuel Smiles, whose classic best-seller *Self-Help*, first published in 1859, was reprinted over fifty times before the First World War. *Self-Help* presented a series of 'illustrations of conduct and perseverance' for the edification of readers. The six figures whose portraits illustrated *Self-Help* offer a representative sample of the personalities lauded by Smiles: the inventor Richard Arkwright, the sculptor John Flaxman, the engineer Isambard Brunel, the medical scientist William Harvey, the sailor Lord Nelson, and the explorer David Livingstone. While lecturing in a northern town, Smiles had been impressed by the commitment to self-improvement displayed by working men and sought to encourage them by 'pointing out that their happiness and well-being as individuals in after life must necessarily depend mainly upon themselves – upon their own diligent self-culture, self-discipline, and self-control – and, above all, on that honest and upright performance of individual duty which is the glory of manly character'.[12]

Smiles's emphasis on *manly* character was deliberate. The index of *Self-Help* listed only two women: the philanthropist Caroline Chisholm and the mother of Lord Langdale, although others, including Florence Nightingale, do occasionally appear in the main text. The work-place was the primary arena for the formation and display of character in the world of Samuel Smiles. Women's access to the activities praised by Smiles (engineering, medicine, armed forces, exploration, and so on) was severely constrained within the dominant ideology of 'separate spheres', which confined women either to domesticity or to a limited range of occupations deemed appropriate to their mental and physical capabilities.

Although Smiles claimed to express an ancient common-sense wisdom, the idea of character was a distinctively nineteenth-century formation. Smiles's emphasis on the work-place as a stage for moral endeavour marked a decisive departure from the eighteenth-century preoccupation with politeness, sociability, and leisure. 'The necessity of labour,' wrote Smiles, 'may indeed, be regarded as the main root and spring of all that we call progress in individuals, and civilization in nations'.[13] This shift reflected the growing influence of the provincial middle classes and critique of aristocratic indolence in Victorian Britain. Smiles reserved his highest admiration for self-made men, who achieved greatness through their own endeavours, not by accident of birth.

David Livingstone embodied the Smilesian virtues and a photograph of Livingstone adorned the frontispiece of *Self-Help* from 1873.[14] Born in a tenement block in Blantyre near Glasgow in 1813, Livingstone's life-story was an archetype of self-improvement. In a famous passage, Smiles describes how, while working in Blantyre Mills, the autodidact Scotsman 'even carried on his reading amidst the roar of the factory machinery, so placing the book upon the spinning jenny which he worked that he could catch sentence after sentence as he passed it'. Sir John Franklin also received praise, described as 'a man who never turned his back upon a danger, yet of that tenderness that he would not brush away a mosquito'.[15]

The Victorian idea of character was rooted in four core qualities: 'self-restraint, perseverance, strenuous effort, courage in the face of adversity'.[16] Smiles himself principally located these qualities amongst the ranks of the industrious middle classes, following *Self-Help* with three volumes on *The Lives of Engineers*. But expeditions to unknown lands also offered an ideal setting for the display of good character, furnishing abundant opportunities for men to demonstrate their hardihood, courage, and endurance as they battled against the forces of nature.

Neither Sir John Franklin, nor the expeditions which searched for him, succeeded in navigating the North-West Passage, but reports of the disaster transformed material failure into moral victory: a triumph of manly character. *Blackwood's Edinburgh Magazine* hailed those Arctic explorers who showed 'human heroism, patience, and bravery, such as imagination could scarcely dream of', while Charles Dickens urged readers to draw inspiration from the explorers' 'fortitude, their lofty sense of duty, their courage, and their religion'.[17] The failure of Franklin's expedition was redeemed by the heroic characteristics which commentators imagined the explorers had displayed in the Arctic. The death of Franklin offered the principal model for the story of Scott of the Antarctic, a discourse of polar heroism which figured death not as disaster, but as heroic sacrifice.

Exploration required not only a journey into an unknown land, but also a journey into the self, which involved writing as much as travel. The encounter between man and nature was staged on the page. Explorers fashioned themselves as heroic figures through the stories they told. In his autobiography, Roald Amundsen describes how he was inspired by tales of exploration which 'thrilled me as nothing I had ever read before. What appealed to me most was the sufferings that Sir John [Franklin] and his men had to endure. A strange ambition burned within me, to endure the same privations . . . I decided to be an explorer.'[18]

The novelist Joseph Conrad also confessed a youthful fascination with the exploits of explorers. In one of his later essays Conrad charts the evolution of geography from the era of 'Geography Fabulous', the medieval age of monsters and strange lands, to the era of 'Geography Militant', in which explorers surged across the globe replacing the 'dull imaginary wonders of the dark ages' with 'exciting spaces of white paper'. Conrad evokes the romance of exploration, describing his passion for Columbus and Cook, Franklin and Livingstone, 'worthy, adventurous and devoted men, nibbling at the edges, attacking from north and south and east and west, conquering a bit of truth here and bit of truth there, and sometimes swallowed up by the mystery their hearts were so persistently set on unveiling'.[19]

Yet Conrad's passion for exploration was tempered with a sense of impending loss. As he was writing in 1923, the era of 'Geography Militant' had already given way to the era of 'Geography Triumphant', in which the mystery of the unknown had been dispelled by the mundane certainties of science.

> No doubt a trigonometrical survey may be a romantic undertaking, striding over deserts and leaping over valleys never before trodden by the foot of civilised man; but its accurate operations can never have for us the fascination of the first hazardous steps of

a venturesome, often lonely, explorer jotting down by the light of his camp fire the thoughts, the impression, and the toil of the day.

For a long time yet a few suggestive words grappling with things seen will have the advantage over a long array of precise, no doubt interesting, and even profitable figures. The earth is a stage, and though it may be an advantage, even to the right comprehension of the play, to know its exact configuration, it is the drama of human endeavour that will be the thing, with a ruling passion expressed by outward action marching perhaps blindly to success or failure, which themselves are often indistinguishable from each other at first.[20]

In a further essay on 'Travel', Conrad observed with regret how 'the days of heroic travel are gone' and explorers 'condemned to make his discoveries on beaten tracks'.[21]

Conrad's essays encapsulated the dilemma which faced the RGS after the death of David Livingstone. The Society had prospered by cultivating the reputations of explorer heroes, but every achievement of a Livingstone or Stanley lessened opportunities for further spectacular feats: the sources of the Nile could only be discovered once. As early as the 1860s, Francis Galton had recognized that the 'career of the explorer will soon inevitably be coming to an end'.[22] The RGS response to this demise would shape the course of British exploration and the expeditions of Captain Scott.

Measuring the World

The days are drawing to a close when one can gain undying geographical renown by struggling against man and beast, fever and hunger and drought, across some savage and previously unknown region, even though little can be shown as the outcome of the journey. All honour to the pioneers by whom this first exploratory work has been so nobly done! They will be succeeded by a race that will find its laurels more difficult to win – a race from which more will be expected and which will need to make up in the variety, amount, and value of its detail, what it lacks in the freshness of first glimpses into new lands.[23]

Archibald Geikie, a young geologist and protégé of Murchison, lectured to the fellows of the RGS in 1879 as part of a new series on the 'special scientific branches of geography'. The lectures attracted little interest and were discontinued, but Geikie had correctly identified a pivotal moment in the history of exploration.

The officers of the RGS responded to the end of the era of Franklin and Livingstone by instituting a comprehensive programme to train the explorers who would follow in the footsteps of the pioneers. A series of reforms transformed every aspect of the Society's activity, to an extent which has been underestimated by previous historians.

Opportunities for pioneering expeditions diminished in the later nineteenth century. But Charles Darwin's writings catalysed a scientific revolution, while the expanding British empire demanded accurate geographical information, opening a distinctive space for geographical science within the growing education system.

In the volatile twenty years after Livingstone's death, a new vision of exploration as a tripartite process of measurement was promoted by the RGS: measuring the world, measuring men, and measuring empire. Three competing motives shaped expeditions. First, expeditions measured the world, recording scientific observations. Second, expeditions measured men, generating tales of heroic adventure. And third, expeditions measured empire, both supplying the geographical information required by imperial administrators and marking the boundaries of imperial power.

These three impulses were mediated through the distinctive institutional structure of the RGS: gentlemen's club, training centre for explorers, platform for heroes, patron of education, forum for scientific debate, and unofficial government archive. Through the provision of training, equipment, instructions, medals, and small grants, rather than direct financial sponsorship, the RGS exerted a decisive influence over the ways in which expeditions produced knowledge, enshrining the accurate measurement of the world as the centrepiece of a geographical expedition.

The transformation of the RGS began in earnest on 26 May 1879, when the newly established scientific purposes committee was asked to prepare a memorandum on a plan for training travellers to make useful scientific observations. The principal author of the report was Clements Markham, fellow since 1854, councillor since 1862, and honorary secretary from 1863.

Born in 1830, four days after the Society's foundation, Markham enjoyed a remarkable career, which included service in the Royal Navy, Inland Revenue, and India Office, and extensive foreign travel, especially in South America. The naval officer and Arctic explorer Albert Markham declared that his cousin cherished two great passions. His first love was for Peru. It was the young Clements who persuaded his superiors in the India Office that the Peruvian cinchona tree, whose bark produced quinine, should be introduced into India. The Peruvian government donated the bust of Clements Markham which still stares forebodingly at visitors to the RGS's Kensington headquarters. His second passion was for polar exploration. Clements had been captivated by the polar regions when he served as a midshipman during the search for Franklin and campaigned for Royal Naval involvement in polar exploration throughout his long career.

More than any other individual, Clements Markham created

a new mould for the explorer hero, a mould from which Scott of the Antarctic, naval officer, scientist, and national martyr, was cast. It was Markham who drove through the reforms which would raise the accurate measurement of the world as the primary goal of the RGS. It was Markham who restored the Society's fortunes after the damaging conflict over women fellows. It was Markham who focused the Society's energies on the exploration of the Antarctic. And it was Markham who chose the young officer who would command the Society's National Antarctic Expedition in 1900.

Markham presented his report on the training of travellers to the RGS council on 9 June 1879. He observed that every year numerous travellers journeyed across the globe, 'yet, for want of necessary training, they travel and return without any or with few results that can be utilized for geographical knowledge'. Markham proposed that the RGS should provide training to 'promote the increase of valuable observations for geographical purposes'. The report identi-fied nine categories of traveller who would benefit: officers in the army and navy; clerks in merchants' houses; planters and settlers; engineers; missionaries; colonial officials; collectors; and sportsmen and ordinary travellers, who visit little-known regions for their own amusement.

Markham suggested that instruction should initially be limited to surveying and mapping, including the fixing of positions by astronomical observations. Training in the use of the sextant, arti-ficial horizon and prismatic compass, he argued, 'is absolutely essential for every traveller who wishes to bring back useful work. It is the groundwork of the acquirements which he ought to possess. A traveller in unknown or little-known regions should be an instructed observer. It is not necessary that he should be a botanist, a zoologist, or a geologist, but he must know how to make and record observa-tions which will be useful as regards those sciences.' [24] John Coles, map curator since 1877, was officially appointed as 'Instructor in Practical Astronomy and Surveying' at the beginning of 1881. While navigating a captured slave-ship to the island of St Helena, Coles had been unable to find his longitude with the available instruments. He knew that if the trade winds caught him he would be carried to Brazil, where the prisoners would be released and he imprisoned. He eventually reached St Helena, but his experiences impressed on him the importance of exact astronomical observations. Coles had lost an eye in the Crimean War, which may explain his skill with single-lensed instruments.

Coles and his assistant, E. A. Reeves, who took over as map curator after Coles's resignation in 1900, supervised the Society's courses for over fifty years. Neither had received any formal training. Indeed, the qualification which secured Reeves's appointment at the age of 16 was a drawing of his home that impressed his neighbour, a certain John Coles.

Markham spelt out the significance of surveying at a meeting of the Geographical Section of the British Association for the Advancement of Science (BAAS) in 1879:

> Our first work as geographers is to measure all parts of earth and sea, to ascertain the relative positions of all places upon the surface of the globe, and to delineate the varied features of that surface. . . .
>
> Accurate maps are the basis of all inquiry conducted on scientific principles. Without them a geological survey is impossible; nor can botany, zoology, or ethnology be viewed in their broader aspects, unless considerations of locality, altitude, and latitude are kept in view.[25]

The Society invested in the new scheme, building an observatory on the roof at Savile Row. The range of courses was broadened in 1884 to include photography, botany, zoology, and geology.

However, all prospective travellers had first to complete Coles's course in surveying.[26] In 1893 Markham proclaimed the course 'the most successful measure that has been adopted by this Society in recent years, and the one which has done most to advance the interests of geography'.[27] Since he was one of the principal architects of the scheme, Markham's assessment was hardly surprising, but the number of students trained was impressive: between 1882 and 1896 Coles gave instruction to 334 pupils, who surveyed every region of the world, from Somalia to Guyana.[28]

The scheme was complemented by the publication in 1883 of a revised edition of the Society's *Hints to Travellers*. The first *Hints to Travellers*, published in 1854, was a 31-page collection of articles designed to answer frequently asked questions about outfit and equipment. Further editions appeared in 1865, 1871, and 1878, but in 1881 the council established a committee to oversee the publication of a fifth edition, to complement John Coles's new course. The fifth edition of *Hints to Travellers* trebled in length to almost 300 pages. The editors explained that the expansion was intended to meet the 'in some ways higher requirements of a new generation of young travellers, many of whom receive scientific instruction in the society's office before leaving England'.[29]

Instead of an assortment of miscellaneous articles, *Hints to Travellers* offered a comprehensive 'How to' manual for the prospective explorer. The section titled 'Surveying, and Astronomical Observations', prepared by Coles, was the principal portion of the work, including a 188-page account of the latest equipment and techniques. The rest of the volume included chapters on meteorology, geology, natural history, anthropology, photography, outfit, and medical advice. The sections on surveying were further expanded in 1889 and 1893, until the Society eventually published *Hints to Travellers* in two volumes in 1901, with a first volume of

425 pages devoted entirely to surveying. The ruler inscribed on the front cover indicated the centrality of accurate measurement to the Society's vision of exploration. Scott's polar expeditions would carry *Hints to Travellers* into the Antarctic.

Detailed instructions were of little use if the explorer did not have access to the latest equipment. In conjunction with the publication of the fifth edition of *Hints*, the council established a committee to oversee the acquisition and loan of instruments to travellers.[30] The Society's loan of instruments increased steadily after the establishment of the committee, with 15 expeditions supplied in the 1860s, 27 in the 1870s, 61 in the 1880s, and 106 in the 1890s. Between 1877 and 1900 the Society supplied instruments to 186 expeditions, ranging all over the world, from Albert Markham's voyage to the Arctic in 1879 to William Conway's exploration of the Himalayas in 1892.[31]

The Society's instructions to explorers, while encouraging systematic observation in a variety of fields, further emphasized the central importance of the production of an accurate survey of an unknown region. The council made the completion of Coles's course an essential prerequisite for sponsorship. The departure of Joseph Thomson's East African Expedition in 1883 was delayed for a month, so that Thomson could receive additional tuition from Coles. Thomson received detailed instructions regarding his route:

> The objects of the expedition are to ascertain if a practicable direct route for European travellers exists through the Masai country from ports on the East African coast to the Victoria Nyanza, and to examine Mount Kenia; to gather data for constructing as complete a map as possible in a preliminary survey, and to make all *practicable* observations on the meteorology, geology, natural history and ethnology of the region traversed. [my emphasis]

Offers of £900 from the BAAS and the Church Missionary Society, which would have covered almost a third of the expedition's costs, were rejected as the council objected to any outside interference over the expedition's route.[32]

Thomson's discoveries earned him the Society's gold medal and in 1888 he applied to the RGS to support a new expedition to southern Morocco and the Atlas Mountains. But when the council pressed for more specific information on his intended route, Thomson replied: 'it seems to me useless to lay down a cut and dried scheme . . . Wherever an opening into new ground presents itself, that I mean to take.'[33] Such vagaries failed to satisfy the expedition committee and Thomson was granted only £100 and the loan of certain instruments, with the promise of an additional £100 if the expedition produced valuable geographical information.[34] The meagre assistance offered to an explorer who had been awarded the Society's highest honour offers a persuasive demonstration of the importance attached to surveying. Mere adventuring in southern Morocco would not secure the Society's full support, no matter the merits of the explorer.

The RGS reinforced its new emphasis on the accurate measurement of the world by reforming the ways in which it distributed geographical information, overhauling its publications, library, map room, and, more controversially, support for education. Clements Markham again played a leading role. Dissatisfied with the Society's existing *Proceedings* as dull and over-formal, Markham proposed a new monthly publication, which would be the leading authority in the world on all subjects relating to geography. Each edition of the new series of the *Proceedings of the Royal Geographical Society* would contain a list of all geographical works published, reviews, news, and a comprehensive index. The Society's new periodical became the largest single item of RGS expenditure. John Scott

Keltie (RGS Librarian, 1885–92) and H. R. Mill (RGS Librarian, 1892–1902) consolidated Markham's improvements and, in 1893, Mill oversaw the replacement of the new series of the *Proceedings* by the *Geographical Journal*, currently approaching its 170th volume.

Official publications were an integral element of the frameworks of professional expertise constructed in a variety of fields in the second half of the nineteenth century. The varied contents of each number (expedition narratives, scientific papers, reviews, reports, diagrams, and maps) articulated both the diverse aims of exploration, from missionary endeavour to commercial expansion, and the wide range of subjects sheltered beneath the umbrella of geography. But the Society's periodical also promoted the accurate measurement of the world as the cornerstone of a geographical expedition: after 1879 every edition contained at least one map, with increasing sums being spent on the preparation of maps for publication.

The financial resources generated by the rapid rise in membership, coupled with the move to larger premises, enabled the RGS to expand its role as an archive of geographical information. Between 1874 and 1896 the Society's library holdings doubled, while the map collection almost trebled from around 23,000 to over 62,000 sheets.[35] The move to Savile Row also facilitated the appointment of the Society's first map draughtsman, W. J. Turner, in 1873, with an assistant added in 1885. By 1890 technological improvements, and the Society's commitment to a vision of scientific exploration centred on surveying, strained the capacity of two full-time specialists.

The last of the reforms instituted to prepare the RGS for the end of the age of the pioneers proved the most controversial: the promotion of geographical education. In 1884 the council appointed John Scott Keltie to investigate the teaching of geography in Britain. Keltie had trained for the Presbyterian ministry in Scotland, but left to pursue a journalistic career; in later years he liked to tell how his former colleagues believed he had lapsed into literature. Keltie's report was highly critical of the standard of British geography teaching compared with France and Germany in particular. The RGS financed an exhibition and lecture series to promote Keltie's report, which has long been regarded as a key moment in the development of geography as an academic discipline in Britain. Keltie's appointment initiated his long association with the RGS, serving first as librarian, and then as secretary. Nearly thirty years later it was Keltie who dealt with the press after the announcement of Scott's death.

The RGS considered a number of proposals to stimulate the teaching of geography in Britain. Most significantly, the council resolved to lobby for the establishment of posts in geography at the universities of Oxford and Cambridge. By the end of 1887, Halford Mackinder had been appointed Reader in Geography at Oxford and agreement had been reached for a lectureship at Cambridge. The RGS agreed to share the costs of the appointments and also funded scholarships to encourage undergraduates to take geography courses. The Society's financial support proved critical in sustaining a geographical presence in the face of both institutional intransigence and disciplinary rivalry, especially with geology.[36]

Two fellows in particular campaigned for the RGS to promote geographical education: first, the long-serving councillor General Richard Strachey, who had spent forty years administering a variety of public works schemes in India; and, second, the keen mountaineer Douglas Freshfield, who had served alongside Clements Markham as joint honorary secretary from 1881.

Markham himself, however, was sceptical of the Society's

educational initiatives, especially financial commitments to Oxford and Cambridge over which the RGS exerted little control. The policy of the doctrinaires, he later complained, 'was to say that there was no longer any occasion for expeditions on a large scale, to starve all exploring work, and to subsidise educational schemes'.[37]

The officers of the RGS sought to redefine the geographical enterprise in the final quarter of the nineteenth century. Markham's reforms trained the explorers who would follow in the footsteps of the pioneers, establishing the accurate measurement of the world as the primary aim of exploration. Freshfield and Strachey also supported the scientific instruction of travellers, but envisaged a more fundamental reorientation of the Society's energies from exploration to education, from the field to the study. Markham became increasingly disillusioned with the educational initiatives that followed the publication of Keltie's report. Strachey's succession to the presidency appeared to confirm the Society's change of direction and so, after twenty-five years' service, Markham resigned his post as honorary secretary of the RGS in 1888.

Speaking after Markham's resignation, Strachey advised explorers to give a somewhat less personal character to their narratives. 'Accounts of personal adventure will always add to the interest that attaches to the exploration of unknown countries,' Strachey acknowledged, 'but from the point of view of geography, the mountains, the deserts, and the seas are the main objects of consideration, rather than the fatigues and perils encountered in crossing them.'[38] Strachey echoed Archibald Geikie's assessment a decade earlier: the age of the pioneers was drawing to a close.

Measuring Manliness

But although the end was in sight, the curtain had not yet fallen on the age of the pioneers: the North Pole remained out of reach and no explorer had even set foot on Antarctica. In 1890 there were still worlds left to conquer.

Indeed, the most distinctive feature of the geographical enterprise supported by the RGS in the last quarter of the nineteenth century was the incorporation of a more scientific approach to exploration *alongside* a romantic conception of the explorer hero. Explorers not only measured the world, they also measured their manliness. This incorporation was revealed most clearly in the annual awards made by the Society. By delineating the criteria on which the RGS awarded its gold medals, a composite picture of the Society's ideal explorer can be constructed, part scientific traveller, part manly hero, the blueprint for Captain Scott.

The Society's gold medal originated in 1831, with an annual gift of fifty guineas from King William IV to encourage geographical science and discovery. In 1839 the council divided the sum between two medals of equal value, the Founder's and the Patron's, awarded annually ever since. The awards were highly prized. The German scholar Ferdinand von Richtofen wrote that the Founder's medal was 'the highest of honours which can be conferred upon any geographer in our time', while H. E. O'Neill, British consul in Mozambique, memorably described the gold medal as 'the Victoria Cross of English travellers'.[39]

The awards reinforced the Society's emphasis on accurate surveying. Between 1876 and 1900 the majority of medals were awarded for the exploration of substantial areas of unmapped territory. Merely to travel long distances, however, was not enough. Explorers also had to demonstrate their skill as scientific travellers: the endurance of hardship would be rewarded only if it were combined with scientific observations. When awarding the Founder's medal to Lieutenant Cameron in 1876, Murchison's successor, the veteran Indian administrator Sir Henry Rawlinson, declared that it was

> not your remarkable exhibition of manly courage and persever-
> ance ... which have on this occasion ... recommended you to
> the favourable notice of the Council. We have selected you to be
> our Medallist, above all other reasons, because you have, amidst
> difficulties and dangers, in failing health, under privation and
> fatigue, steadily kept in view the paramount claim on your
> attention of Scientific Geography, and have thus brought back
> with you from the interior of Africa a Register of Observations
> for Latitude, Longitude, and Elevation, which, for extent and
> variety – and we are authorised by the Report of the Greenwich
> authorities to add for judicious selection and accuracy of result –
> may favourably compare with the finished work of a professional
> survey.

Rawlinson raised Cameron as a model to future travellers.[40]

Accurate survey work became an essential prerequisite for receipt of an RGS award. When awarding the Patron's medal to G. Grenfell in 1887, Strachey observed that during his trek through West Africa, 'amidst the anxieties and dangers of journeys through countries peopled by distrustful or hostile savages, you never lost sight of the need of geographical precision. Your course was plotted from hour to hour by an uninterrupted system of dead reckoning and compass bearings, corrected by frequent observations for latitude.'[41]

Admiration persisted, though, for the manly qualities displayed by explorers in the face of danger. Geographical knowledge was still won in the field, through the contest between man and nature. The character displayed during the collection of geographical information was highlighted in almost every award. In 1886 the Liberal statesman Lord Aberdare, who served two terms as President in the 1880s, presented a gold medal to the US Army Lieutenant Adolphus Greely. Greely's recent Arctic expedition had taken an extensive range of observations and set a new 'farthest north' record of 83° 24'. But eighteen of the twenty-five-man crew had starved after they were forced to abandon their base camp and head south in search of relief, and the press had been filled with reports of cannibalism among the survivors. Aberdare welcomed Greely back 'from the very gates of death', praising his 'magnificent courage' and 'willingness to endure any hardship for one step in the enlargement of scientific survey'.[42]

Clements Markham was especially anxious to pass the mantle of heroism to the generation of explorers who followed in the footsteps of the pioneers. Stories of heroic devotion, declared Markham,

> true deeds of knight errantry, long and tried services, are recorded of our geodesists and rigorously accurate surveyors, as well as of our explorers and discoverers . . . The danger of surveying service in the jungles and swamps of India . . . is greater than the chances against one man on a battlefield; the percentage of deaths is larger, while the sort of courage that is called forth is of quite as high an order. When the stories of the Ordnance Survey in Great Britain, and of the Great Trigonometrical Survey of India are fitly told, they will form some of the very proudest pages in the history of our nation.[43]

Markham liked to tell the story of Captain Basevi struggling to take observations in freezing temperatures 17,000 feet above sea level, who died at his post a 'martyr to science'.[44] David Brewster had popularized this phrase in his mid-century study of Galileo, Kepler, and Tycho Brahe, and nearly forty years later Captain Scott and his companions would be hailed as martyrs to science.

Both race and gender, however, excluded many from the Society's vision of the explorer hero. Between 1831 and 1917 only two women received the Society's gold medal, but not for exploration in the field. Lady Franklin was honoured for her devotion to her husband, receiving the Founder's medal in 1860 in 'admiration of her noble and self-sacrificing perseverance in sending out, at her own cost, several searching expeditions, until at length the fate of her husband has been finally ascertained'.[45] Mary Somerville received the Patron's medal in 1869 for her geographical textbooks, and was praised for her excellence 'in the arts of painting, music, and all feminine accomplishments'.[46] The qualities of the explorer – scientific training, courage in the face of danger, the endurance of hardship – were considered exclusively masculine. No female explorer would be honoured by the RGS until Gertrude Bell in 1918.

The men who received the Society's medals were almost all white Europeans or Americans. Nain Singh was the principal exception. The most famous of those native surveyors (Pundits) who worked in secret on the Indian frontier, Nain Singh received the Patron's medal in 1877 for his exploration of Tibet. But even he was denied full recognition as an explorer hero. Although Rutherford Alcock praised Nain Singh's noble qualities of loyalty, courage, and endurance, the Society's President emphasized that the Pundit had worked in parts of Asia which no European could explore, while Colonel Yule, who received the award on behalf of Nain Singh, paid special praise to the British officer who had trained the Pundit, Colonel Montgomerie.[47]

General J. T. Walker, former Surveyor-General of India, qualified the achievements of native surveyors in similar fashion when describing the Tibetan journeys of Pundit A——k in 1885 (real names were suppressed while Pundits continued working for the Indian Survey). Walker emphasized that native surveyors were only partially educated. Neither A——k nor Nain Singh could have acquired the art of determining absolute longitudes, which many Europeans found difficult, and A——k was purposely not taught to plot maps from the information he gathered, as the only guarantee of his observations was to have his findings worked out at headquarters.

Pundit A——k was reduced to an instrument of General Walker's own scientific training and good character. Summing up after the paper, Sir Henry Rawlinson emphasized that

> A——k was really General Walker's own creation; for they were indebted to the General, not only for the scientific preparation of the individual and for the organisation of the expedition, but also for the utilisation of the results. Without an experienced and commanding head to have reduced those rough notes and books to order, all this exploration and this expenditure of skill, of industry, and of courage, would have been in vain.[48]

Forbidden from representing his own experiences on the page, A——k's status as a heroic explorer was denied.

Measuring Empire

The treatment of native surveyors exposes the imperial dimension of the RGS's history. The world which explorers measured was not empty. Founded to promote 'the welfare of a maritime nation', the RGS was intimately bound up with the expansion of the British empire. Beneath the disinterested language of scientific progress, lies a history of imperial expansion and exploitation.

The British empire underwent an astonishing transformation through the nineteenth century, with the steady growth of the 'white Dominions' of Canada, South Africa, Australia, and New Zealand, and the imposition of direct or indirect rule over vast new territories, particularly in Africa. Large sections of the political elite and the public were hostile to empire in the 1850s and 1860s. Heartened by the nation's escape from the worst excesses of the 1848 revolutions, many celebrated the freedoms guaranteed by British constitutional arrangements, and condemned the excessive expenditure necessitated by imperial entanglements. But Prussia's defeat of France in 1870 and the fall of Napoleon III upset the balance of power in Europe, inaugurating a decisive shift in both policy and attitudes. Between 1874 and 1902 alone 4,750,000 square miles of land inhabited by nearly 90 million people were added to the British empire.

The causes of this shift were complex. The variegated processes of imperial expansion remain the subject of fierce debate, but we can at least line up a familiar list of suspects: international competition; commercial opportunity; missionary ambition; technological developments in medicine, transport, and communications; the decline of confidence in British constitutional arrangements resulting, in part, from conflict over Ireland; the rise of social Darwinism and hardening of racial language; loss of faith in the pacific effects of free trade; and the cultivation of popular imperialism to appeal to newly enfranchised voters.

Geographical knowledge supported imperial expansion in two ways. First, detailed topographical information was an essential prerequisite of both commercial activity and effective colonial administration. At a dinner to honour Stanley in 1890, the colonial administrator and naturalist Harry Johnston confessed he had no ambition to become a great explorer. He called instead for a 'series of *exploiters*, of practical, resolute men who shall turn to the advantage of the British Empire – and the advantage of the

British Empire is the advancement of civilisation and the benefit of the world at large – the discoveries, the experiments, the sufferings, the knowledge, often so cruelly and dearly acquired, of those great explorers who have passed away'.[49]

Second, and less obviously, apparently disinterested forms of scientific enquiry also participated in the construction of imperial authority. In his seminal study, Edward Said defined 'Orientalism' as 'a western style for dominating, restructuring, and having Authority over the Orient'.[50] Drawing on the writings of the French thinker Michel Foucault, Said mapped the construction of an Orientalist discourse, a set of rules and techniques conditioning the representation of colonized peoples and spaces, which legitimized European oppression by, for example, portraying natives as intellectually inferior. Geographers were in the vanguard of European imperialism, appropriating native space and opening the way for colonial exploitation.

Much recent scholarship has investigated the construction of native 'others' in geographical texts, negative stereotypes of sex, race, health, and illness to contrast with European 'norms'. Many of the RGS's officers, from Francis Galton to Leonard Darwin, were closely involved in the rise of anthropology, ethnography, and eugenics. Harry Johnston's *British Central Africa* (1897), for example, used photographs to back up theories about the inferiority of what he called 'the negro race', and its improvement under British rule. An examination of the representation of native peoples in tales of exploration is beyond the remit of this book. But the delineation of racial difference was a central facet of the measurement of empire.

The institutional focus of the RGS, though, was trained on the accurate measurement of the natural world throughout this period. The 1886 edition of *Hints to Travellers* devoted 225 pages to 'Surveying and Astronomical Observations' and only 35 pages to

'Anthropology'. Commentary on the customs and practises of native peoples can certainly be found within the Society's publications, but the volume of material devoted to topographical information, to drainage systems and soil characteristics, was far greater.

The classification of natural phenomena also bore the imprint of empire, however: 'empire helped to shape the cognitive content of the field sciences.'[51] Sir Roderick Murchison's schemes of geological classification deployed imperial terminology, while discussions of climate were pervaded with assumptions about the relationship between race and place. Maps are not neutral reflections of the earth's surface, but complex systems of representation incorporating a plethora of choices about what features to include and how to depict them.

The rapid expansion of the British empire in the final quarter of the nineteenth century catalysed the RGS's promotion of a more scientific approach to exploration. Travellers' tales were of little use to Britain's growing army of colonial officials. Governments had long approached the RGS for information and advice. The RGS secretary received a letter from the Foreign Office in the 1860s, preparing for a parliamentary question concerning Casablanca. Although the civil servants knew they had a consul stationed in Casablanca, they were not certain of the city's location and presumed it was in Italy.[52]

RGS officers worked hard to fulfil Murchison's prediction that the Society's map room would become the 'Map Office of the Nation'. Clements Markham recorded that the map room was constantly utilized by the War Office and other government departments. The RGS provided maps for the British representatives at the Berlin West Africa Conference in 1884, traditionally portrayed as the beginning of the 'scramble for Africa'.[53] In return for such services, both the library and map room received regular donations from a number of government departments.

John Coles's surveying course was specifically directed towards colonial officials. In 1892 the former Liberal MP and Governor of Madras, Sir Mountstuart Elphinstone Grant Duff, reported that forty-eight government servants, twenty-one of whom were employed on special service and boundary commissions, had recently taken Coles's course. When Coles asked for a raise in 1885, it was noticeable that he justified his request by referring to the valuable assistance he offered officials of the Foreign Office, War Office, Colonial Office, and Admiralty, rather than the Society's fellows.[54] When the Society stepped up its search for new premises in the 1890s, the council resolved that any new site should be close to the offices of government, and Grant Duff hoped that a room might be provided where MPs and civil servants could be supplied with information on 'any of the innumerable questions where politics and administration cross the frontiers of geography'.[55]

Links were particularly strong with the armed forces and colonial officials. Of the twenty-one council members in June 1885, at least nine had practical surveying experience, at least ten had spent considerable time on the Indian subcontinent, and eight were high-ranking officers in the armed forces, including Admiral Leopold McClintock, the discoverer of Franklin's fate, and the new Hydrographer to the Navy, W. J. L. Wharton. Nearly 700 of the Society's 4,031 fellows in 1900 were officers in the armed forces.[56]

The reform of the RGS after Livingstone's death was driven in part by the requirements of British imperial expansion. Scientific instruction was targeted at colonial officials, while imperial rhetoric infused the Society's activities, from the promotion of education to the funding of the map room.

But the RGS was not simply an instrument of British imperial expansion. This distinctive hybrid institution generated a range of impulses, some complementary, some contradictory. Said and others have quite rightly questioned the disinterestedness of scientific research: all systems of knowledge bear the imprint of their conditions of production. The history of science and the history of empire were intimately connected through the nineteenth century, their relationship mediated through institutions like the RGS. But the two histories were not identical. The imperial utility of geographical information varied widely, and the interests and agendas of the Society's officers and fellowship frequently diverged. The measurement of the world and the measurement of manliness could propel explorers away from the measurement of empire, as we shall see.

During a series of influential lectures in 1883, the Cambridge historian J. R. Seeley criticized those explorers who 'naturally but unfortunately turned their attention to the Polar regions, and so discovered nothing but frozen Oceans, while their rivals were making a triumphal progress'.[57] A decade later the RGS would launch a campaign for a British Antarctic Expedition, culminating in the launch of the ship *Discovery*, with Captain Scott at the helm. The conquest of the South Pole would serve as a potent symbol of Britain's global influence, but the needs of the empire cannot explain why, at the high point of the scramble for Africa, the RGS made the most substantial grant in its history for an expedition to a region of negligible strategic or commercial value. To understand the origins of the campaign that was to send Scott to the South Pole, we must turn our attention to a dispute which threatened to tear the Society apart.

· CHAPTER TWO ·

THE RACE TO THE SOUTH POLE

ON 12 May 1876 Lieutenant Albert Markham planted the Union Flag farther north than anyone had ever stood before. British interest in polar exploration had diminished after the excesses of the search for Franklin, but, thanks in no small measure to the efforts of Albert's cousin Clements, the Royal Navy had been persuaded to send two ships to the Arctic in 1875, *Alert* and *Discovery*, under the command of George Nares. Markham reached 83° 20′ N when, blighted by scurvy, his party was forced to turn back with the North Pole still 400 miles distant. On reaching Ireland, Nares sent a telegram to London declaring 'NORTH POLE IMPRACTICABLE'. The Admiralty subsequently decided that further attempts on the Pole would be dangerous, expensive, and most probably futile. Americans, Norwegians, Swedes, and Italians, from Robert Peary to Fridtjof Nansen, Nils Nordenskjöld to the Duke of Abruzzi, would make their name in the Arctic over the next forty years. But never again would a British explorer lead the race for the North Pole.

By 1890 British involvement in polar exploration was at its lowest ebb since John Barrow directed the Royal Navy to the ends of the earth after the Napoleonic Wars. Although a group of New England sealers may have reached land as early as 1821, no confirmed landing on the Antarctic continent had yet been made. Southern expeditions proposed by Australian scientific societies, the BAAS, and the Royal Society of Edinburgh, how-ever, failed to secure adequate support. And the most vocal British champion of polar endeavour, Clements Markham, no longer held sway over the unofficial headquarters of global exploration, the RGS.

But then there was an argument, an argument over a lady, or, to be more precise, an argument over twenty-two ladies. A rancorous dispute about the admission of women as fellows of the RGS erupted unexpectedly in November 1892, dividing the fellowship and inviting public ridicule. In the aftermath, several prominent figures turned down the presidency and the council looked in desperation to Clements Markham. After the educational reforms of Strachey and Freshfield, Markham would return the Society's focus to the exploration of unknown lands, fixing on a grand Antarctic expedition to reconcile the warring factions and restore the Society's reputation.

By installing Clements Markham at the helm of the RGS, the dispute over the admission of women changed the course of British exploration. For without Markham's polar obsession, it is both quite possible that Britain would not have played a leading role in the exploration of the Antarctic, and almost certain that Robert Scott would not have become the pre-eminent hero of his generation.

'A Traveller in Skirts?'

'I have only one formidable rival in Isabella's affections,' reflected Dr John Bishop on the sentiments of his wife, 'and that is the high tableland of Central Asia.'[1] Isabella Bird Bishop proved one of the most accomplished women travellers of the nineteenth century, journeying throughout Asia and America, and dying on the eve of her seventy-third birthday with her luggage packed and labelled for her next expedition. She sailed for India in 1889 to found mission hospitals in memory of her late husband and sister, touring western Tibet and joining an Indian Army reconnaissance of south-west Persia. On her return, she lectured at the annual meeting of the BAAS in August 1892, but declined the RGS's invitation, explaining she did not wish to read a paper to a society which would not admit her as a fellow. She spoke instead to the new London branch of the Scottish Geographical Society, which had admitted women from its foundation in 1884.

Richard Strachey had proposed the admission of women to the RGS in 1887, but, although no legal obstacle was found, no decision had been taken. The new London branch of the Scottish Geographical Society forced the council's hand and the August 1892 issue of the Society's *Proceedings* announced that women would be eligible for the fellowship on the same terms as men. The council explained that women's work as travellers, teachers, and students of geography compelled their admission. But the council's primary motive was financial: to attract subscriptions to fund both new educational initiatives and a move to larger premises. The Society's secretary, Douglas Freshfield, wrote to the President, Grant Duff, that 'the acceptance of Lady's certificates need not be postponed . . . the opposition will collapse or be insignificant. The step is a popular one.'[2]

Freshfield's misjudgement proved catastrophic. Two veterans of the search for Franklin, Admirals Halliday Cave and Leopold McClintock, expressed their opposition at the end of November, when Miss Maria Eleanor Vere Cust, daughter of the distinguished academic Robert Cust, was elected as the first female RGS fellow.

A bitter dispute raged over the following months, with senior naval officers leading the opposition to the twenty-two women elected to the fellowship. Some were motivated primarily by concerns about overcrowding and the availability of tickets for Society functions, while others feared an increasing emphasis on enter-tainment. 'We already have magic lanterns and dissolving views,' announced one disgruntled fellow, 'in a short time we should probably have a piano.'[3] But the dispute was not simply another manifestation of broader late-Victorian debates about the involve-ment of women in public life. It was a more specific contest about the identity of the RGS, and the proper balance between education and exploration, the study and the field. The outcome of the dispute would determine whether the RGS played a leading role in the exploration of the Antarctic.

Strachey, Freshfield, and Grant Duff sought to reorient the Society away from exploration. They had showered unprecedented honours on H. M. Stanley in 1890, after his completion of the geography of the Nile sources, hiring the Royal Albert Hall for the first time and creating a new award, the Society's special gold medal, in recognition of his achievements. The cultivation of Stanley's reputation helped attract almost 300 new fellows and unprecedented entrance fees. But Strachey believed it was now almost time to declare that 'the possibility of further geographical discovery in the old sense of the words is at an end'.[4] He showed little interest in Antarctic exploration. The admission of women would symbolize the Society's new direction.

Those opposed to the admission of women disagreed. They believed that the promotion of exploration should remain the Society's core activity, that the progress of geography still required the hardihood, courage, and endurance of explorer heroes prepared to suffer in the cause of scientific progress.

Clements Markham had detached himself from the Society's affairs, so the case against the admission of women was most force-fully expressed by a rising star of English public life, the young Tory MP George Nathaniel Curzon. Between 1887 and his marriage in

1895, Curzon embarked on a series of journeys which established him as an expert on Asian affairs. After the Conservative Prime Minister Lord Salisbury's narrow defeat in the election of July 1892, Curzon set out on a tour of Japan, Korea, and China, returning to England the following March to lead the campaign against the admission of women.

Curzon engaged in a vitriolic argument with Douglas Freshfield in the letters pages of *The Times*. Responding to a letter from a 'A *bona fide* traveller', almost certainly Freshfield,[5] Curzon announced he contested '*in toto* the general capability of women to contribute to scientific geographical knowledge. Their sex and training render them equally unfitted for exploration; and the genus of professional female globe-trotters with which America has lately familiarised us is one of the horrors of the latter end of the 19th century.' Curzon conceded that many men did not deserve the initials FRGS, but Isabella Bishop was an exception, and the general admission of women would further dilute the Society's character. 'If scholarship were merely required in geography, and the female FRGS were a student who worked in a library, the parallel of the Asiatic Society, which admits ladies, might be apposite . . .' Curzon argued. 'But the Royal Geographical Society has a far wider and more cosmopolitan reputation to sustain'.

Freshfield mocked Curzon's suggestion that women should be excluded as few would prove hardy explorers. 'Scientific geographers are employed in the study as well as in the field . . . In fact, but a comparatively small proportion of our Fellows can be makers of knowledge; most of us are content to be receivers and transmitters only.' Curzon closed the debate by reiterating his belief that women would contribute nothing but their guineas to geography.[6]

Such hostile exchanges damaged the Society's reputation.

Punch published a poetic reply 'To the Royal Geographical Society', in which an Admiral exclaimed:

> A lady an explorer? a traveller in skirts?
> The notion's just a trifle too seraphic:
> Let them stay and mind the babies, or hem our ragged shirts;
> But they mustn't, can't and shan't be geographic.

Judy mocked the RGS in print and pictures (**Fig. 2.1**). The *Daily Telegraph* suggested Curzon, 'who also has the disadvantage of being a bachelor, has in the course of his travels in the East, become too strongly imbued with Mohameddan notions on the subject of the gentler sex'.[7]

THE ROYAL GEOGRAPHICAL SOCIETY LADIES NOT ADMITTED.

2.1 'Ladies Not Admitted'. The Royal Geographical Society was widely ridiculed in the press during the internal dispute over the admission of women as fellows.

But, although a ballot of the fellowship was overwhelmingly in favour of the admission of women, Curzon had the last laugh. The Society's constitution decreed that the vote of a special general meeting took precedence over any ballot and, at the crucial gathering on 3 July 1893, a motion to admit women was narrowly defeated by 172 votes to 158.[8] Rather than prolong the embarrassing conflict, the council agreed not to press the matter further. No more women were elected to the fellowship of the RGS for twenty years.

In the wake of the dispute, Grant Duff resigned the presidency, Freshfield resigned as secretary in 1894 and Strachey remained as vice-president, but was retired for non-attendance in 1898. The principal proponents of the Society's new educational initiatives had gone. Curzon, in contrast, would receive the Society's gold medal in 1895, an honour he valued 'more highly than any non-political compliment or distinction that I have ever received'.[9]

The presidency proved difficult to fill after Grant Duff's resignation. The council approached a number of prominent public figures, before Clements Markham finally accepted.[10] Markham proved acceptable as he had kept his personal reservations about the admission of women private, but his position was clear: 'The chief work of the Society should be the encouragement and assistance of exploration and discovery, by grants of money and assistance to travellers'.[11]

On 27 November 1893, in the first session of Markham's presidency, John Murray presented a paper on 'The Renewal of Antarctic Exploration' to a packed meeting of the RGS. Murray had served as a biologist on the global oceanographic voyage of HMS *Challenger* in the 1870s. The results of what was probably the greatest research expedition mounted before the twentieth century took twenty years to publish in fifty volumes. Although the crew never sighted Antarctica, geological specimens carried out to sea by glacial movement first proved beyond reasonable doubt the existence of a separate Antarctic continent. Murray examined how a range of disciplines, including botany, geography, meteorology, oceanography, and the study of terrestrial magnetism, would benefit from an Antarctic expedition, concluding that 'the results of a well-organised expedition would be of capital importance to British science'.[12] The nation's premier scientific society and the oldest scientific body in the world, the Royal Society, fully supported Murray's proposal and joined with the RGS in appointing a committee to campaign for a British Antarctic expedition.

Markham predicted that Murray would 'stir up our enthusiasm as geographers and our patriotism as Britons'.[13] A polar expedition that did both could unite the RGS after the recent turmoil. Scientists clamoured for information regarding a continent on which no recorded landing had been made, while the prospect of a Royal Naval expedition appealed to the admirals who had played such a prominent role in the opposition to women fellows.

In November 1911, just a few days after Captain Scott left on his final journey to the South Pole, Clements Markham wrote to Curzon to explain why he had campaigned for a British Antarctic expedition after assuming the presidency in 1893.

> I believed, rightly or wrongly, that the only way to restore the Society's credit was to undertake some great enterprise in the cause of geography. I chose the Antarctic regions. It was a risk, for failure would leave us worse than before. All depended on the leader of the expedition. Scott was selected with great care . . . He secured for our expedition complete success, which to us was so important. For this we owe him an immense debt of gratitude. It restored our credit to us, lost by the mismanagement of the female trouble.[14]

By restoring Clements Markham's influence, and directing the focus of the RGS back to the exploration of unknown lands, the dispute over the admission of women as fellows set in motion the chain of events which would send Scott to the South Pole.

The National Antarctic Expedition, 1901–1904

Although the two leading scientific societies in the land had joined the campaign, the prospects for a British Antarctic expedition were still uncertain. Other nations would take the lead, but Clements Markham's determination never wavered and the expedition which set out in 1901 was, in the words of Markham's biographer, 'the creation of his brain, the product of his persistent energy'.[15]

Markham's commitment came at a price, however. The expedition would carry Markham's prejudices into the Antarctic, most importantly his obsession that the manhauling of sledges was the most noble form of polar travel. The price would be paid, not by Markham, but by those who ventured south.

Markham's campaign received great impetus when the RGS hosted the sixth International Geographical Congress in 1895, with over 1,500 representatives from thirty foreign governments and ninety scientific societies. One of the high points came when Carsten Borchgrevink spoke about his recent voyage on board the whaling ship *Antarctic*. Born in Christiania (Oslo) of a Norwegian father and English mother, Borchgrevink had leapt from the vessel to claim the first confirmed landing on the Antarctic continent at Cape Adare on 24 January 1895.

At the suggestion of the RGS librarian H. R. Mill, the Congress famously passed a unanimous resolution that the exploration of the Antarctic Regions is the greatest piece of geographical exploration still to be undertaken. That, in view of the additions to knowledge in almost every branch of science which would result from such a scientific exploration, the Congress recommends that the scientific societies throughout the world should urge, in whatever way seems to them most effective, that this work should be undertaken before the close of the century.[16]

But the British government remained unmoved. Attempts to exploit Queen Victoria's Diamond Jubilee in 1897 by soliciting pledges from colonial premiers met with limited success. The RGS appealed directly to Lord Salisbury, but the Prime Minister replied that the Society should not expect the government to embark on an undertaking of such magnitude. Markham did persuade the RGS council to pledge £5,000, and received a similar sum from the newspaper magnate Alfred Harmsworth, who had financed Frederick Jackson's recent Arctic expedition. Yet by the end of 1898 Markham had raised only £13,000 towards the £50,000 required.

While Markham was frustrated, others made progress. The Brussels Geographical Society launched a Belgian expedition led by Adrien de Gerlache, which sailed from Antwerp in 1897. The crew, including a young Roald Amundsen, became the first to endure an Antarctic winter on board ship, after their vessel the *Belgica* inadvertently became trapped in pack ice in the Bellinghausen Sea. Harmsworth's great rival George Newnes, publisher of *Tit-bits* and the *Strand Magazine*, dealt a further blow to Markham's hopes by committing £40,000 to his own expedition. The *Southern Cross*, commanded by Borchgrevink, became the first expedition to winter on the Antarctic continent itself in 1899, making camp at Cape Adare. Newnes insisted that the ship sail under a British flag, even though all but three of her crew were Norwegian. Markham viewed Borchgrevink as an unwelcome competitor for public funds and chastised Mill for attending the launch of the *Southern Cross*.

A donation of £25,000 by a wealthy paint manufacturer and RGS fellow, Llewellyn Longstaff, in March 1899 changed everything. Longstaff's pledge prompted renewed approaches to Lord Salisbury and on 3 July the government finally offered £45,000 to the expedition, provided an equal sum was raised by private sponsorship. Salisbury's change of heart was influenced by foreign competition. Two new expeditions had recently been announced, one Swedish, led by Otto Nordenskjöld, to be financed privately, and one German, led by Erich von Drygalski and paid for by the German government. With finance for the dispatch of a single ship secured, Markham commissioned the Dundee Shipbuilders Company to construct a vessel specially designed for Antarctic research, christened the *Discovery*.

The RGS provided £8,000 towards the National Antarctic Expedition (NAE), the Society's largest contribution to any expedition between its foundation in 1830 and the outbreak of the First World War (**Fig. 2.2**). The expedition was the hidden legacy of the Society's expansion in the age of Murchison, Livingstone, and Stanley, and a testament both to Clements Markham's personal obsession and to the unique appeal of Antarctica as a locus of geographical exploration at the turn of the century.

Now, at last, Robert Falcon Scott, a torpedo lieutenant in the Royal Navy, enters our story, to take a leading role in Clements Markham's Antarctic drama. Con, as he was affectionately known, was born in Devon in 1868 to a family with strong naval connections. His mother Hannah was the sister of a naval captain and niece of a vice-admiral, while his grandfather had purchased a

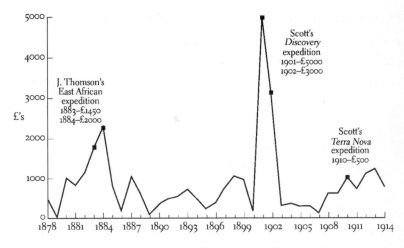

2.2 Royal Geographical Society Expenditure on Expeditions, 1878–1914.

small brewery in Plymouth with prize money earned during the Napoleonic Wars. Hannah and John Scott decided on careers in the armed forces for their two sons, and Con was sent to Foster's Naval Preparatory School at Stubbington House, Fareham. After successfully passing his cadetship exam on his thirteenth birthday, he joined the naval training ship *Britannia*, moored on the River Dart, and rose steadily through the ranks of the Royal Navy.

Financial uncertainty dogged the family through the 1890s, however. John Scott sold his brewery in 1894 and, aged 63 and in poor health, was forced to take a job managing another establishment in Somerset. He died three years later, leaving Hannah Scott and her four daughters, Ettie, Rose, Grace, and Katherine, dependent on Con and his younger brother, Archie. Archie had prospered, serving for a time as private secretary to the Governor of Lagos, Sir Gilbert Carter. When Archie visited Britain in 1898, Con predicted a glittering career for his brother: 'Commissioner, Consul and Governor is the future for him I feel sure.' But a little over a week later, Archie was dead. Having survived the dangers of disease in West Africa, he contracted typhoid fever after playing golf in Kent.

Polar exploration had provided opportunities for ambitious seamen throughout the nineteenth century and the Antarctic offered Lieutenant Scott the prospect of advancement. Clements Markham had seen the young midshipman win a service cutter race off the island of St Kitts in 1887, and he included Scott in his copious notes on promising naval officers. A chance encounter on a London street prompted Scott to apply to lead the NAE. His hopes were swiftly realized when, a month after his appointment on 25 May 1900, he was promoted to Commander.

Disagreements between the Royal Society and the RGS, however, damaged the expedition. J. W. Gregory, head of the geographical department of the British Museum, had been appointed the expedition's scientific director. The Royal Society's representatives proposed that Gregory take command from Scott after the expedition disembarked in the Antarctic. Markham and the RGS representatives, on the other hand, argued that Scott required a completely free hand in making decisions that might effect the safety of his crew. Gregory resigned, protesting that were he to cede command of the shore-party to a naval officer 'there would be no guarantee to prevent the scientific work from being subordinated to naval adventure'.[17] Many polar historians have agreed with Gregory, and argued that his resignation changed the course of polar exploration in Britain. 'Science', in the words of T. H. Baughman, 'was made the handmaiden of adventure.'[18]

Disputes between scientists and seamen had long been a feature of voyages of exploration, but the presentation of scientific research and naval adventure as diametrically opposed objectives is misleading. Markham certainly drew his principal inspiration from the Royal Naval Arctic expeditions of Franklin, McClintock, and Nares.

Throughout his life, he consistently argued that polar exploration offered the 'true and best work for the navy in times of peace'.[19] But if Markham had solely been interested in naval adventure, why did he not recreate the expeditions he so admired by mounting an attempt on the North Pole? The answer lay in the relative scientific benefits of Arctic and Antarctic exploration.

In 1894 Markham observed that the RGS council 'has always consistently maintained that merely to reach the North Pole, or to attain a higher latitude than someone else, were objects unworthy of support. In our view, the objects of Arctic exploration are to secure useful scientific research'. Between 1893 and 1896, Fridtjof Nansen's famous drift on board the *Fram* had proved that the North Pole was located on neither an open sea nor a stable cap of ice, but on a shifting changeable pack. When he realized the *Fram* would not drift across the Pole itself, Nansen set out from the ship with Hjalmar Johansen, setting a new record farthest north of 86° 10' N, 230 miles from the Pole. The RGS council honoured Nansen by hiring the Royal Albert Hall and minting a special medal for only the second time in its history. Markham subsequently declared that, although the North Pole had still to be reached, the 'whole problem of Arctic geography has now been solved. There are many isolated pieces of work that I should like to see undertaken . . . But there are none which would justify the dispatch of an expedition on a large scale.'[20] An expedition to Antarctica, on the other hand, proved so attractive because it offered the opportunity to *combine* scientific research, heroic endeavour, and imperial theatre.

The dispute over the leadership and objectives of the NAE was a contest for authority between two competing institutions, not a simple choice between science and adventure, but a dispute over the appropriate balance of the expedition's myriad aims. While Markham and the RGS were determined that the Royal Navy should take the lead, the Royal Society sought both to subordinate naval officers to the authority of scientists, and to relegate surveying to an inferior status beneath analytical forms of knowledge. Gregory's resignation marked a victory for the tenacious Markham, ensuring that scientific research and heroic adventure would both be pursued in the Antarctic.

Five scientists were appointed to winter in the south: the physicist, Louis Bernacchi; geologist, Hartley Ferrar; biologist, Thomas Hodgson; surgeon and botanist, Reginald Koettlitz; and surgeon and zoologist, Edward Wilson. George Murray, head of the botanical department of the British Museum, replaced Gregory as scientific director, but agreed to travel with the *Discovery* only as far as Melbourne. Following the practice adopted before the Nares Arctic expedition, Markham initiated the production of an *Antarctic Manual*, a customized *Hints to Travellers* for the crew of the *Discovery*. Edited by Murray, the *Manual* included instructions on tidal, wave, ice, and pendulum observations, on terrestrial magnetism, climate, the aurora, atmospheric electricity, geology, volcanic action, rock collecting, and botany.

The *Discovery* sailed from East India Docks at noon on 31 July 1901. The 'Instructions' signed by the Presidents of the RGS and the Royal Society placed Scott in full command of all aspects of the expedition, which was intended 'for scientific discovery and exploration'.

> The objects of the expedition are (a) to determine, as far as possible, the nature, condition and extent of that portion of the south polar lands which is included in the scope of your expedition; and (b) to make a magnetic survey in the southern regions to the south of the 40th parallel, and to carry on meteorological, oceanographic, geological, biological, and physical investigations and researches. Neither of these objects is to be sacrificed to the other.[21]

This combination of a detailed survey of an unknown region, with observations in a range of fields, articulated the familiar pattern promoted by the RGS from the late 1870s.

Before leaving British waters, the *Discovery* stopped over at the royal regatta at Cowes. The new king, Edward VII, declared that he had 'often visited ships in order to say farewell when departing on warlike service; but you are starting on a mission of peace, and for the advance of knowledge. The results of your labours will be valuable not only to your country, but to the whole civilised world.'[22]

The expedition spent two winters in the Antarctic between January 1902 and February 1904. Sailing farther east along the Great Ice Barrier than any previous vessel, the expedition sighted a vast new land which was named after King Edward VII. Working from the tables in *Hints to Travellers*, the explorers conducted nearly thirty sledge journeys, charting the range of mountains sighted by Ross in Victoria Land as far south as the 83rd parallel.[23] Observations were collected in a variety of fields, including two years' continuous meteorological and magnetic records. One seaman, George Vince, died during an abortive mission led by Charles Royds to leave messages for a relief ship at Cape Crozier.

The expedition's most newsworthy achievement was a new 'farthest south' record of 82° 17′ S, 480 miles from the Pole, by a sledging party of Commander Scott, Lieutenant Ernest Shackleton, and Dr Edward Wilson. Christian faith was at the core of Edward Wilson's being. He worshipped God by observing the natural world, in the tradition of Turner and Ruskin. After reading Natural Sciences at Cambridge, Wilson moved to London to study medicine. He had been weakened by a bout of tuberculosis contracted while working for a Cambridge mission in Battersea, but his uncle, Major-General Sir Charles Wilson of the Royal Engineers, wrote directly to Clements Markham to secure his nephew's appointment.

Wilson secured the respect of his peers through his patience, empathy, and selflessness, complementing Scott's aloof leadership.

If Scott sailed south to advance his career and Wilson to observe the wonders of God's creation, then Ernest Shackleton sought fame and adventure. His Anglo-Irish father, Henry, had sold the family land on the outskirts of Dublin and moved to London in 1884. Henry would have preferred his son to read medicine, but Ernest was eager to live, not study. Like so many Victorian school-boys, he became entranced by the prospect of a life at sea. When Shackleton left Dulwich College in 1890, his father sent him to work on the sailing ship *Hoghton Tower*, hoping to cure the adolescent romantic of his predilection for maritime adventure. Relishing his freedom, Shackleton spent ten years in the merchant marine, serving on the troop ship *Tintagel Castle* during the South African War. Stirred by the camaraderie of the soldiers and bored with the routines of the merchant fleet, the restless dreamer applied to join the NAE.

Scott, Shackleton, and Wilson initially harboured ambitions of reaching the Pole, but struggled to gain the 82nd parallel, covering 960 miles in ninety-three days. In retrospect, the party appears appallingly ill-prepared. Equipment and provisions proved woefully inadequate, and all three developed symptoms of scurvy. Wilson suffered badly from snow blindness from unwise sketching. The three men took dogs and skis, but showed little competence in the use of either. None was an accomplished skier. Nineteen dogs were harnessed in a single trace to five awkwardly loaded sledges. Suffering from deficient food and poor handling, the dogs died, forcing the British explorers to manhaul their sledges. Supply depots were placed too far apart and to eke out their meagre provision on their return, the explorers reduced their lunch to a biscuit and a half, eight lumps of sugar, and a piece of seal meat. Shackleton suffered most, unable to haul and occasionally sitting on the sledge to act as a brake. They were fortunate to survive, but had at least succeeded in travelling over 300 miles further south than anyone before them, furnishing the expedition with a suitably sensational headline.

Almost as soon as the *Discovery* had sailed, Markham began to campaign for funds to finance a relief ship. But he had failed to include the costs of relief in his original estimates and an angry Prime Minister, Arthur Balfour, refused to contribute. The relentless Markham raised £22,600 to equip the Norwegian whaler *Morning*, which relieved the ice-bound *Discovery* in early December 1902. A further £15,000 was needed to equip the *Morning* to return the following year, however, and Markham kept up the pressure, declaring that the government was directly responsible for the crew.

Markham eventually persuaded the President of the Royal Society, Sir William Huggins, to participate in a joint approach to the government in May 1903. An outraged Balfour finally agreed to intervene, but castigated the mismanagement of the expedition, declaring in the House of Commons that governments could only support scientific societies if they had absolute confidence in the estimated costs. 'That confidence', Balfour ominously declared, 'has been rudely shaken by the present case.'[24] The officers of the Royal Society swiftly arranged a meeting with Balfour, placing the blame squarely on Markham and the RGS.

The government assumed control of relief operations, humiliating the RGS by insisting that ownership of the *Morning* be transferred to the Admiralty. The Admiralty purchased a Dundee whaling ship, the *Terra Nova*, skippered by the highly experienced Captain Harry McKay. The *Morning* and *Terra Nova* reached the *Discovery* on 5 January 1904, carrying orders for Scott to abandon ship if he could not release the *Discovery* by the end of February. After an anxious wait, during which charges and ice-breaking manœuvres co-ordinated by McKay broke up the ice, the *Discovery* was finally freed on 14 February 1904 and Scott was able to sail back to Britain.[25]

Science and Adventure

The expedition was hailed as a success after the *Discovery* entered Stokes Bay, near Southsea, at 11.00 a.m. on 10 September 1904. The *Pall Mall Gazette* declared the NAE had done 'exceedingly well in the cause of science', while *The Times* opined that the expedition 'has been one of the most successful that ever ventured into the Polar regions, north or south'.[26] Scott was promoted to Captain and invited to Balmoral to lecture to an audience that included King Edward and Queen Alexandra, and the Prince and Princess of Wales.

On 7 November Scott followed Stanley and Nansen in lecturing to the fellows of the RGS from the stage of the Royal Albert Hall. He then embarked on a national lecture tour, passing through Manchester, Newcastle, Middlesbrough, and Edinburgh, where 2,300 people packed the Synod Hall to hear him speak. An exhibition at the Bruton galleries in Bond Street attracted such crowds, reported the *Daily Express*, 'that it was necessary to close the doors a quarter of an hour before the opening . . . Hundreds drove away. The proprietor of the galleries estimated the number of persons who came to the door at 10,000'.[27]

Scott took leave to write an account of the expedition for Smith, Elder. *The Voyage of the Discovery*, published on 12 October 1905, was a hit, exhausting its first edition before Christmas, and eventually selling around 3,500 copies. The *Spectator* proclaimed the book 'the ablest and most interesting record of travel to which the present century has yet given birth'.[28]

The NAE encapsulated the vision of exploration as a tripartite process of measurement promoted by Clements Markham since the 1870s: measuring the world, measuring manliness, and measuring empire. In the absence of either native peoples or natural resources to exploit, the NAE should be distinguished from the African expeditions of Livingstone and Stanley, not so much an imperialist enterprise, but, rather, the expression of an imperial nation. The *Discovery* marked out the boundaries of empire, sailing down an imperial corridor via South Africa and New Zealand to reach the Antarctic, while the raising of the flag at the southernmost point yet reached on earth offered a compelling emblem of the extent of British power.

The measurement of empire tested the manliness of the explorers and several commentators emphasized how they had endured hardship in the cause of scientific research. *The Times* hailed the 'example of "grit" and self-sacrifice in the service of science shown by Captain Scott and his companions'. At a reception in London's Criterion restaurant, Scott himself praised 'Mr. Hodgson, staggering in with his arms full of frozen specimens, and distributing them over the ward-room table; [and] Mr. Royds, who had every morning to change his records with frost-bitten fingers'.[29]

The NAE did indeed make a contribution to contemporary knowledge about Antarctica. The expedition surveyed large portions of unknown territory, and demonstrated that the Great Ice Barrier was a floating ice shelf. A journey along the Ferrar Glacier led to the discovery of the Taylor Valley, the first of the snow-free oases unique to Antarctica, which have featured prominently in recent research.

The expedition was the first to discover a nesting colony of the emperor penguin, and Wilson composed a groundbreaking study of the life-cycle of this most mysterious Antarctic native.

The expedition also gathered detailed observations of natural phenomena and vast collections of samples. In the absence of funds to employ the crew to work up the results, however, the records were handed over to other experts through the Royal Society and British Museum, and published in a series of volumes between 1907 and 1913. Criticisms were voiced in some quarters. Gregory predictably complained about the paucity of oceanographic data, a snipe at Scott's decision to allow the *Discovery* to winter in the Antarctic. Dr Napier Shaw, director of the Meteorological Office, was highly critical of the meteorological results, complaining about the lack of training of certain individuals. Scott was indignant, as Shaw had made no effort to contact the crew members involved to clarify their findings. David Yelverton's recent study has defended the expedition's record, highlighting errors in Shaw's own report.[30] Shaw's criticisms marked the revenge of the scientific establishment on the decision to appoint a naval officer ahead of his friend Gregory.

The claim that the NAE returned with 'the richest results, geo-graphical and scientific ever brought from high southern latitudes', should certainly be treated with caution, as the expeditions of William Bruce, Jean Charcot, Otto Nordenskjöld and Erich von Drygalski, also produced a wealth of information about Antarctica.[31] But the proposition that Scott's appointment marked the triumph of adventurers over scientists cannot be sustained. The historian of Antarctic science, G. E. Fogg, has argued that Gregory's appoint-ment would not have guaranteed higher scientific standards. Scott was consistently praised by his colleagues, both for facilitating their research and for his own scientific understanding.[32]

Ironically, Clements Markham's influence ultimately hindered geographical exploration more than scientific research. Markham's romantic attachment to Victorian methods prejudiced the British against the use of dogs and skis. Markham hailed the manhauling of sledges as the noblest form of polar travel, praising the NAE for achieving 'excellent results mainly without the aid of dogs; by sheer hard work, by a strong sense of duty, and by that indomitable pluck which has ever characterised the British sailor.' In a widely quoted passage from *The Voyage of the Discovery*, Scott concurred that the use of dogs

> must and does rob sledge-travelling of much of its glory. In my mind no journey ever made with dogs can approach the height of that fine conception which is realised when a party of men go forth to face hardships, dangers, and difficulties with their own unaided efforts, and by days and weeks of hard physical labour succeed in solving some problem of the great unknown. Surely in this case the conquest is more nobly and splendidly won.[33]

But the voyage of the *Discovery* heralded not the domination, but the demise of Royal Naval involvement in polar exploration. The NAE was the last great naval expedition in the tradition of Franklin and Nares. Sir John Fisher, whose reforms would transform the Royal Navy, had little interest in polar exploration. Scott used his personal contacts to ensure a strong naval presence on his last expedition, but the Admiralty allowed only one officer to join Shackleton's Imperial Trans-Antarctic Expedition in 1914. Never again would the provision of opportunities for officers 'to perform deeds of derring do' be cited as the principal motive of a polar expedition. Scott did not mention the value of polar exploration as training for the Royal Navy in either the prospectus for his last expedition, or his speech to the RGS setting out his plans.

Scott's endeavours brought promotion, medals, membership of

the French Légion d'honneur and appointment as a Commander of the Royal Victorian Order. But Balfour had his revenge by denying the expedition any government recognition. In 1940 Sir Richard Gregory, editor of *Nature* and President of the BAAS, expressed his dismay at the absence of official recognition: 'I have no doubt it was the attitude of the Royal Society and Balfour that was the cause. The injustice was an insult to science and to human achievement, and an example of an indifference unworthy of an enlightened people.'[34]

Thirty five years earlier, a guest at a reception for the crew had written to the *Daily Mail* to call for some national acknowledgement of the expedition's achievements. 'Had the ship's crew perished in the Antarctic,' the correspondent suggested, 'we doubtless should have raised a national memorial to them. It seems to be a pity that we should suffer their deeds to pass to oblivion because they have returned safe and sound.'[35] Such observations would prove prescient.

Preparing to Return

Scott still harboured Antarctic ambitions when he returned to the sea in August 1906 as flag-captain to Rear-Admiral Sir George Egerton. On shore he courted a cosmopolitan sculptor, Kathleen Bruce, who had trained with Auguste Rodin in Paris. Kathleen was a remarkable woman, charismatic, talented, and possibly unique in including both the infamous magus Aleister Crowley and the Liberal Prime Minister Herbert Asquith among her numerous admirers. Kathleen chose Scott over a rival suitor, the tempestuous writer Gilbert Cannan, and the couple were married at the Chapel Royal, Hampton Court Palace, on 2 September 1908. Cannan was later institutionalized, suffering from delusions which included the belief that he was the famous British explorer, Captain Scott.

Six months later news reached London that Ernest Shackleton had led an expedition to within a hundred miles of the South Pole, before being forced to turn back due to lack of provisions. Explaining his decision to return when so tantalizingly close to his goal, Shackleton told his wife Emily that 'a live donkey is better than a dead lion, isn't it?' Press and public lavished praise on Shackleton through the summer of 1909. 'What they honour,' declared the *Daily Graphic*, 'is the indomitable spirit of the man who strove with amazing pluck and resourcefulness to do what no other man had done before'.[36]

Shackleton's expedition had been largely financed by the ship-builder William Beardmore. Influenced by Markham's loyalty to Scott, the RGS had offered him little encouragement, contributing only the loan of three chronometers. Yet, mindful of the need to cultivate explorer heroes, the Society embraced Shackleton on his return and he followed Stanley, Nansen, and Scott as only the fourth explorer to address the RGS in the Royal Albert Hall. Keltie later observed that the Society had 'rather cold-shouldered it [Shackleton's expedition], but I think it is desirable that the Society should have a direct interest in every great expedition similar to this'.[37]

Shackleton's spectacular and largely unexpected success earned him a knighthood and stung Scott into action. The relationship between the two men had deteriorated since the voyage of the *Discovery*. Scott had requested that Shackleton not disembark in McMurdo Sound, leaving the area free for his own future expedition. But adverse weather conditions forced an extremely reluctant Shackleton to go back on his word, directing his ship *Nimrod* into McMurdo Sound and making camp near the *Discovery*'s old base.

In September 1909, Scott wrote to the RGS President, Major Leonard Darwin, to outline his proposal for a new expedition. The Society's officers had already expressed their disapproval of any expedition whose sole objective was to reach the Pole. Scott emphasized that, in addition to the attainment of the Pole, his plan provided 'for the scientific exploration of a considerable extent of the Antarctic continent and will therefore I hope commend itself to the Royal Geographical Society'.[38] Scott's second Antarctic expedition was formally announced on 13 September 1909. The following day Kathleen Scott gave birth to a boy, who was named Peter after J. M. Barrie's *Peter Pan*.

Scott outlined his expedition's objectives at a meeting of the RGS.[39] In a riposte to those who saw no value in polar exploration, Scott declared

> that the effort to reach a spot on the surface of the globe which has hitherto been untrodden by human feet, unseen by human eyes, is in itself laudable; and when the spot has been associated for so long a time with the imaginative ambitions of the civilized world, and when it possesses such a unique geographical position as a pole of the Earth, there is something more than mere sentiment, something more than an appeal to our sporting instinct in its attainment; it appeals to our national pride and the maintenance of great traditions, and its quest becomes an outward visible sign that we are still a nation able and willing to undertake difficult enterprises, still capable of standing in the van of the army of progress.

From the outset, then, Scott raised the conquest of the South Pole as the expedition's primary aim.

Yet crucially Scott went on to argue that it was the

> plain duty for the explorer to bring back something more than a bare account of his movements; he must bring back every

possible observation of the conditions under which his journey has been made. He must take every advantage of his unique position and opportunities to study natural phenomena, and to add to the edifice of knowledge those stones which can be quarried only in the regions he visits . . .

I have arranged for a scientific staff larger than that which has been carried by any previous expedition, and for a very extensive outfit of scientific instruments and impedimenta . . . to achieve the greatest possible scientific harvest which the circumstances permit.

Although an independent venture, Scott's last expedition bore the imprint of the template forged by the RGS after the death of Dr Livingstone, as Scott planned to reap a scientific harvest while engaged on a heroic quest in the service of the nation.

The execution of a carefully planned research programme was an integral part of the expedition. Edward Wilson explained to his father that we 'want the Scientific work to make the bagging of the Pole merely an item in the results'.[40] The meteorologist George Simpson, physicist Charles Wright, biologists Dennis Lillie and Edward Nelson, and geologists Frank Debenham, Raymond Priestley, and Thomas Griffith Taylor, shared Wilson's perspective. All were professional scientists, who had staked their careers on the integrity of the expedition.[41]

The RGS had benefited from Clements Markham's passion for polar exploration. The Society's fellowship rose by over 1,000 during his presidency to reach 4,500 in 1905, and had passed 5,000 by 1914. Yet the extravagant expenditure on the *Discovery* and the relief-ship debacle damaged both the Society's reputation and finances. After Markham's retirement, the imperial administrator George Taubman Goldie presided over a period of retrenchment and careful diplomacy, which was continued by his successor, Leonard Darwin.

Scott's second expedition was awarded £500, the largest grant of the period, yet only a fraction of the sum given to the NAE. A subscription list circulated among the Society's fellows raised an additional £1,130, but Scott would have difficulty raising the £40,000 necessary to finance an expedition.[42]

A lecture tour failed to attract substantial donations and several periodicals printed letters attacking the expedition. 'Everything of value concerning life in low temperatures has already been discovered', insisted *Vanity Fair,* 'and the search for the Pole itself is utterly profitless.' Scott's second-in-command, the Royal Naval Lieutenant E.R.G.R. 'Teddy' Evans, who was persuaded to shelve his own plans for a Welsh Antarctic expedition and join forces with Scott, believed 'we should never have collected our expeditionary funds from the scientific point of view'.[43] The largest single donation, from the city financier Edgar Speyer, came to only £1,000. In the absence of a Longstaff or a Beardmore, Evans's more aggressive approach, appealing to patriotism and civic pride, proved invaluable. The citizens of Bristol contributed £750, of Manchester and Liverpool £2,000 each, and of Cardiff both £2,500 and numerous free supplies, thanks largely to Teddy Evans.

Commercial sponsorship and media rights also generated essential revenue. Many of the most famous names in British industry donated supplies, including Colman's mustard, Fry's chocolate, and Huntley & Palmer's biscuits. Scott hired a photographer of international renown, Herbert Ponting, and signed an agreement with the Gaumont Company, which ran the most extensive film-hiring operation in Britain, to distribute films of the expedition. Schools proved among the most enthusiastic donors, with over a hundred contributing either £5. 12s. 6d. for one sledge, £5 for one pony, £3. 3s. for one dog, or £2 for one sleeping bag.

Between 6,000 and 8,000 men applied for posts on the expedition, indicating the hold of the great white south over the popular imagination.[44] Those selected included Petty Officer Edgar 'Taff' Evans, a veteran of the *Discovery*, and Lieutenant Henry 'Birdie' Bowers, an indefatigable Royal Indian Marine. Two men purchased their places by matching Speyer's contribution: a young landowner, Apsley Cherry-Garrard, and Captain Lawrence 'Titus' Oates of the 6th Inniskilling Dragoons, who had seen action in the South African War.

The Liberal government eventually announced a grant of £20,000, matching the sum awarded to Shackleton. With the *Discovery* unavailable, Scott purchased the old whaling ship *Terra Nova*, which had relieved the NAE in 1904. By the summer of 1910 the campaign had raised a further £14,000, enough to underwrite the launch.

On 31 May the RGS entertained the officers of Scott's last expedition to lunch at the King's Hall restaurant, Holborn. The president, Major Darwin, proposed the toast to Captain Scott and his gallant companions:

> they mean to do or die – that is the spirit in which they are going to the Antarctic . . . I have not the slightest doubt that a rich harvest of facts will be reaped . . . Captain Scott is going to prove once again that the manhood of the nation is not dead, and that the characteristics of our ancestors, who won this great empire, still flourish amongst us; and although we, who stay at home, have no right to share in a particle of the glory, yet the self-respect of the whole nation is certainly increased by such adventure as this.[45]

Darwin's speech articulated the tripartite process of measurement on which the expedition was engaged, gathering a scientific harvest, displaying the vitality of the empire, and testing the manhood of the crew.

Scott's Last Expedition

The *Terra Nova* set sail from Cardiff on 15 June 1910, in honour of the city's contribution to the expedition. Scott continued to campaign for funds as the ship headed south, raising money in South Africa, New Zealand, and Australia. But in Melbourne he received a fateful telegram: 'Beg leave to inform you *Fram* proceeding Antarctic. Amundsen.' At a stroke, Scott's hopes for priority at the Pole were placed under serious threat. He now faced a formidable rival: Roald Amundsen.

Born near Christiania on 16 June 1872, Amundsen first sailed to the Antarctic as second mate on the *Belgica*. He established his reputation as one of the most accomplished explorers of the age between 1903 and 1906, when he led the first complete expedition through the North-West Passage on board the 47-ton sloop *Gjøa*. Amundsen honed his skills as a polar traveller during the passage, learning much about equipment and the driving of dog-sledges from native Inuits. After his return, Amundsen secured Nansen's famous ship *Fram* for an Arctic expedition, but, when Frederick Cook and Robert Peary both claimed to have reached the North Pole in September 1909, the Norwegian turned his attention south.

Amundsen appears to have taken the decision just before Scott announced his new expedition, but still concealed his plans from almost everybody, concerned that opponents would prevent his departure. In March 1910 Scott telephoned a hotel in Christiania, eager to discuss his plans with the respected Norwegian. Anxious not to lie directly to Scott, Amundsen instructed the concierge to apologize that he was unavailable. Later in the month, Scott travelled to Norway to test the motor sledges he hoped would win him the Pole. He discussed his plans with Nansen, who was also unaware of Amundsen's volte-face. But when Scott travelled to Amundsen's house at Bundefjord, the Norwegian simply disappeared. Gustav Amundsen told Scott that his brother had been informed that he wished to speak to him, but the Norwegian explorer failed to return. Scott waited for an hour and left.[46] Amundsen's duplicity would come back to haunt him.

The *Terra Nova* finally reached the Antarctic in January 1911, with a shore-party of thirty-three men, comprising seven officers (five from the Royal Navy), a scientific staff of twelve, twelve naval seamen, and two young Russian animal handlers.[47] Seventeen ponies, thirty dogs, and two tracked motor sledges were disembarked in delightfully sunny weather. A third motor sledge crashed through the ice and sank to the bottom of McMurdo Sound.

The attempt to reach the Pole was part of an extensive programme of scientific experiments and explorations. From the base camp hut erected at Cape Evans, the scientific staff conducted investigations in a wide range of fields, including pioneering meteorological research co-ordinated by George Simpson. Griffith Taylor also led a small group on a geological survey of Victoria Land's mountains and glaciers.

The *Terra Nova* left Cape Evans to carry a party of six, led by Victor Campbell, east to explore the coast of King Edward VII land. En route, however, the ship encountered Amundsen's *Fram* in the Bay of Whales and the two crews exchanged hospitality in strained circumstances. Amundsen had gambled on making camp directly on the Great Ice Barrier, 60 miles closer to the Pole than Scott. The Norwegians had brought 110 dogs to the Antarctic and Amundsen staged a formidable display of dog-driving, impressing the British. With individual cabins for its crew of nineteen, the *Fram* had also provided far more comfortable accommodation on the journey south than the sixty-five men on the *Terra Nova* had enjoyed: 'mustard' had always been plentiful on the seamen's mess table, which was located directly below the pony stalls. Relieved that the *Terra Nova* did not carry a wireless enabling the British to communicate any news first, Amundsen was, however, increasingly concerned that Scott's motor sledges would rob him of success.

With Campbell unwilling to make camp near the Norwegians, the *Terra Nova* returned to Cape Evans, confirming Amundsen's presence to Scott. Campbell's party chose now to explore to the north. Deteriorating conditions forced the *Terra Nova* to deposit the six men at Cape Adare, where Carsten Borchgrevink had spent the first Antarctic winter a decade earlier. The ship then sailed back to New Zealand for refitting, carrying the first reels of Herbert Ponting's film. The *Terra Nova* would return to Cape Evans in January 1912, in the hope of receiving news of Scott's triumph.

The attainment of the Pole lay at the symbolic heart of the British expedition and the summer months, from January to April 1911, were occupied with the laying of depots. Sledge parties established supplies of fuel and provisions roughly every 80 miles along the route to the Pole. Scott proposed to follow Shackleton's path, ascending the perilous terrain of the glacier which Shackleton had discovered and named after William Beardmore, to reach the summit plateau. The journey can be divided into three stages: first, 425 miles over the Great Ice Barrier; second, 125 miles up through the Beardmore Glacier, rising to a height of 8,000 feet above sea level; and finally about 350 miles along the summit plateau to the geographical South Pole itself, at a continuous altitude of between 9,000 and 10,500 feet.

Scott had learned some important lessons. The men used green-tinted goggles to combat snow-blindness. Scott had also realized that skis were essential for efficient polar travel and included a Norwegian ski expert introduced to him by Nansen, Tryggve Gran, to train the crew. Scott planned to deploy a mixture of ponies, dogs,

CAPTAIN SCOTT'S TOMB NEAR THE SOUTH POLE.

The Daily Mirror 24 Pages

THE MORNING JOURNAL WITH THE SECOND LARGEST NET SALE.

No. 2,987. | Registered at the G.P.O. as a Newspaper. | WEDNESDAY, MAY 21, 1913 | One Halfpenny.

 THE MOST WONDERFUL MONUMENT IN THE WORLD: CAPTAIN SCOTT'S SEPULCHRE ERECTED AMID ANTARCTIC WASTES.

 It was within a mere eleven miles of One Ton camp, which would have meant safety to the Antarctic explorers, that the search party found the tent containing the bodies of Captain Scott, Dr. E. A. Wilson and Lieutenant H. R. Bowers. This is, perhaps, the most tragic note of the whole Antarctic disaster. Above is the cairn, surmounted with a cross, erected over the tent where the bodies were found. At the side are Captain Scott's skis planted upright in a small pile of frozen snow.—(Copyright in England. Droits de reproduction en France reservées.)

1. Captain Scott's tomb. This photograph of the cairn which the search party built over the bodies of Scott, Bowers, and Wilson was first published on the front page of a special memorial edition of the *Daily Mirror* on 21 May 1913. The edition was one of the best-selling issues of any daily newpaper published in Britain before the First World War.

2. Motor sledge. Seaman William Lashly, engineer Bernard Day, Lt. Teddy Evans and steward Frederick Hooper (l. to r.) stand in front of a motor sledge flying a heraldic banner. While engine problems proved an insurmountable obstacle, the new caterpillar tracks were highly successful and Scott's motor sledges pointed the way towards the development of the tank during the First World War. (TOP LEFT)

3. David Livingstone's coffin. Livingstone's body rested in a coffin of English oak in the Map Room of the Royal Geographical Society before his burial in Westminster Abbey in April 1874. Jacob Wainwright was the only African to attend the funeral service. He had served the explorer for barely a year, but had been a pupil at a Church Missionary Society school, and the CMS paid his passage to England to raise publicity. (BOTTOM LEFT)

4. *Sir Clements Markham* (1913). George Henry's portrait of Captain Scott's principal patron, shows Clements Markham beside a painting of the Cinchona plant which Markham introduced to India, and a silver statuette, which Markham was given by the officers of the *Discovery* and *Morning* in 1904. The statuette shows a man pulling a sledge. (ABOVE)

5. The polar martyrs. The death of Sir John Franklin in 1847 during his voyage in search of the North-West Passage provided a frequent reference point for reports about Scott's last expedition. (LEFT)

6. Shackleton, Scott, and Wilson (l. to r.) set out for the Pole, November 1902. Clements Markham designed heraldic sledge flags for the officers of the National Antarctic Expedition, 1901–4. The *Discovery* expedition would be seriously hampered by Markham's attachment to nineteenth-century methods. (BELOW)

ST. JAMES'S HALL,

PICCADILLY.

The Lecture Agency, Ltd., begs to announce that

Captain SCOTT, R.N.

COMMANDER OF THE

British Antarctic Expedition,

WILL GIVE HIS

FIRST PUBLIC LECTURE

ENTITLED—

"FARTHEST

SOUTH,"

ON

Tuesday, November 8th,

AT 8.30

The Lecture will be copiously illustrated by photographs taken by the Expedition, and shown on the screen by the oxy-hydrogen light.

The chair will be taken at 8.30 by the

Rt. Hon. Sir GEORGE T. GOLDIE,
K.C.M.G.

CARRIAGES AT 10.30.

Photo by Messrs. Thomson, 141 New Bond Street, W.

Platform, 21/-; Sofa Stalls and First Row of Balcony, 10/6; Reserved Balcony and Area, 5/-; Unreserved Balcony and Area, 2/6; Gallery, 1/-

Tickets from Whitehead's Box-Office, St. James's Hall; Chappell & Co., Ltd., 50 New Bond Street, and Box-Office, Queen's Hall; Ashton, 38 Old Bond Street, 35 Sloane Street, S.W., and 34 Lime Street, E.C.; Alfred Hays, 4 Royal Exchange Buildings, E.C., and 25 Old Bond Street, W.; Keith, Prowse & Co., 48 Cheapside, E.C., and all branches; Mitchell, 33 Old Bond Street, W., 16 Gloucester Road, S.W., and 5 Leadenhall Street, E.C.; Cecil Roy, 15 Sussex Place, South Kensington; Webster & Waddington, 304 Regent Street; Lacon & Ollier, 168 New Bond Street; and of

THE LECTURE AGENCY, Ltd., The Outer Temple, Strand.

Telegrams: "Lecturing, London." Telephone: 2899 Gerrard.

7. Captain Scott's 'Farthest South'. Scott embarked on an extensive national lecture tour following the return of the *Discovery* in 1904. The London lecture advertised in this poster was chaired by Sir George Taubman Goldie, the 'founder of Nigeria', who succeeded Clements Markham as President of the Royal Geographical Society in 1905.

8. The Dishcover Minstrel Troupe. The crew carried the cultural practices of an imperial nation to the Antarctic. Theatrical shows proved popular, and 6 August 1902 witnessed a performance of the 'Dishcover Minstrel Troupe' at the Royal Terror Theatre, surely the most southerly minstrel show ever. (ABOVE)

9. Wolsey underwear in the Antarctic. Many well known firms sponsored polar expeditions, and used them in their advertising. The demanding Antarctic environment proved particularly attractive to food and clothing manufacturers, from Shippams' potted meats to Jaeger boots. Extensive media coverage of expeditions inevitably generated widespread exposure for products. (LEFT)

10. Advertisement for 'Shell' Motor Spirit. Scott's experiments with motor sledges projected the image of an expedition at the forefront of modern technology. (TOP)

11. The *Terra Nova* sails south. A heavily laden *Terra Nova* departed Port Chalmers, New Zealand, for the Antarctic on 29 November 1910. Thirty dogs brought from Siberia by Cecil Meares were berthed on deck.

12. The Tenements. Apsley Cherry-Garrard, Henry Bowers, Lawrence Oates, Cecil Meares (top), and Edward Atkinson (bottom) (l. to r.) in the hut at Cape Evans. (ABOVE)

13. 'Capt. Scott, R.N., Has Reached The South Pole!!'. The Gaumont Company predicted massive demand for Herbert Ponting's film of the *Terra Nova* expedition, when news arrived in London that Scott had reached the South Pole. Amundsen would cable news of his victory in the race for the Pole around the world two months later. (LEFT)

and motor sledges to reach the Pole. A Russian dog-driver, Dimitri Gerof, accompanied the expedition, but none of the crew mastered the difficult skill of dog-driving as effectively as the Norwegians. Influenced by Shackleton, Scott placed more faith in ponies than dogs, but the ponies which Cecil Meares had purchased for the expedition in Siberia were in poor condition The beasts on which so much depended caused continual anxiety to the moody Scott, and, in spite of the cavalry officer Oates's strenuous efforts, a number died before the southern journey assault had even begun. Assessing the expedition's prospects of reaching the Pole, Oates considered that the Norwegians 'have a jolly good chance of getting there if their dogs are good and they use them properly . . . with the rubbish we have it will be jolly difficult and means a lot of hard work'.[48]

Scott, though, doubted whether dogs or ponies, let alone motor sledges, would be of much help during the ascent of the Beardmore Glacier. Ponies might make some headway, but he considered the terrain simply too tortuous for the effective use of dog-teams. He believed that for a considerable portion of the march, the explorers would have no option but to haul their own sledges, not because it was more noble, but because there was no other way.

On 23 April the sun rose for the last time before the onset of the Antarctic winter. Darkness and extreme cold confined the crew to the environs of their hut for the next four months. Officers and men passed the time with scientific research, preparations for the southern journey, gramophone records, slide shows, reading, smoking, cards, chess, football games in the half-light, and even the printing of a newspaper, the South Polar Times, a light-hearted collection of articles, poems, and sketches, which proved the highlight of celebrations on Midwinter Day. Such activities foreshadowed the vibrant trench culture which, it has been argued, helped sustain the British army during the First World War.[49]

Most notably, Wilson persuaded Scott to allow him, Bowers, and Cherry-Garrard to undertake the first sledge journey ever attempted during an Antarctic winter, to the emperor penguin rookery at Cape Crozier he had located on the *Discovery* expedition. The three men dragged themselves back to Cape Evans at the beginning of August, after five weeks of the worst sledging conditions any man had yet endured. At one point the temperature fell to an unimaginable −77.5°F. 'This journey had beggared our language,' Cherry-Garrard later wrote, 'no words could express its horror.' But, in less than two months, Bowers, Cherry-Garrard, and Wilson would don their harness once again. The prize for their suffering was three emperor penguin eggs.

Intensive preparations for the southern journey occupied September and October, as the sun slowly returned in the spring. Scott, though, feared departing too early, as harsh weather would further debilitate the ponies. An advance party of four, led by Teddy Evans, started with the motor sledges in the last week of October, to carry supplies as close to the Beardmore as possible. Finally, an initial party of ten men and ten ponies set out for the Pole a week later, on 1 November 1911. 'The future is in the lap of the gods', Scott wrote the night before departure. 'I can think of nothing left undone to deserve success.' However, he forgot to take with him the Union Flag presented by Queen Alexandra for the Pole. Fortunately, he was able to use a telephone connection between the *Discovery*'s old winter quarters at Hut Point and the base at Cape Evans, to ask Tryggve Gran to bring the flag up to the southern party. As Scott waited at Hut Point for a Norwegian to retrieve his country's flag, the five men, four sledges, and forty-eight dogs of Gran's compatriots had already been heading south for almost two weeks.

Back in London at this time, Kathleen Scott was adding another Norwegian, Fridtjof Nansen, to her impressive roll-call of male admirers. Kathleen attended Nansen's first London lecture on the Norse discovery of America, and the pair met regularly until he left England. Nansen invited Kathleen to a book launch in Germany, and the two spent a week together in the same Berlin hotel. Nansen was smitten. 'I lived away from the world for so long now, that I fall in love so easily', he confessed in a string of letters. 'The only star I see now is you'. That Nansen was married and also had a mistress at this time indicates the appetite of the great Norwegian. Kathleen was undoubtedly attracted to powerful men, and drawn to someone who understood the trials her husband was facing. But, while Nansen's infatuation is clear, evidence for an extra-marital affair is thin, and a recent authoritative biography of the Norwegian does not repeat earlier allegations. In the British press, Nansen quietly suggested Amundsen's superior knowledge of 'Eskimo methods' with dog and skis would bring victory in the race to the Pole.[50]

A little over a fortnight after the departure of the southern party, Kathleen joined a crowd of 1,500, including Ernest Shackleton and George Bernard Shaw, in the London Coliseum to view the first series of Herbert Ponting's film *With Captain Scott, RN, to the South Pole*. The film displayed twenty scenes, showing the departure of the *Terra Nova* from New Zealand, the voyage south, and the establishment of the expedition's base camp. The first series proved a tremendous hit, playing in more then eighty towns and cities throughout Britain. Shackleton had exposed 4,000 feet of film during his *Nimrod* expedition, but Ponting raised polar cinematography to new heights. The *Bioscope* reported that Ponting's images were 'bringing great business to the houses where they are being featured, invariably arousing the keenest interest and comment. Indeed, at some of the suburban music-halls the films are being "starred", with the result that the bioscope "turn" is proving more than usually attractive. Congratulations to Messrs. Gaumont!'[51]

The first stage, to the base of the glacier, was completed by 10 December, about a week behind schedule. The two motor sledges broke down barely 50 miles from Cape Evans. Their caterpillar tracks proved successful, but the engines were simply unable to sustain heavy work rates in the harsh conditions. Although temperatures were not extreme, a series of blizzards delayed the party, and took a serious toll on the ponies. 'We men are snug and comfortable enough,' Scott wrote, 'but it is very evil to lie here and know that the weather is steadily sapping the strength of the beasts on which so much depends.' An unusually wet blizzard detained the party at the bottom of the Beardmore for four days, further sapping morale. Scott had taken thirty-eight days to cover 380 miles. Amundsen had taken only twenty-nine days to cover the same distance.

The five remaining ponies were slaughtered for food at the foot of the glacier, and Scott sent the dog-teams back to Cape Evans, to rest, he hoped, before coming out again to assist the returning polar party in March. Earlier than he had planned, then, the entire weight of the expedition's three 500-pound sledges was dragged by the men alone. Pony meat at least provided some extra nourishment. Each man hauling a sledge probably burned around 6,000 calories per day, but the sledging ration of tea, cocoa, butter, sugar, Huntley & Palmer's special biscuits, and pemmican (lean meat, dried and ground to a powder, mixed with lard and cast into blocks), produced only 4,500 calories. They were slowly starving.

Twelve men toiled up the Beardmore Glacier to a height of 9,000 feet, in appalling conditions over tortuous terrain, slashed through with crevasses. The sledges regularly sank over a foot into the snow. Scott selected the first team of four men to return to Cape Evans on 20 December: Surgeon Edward Atkinson, Apsley

Cherry-Garrard, Canadian physicist Charles Wright, and naval seaman Patrick Keohane. Cherry-Garrard was particularly disappointed to leave his companions from the winter journey. 'There is a very mournful air tonight,' he wrote, 'those going on and those turning back.'

On Christmas Day Teddy Evans's sledge team was nearly lost in a crevasse, when William Lashly fell to the full length of his harness. But the eight remaining men celebrated in high spirits after improvements in both weather and terrain had speeded their progress. The explorers hoped that the worst was over after ascending the glacier. The Pole was in sight and tension mounted over whom Scott would select for the final assault.

On New Year's Day, Scott ordered Teddy Evans's team of Henry Bowers and the seamen Thomas Crean and William Lashly to depot their skis to save weight. But it seems likely Scott was also preparing the ground for his final selection as, on 3 January, Teddy Evans, Lashly, and Crean were sent back to base. At the very last moment Scott changed his plans and took an extra man from Evans's team for the assault on the Pole: Bowers. Teddy Evans acquiesced. He could hardly refuse a direct request from his leader, but this impulsive decision would disturb the careful arrangement of the supply depots, increase the time needed for cooking, and left Bowers to trudge through the snow without skis for over 300 miles.

By the end of January, Teddy Evans's limbs were swollen and his gums bleeding: any disappointment at his omission from the polar party had been forgotten, as he was suffering severely from scurvy. Evans only survived thanks to the heroic efforts of his two companions. Crean left Lashly to nurse Evans and marched alone for over 35 miles to get help, nourished only by a few biscuits and a small bar of chocolate. A support party from the expedition's base managed to rescue Evans, who returned to New Zealand with the *Terra Nova* to convalesce, before the onset of the expedition's second Antarctic winter.

Scott, Bowers, Edgar Evans, Oates, and Wilson journeyed on to the Pole, manhauling on difficult surfaces, with minimum temperatures averaging −23°F. 'It takes it out of us like anything', Scott wrote. 'None of us ever had such hard work before.' But hopes were high on 9 January, when the five explorers marched 'beyond the record of Shackleton's exaggerated walk'. The word 'exaggerated' would be omitted from Scott's published journal.

But then, just seven days later, 'the worst has happened, or nearly the worst'. Bowers detected what he thought was a cairn on the horizon. A black flag tied to a sledge shook in the wind. Scott's party had been beaten to the South Pole. Further on, they found a tent containing a record of the five Norwegians, Roald Amundsen, Olav Bjaaland, Helmer Hanssen, Sverre Hassel, and Oscar Wisting, who had arrived at the Pole over a month before, on 15 December 1911. The clear prints of dogs' paws in the snow, many dogs, marked the origin of Amundsen's success.

'It is a terrible disappointment, and I am very sorry for my loyal companions', Scott wrote in his journal. 'He has beaten us in so far as he made a race if it', wrote Wilson, a touch of chagrin discernible even in the most selfless of the polar pioneers. 'We have done what we came for all the same and as our programme was made out.' Oates paid tribute to Amundsen, who 'must have had his head screwed on right. The gear they left was in excellent order and they seem to have had a comfortable trip with their dog teams very different from our wretched man-hauling.' Scott handled the defeat much better than Oates had expected.[52] Even then, Scott still hoped he might reach the *Terra Nova* and get the news through first. 'Well we have turned our back now on the goal of our ambition with sore feelings, and must face our 800-miles of solid dragging – and goodbye to most of the day-dreams!'

Amundsen's Victory

The *Fram* sailed into harbour at Hobart, Tasmania, on 7 March 1912, bringing news of a Norwegian triumph. ' "South Pole Dash" was the heading given by the *Evening Standard* to its account of Captain Amundsen's achievement', reported *Punch*. 'We fancy that "Dash" will prove to be a remarkably euphemistic version of Captain Scott's remark on hearing the news.'[53] As Amundsen's victory echoed around the world, Edgar Evans had already been dead for three weeks. 'One feels that for poor Oates the crisis is near,' wrote Scott, 'but none of us are improving'. Of the four surviving Britons, only Scott still kept up his journal.

On the very same day, having delayed as long as possible and oblivious of Amundsen's triumph, the *Terra Nova* left the increasingly treacherous waters around Cape Evans. Scott had expected he might not get back in time before ice forced the ship to depart, and left orders for a pre-arranged message to be sent to London when the *Terra Nova* reached the cablehead in New Zealand: 'I am remaining in the Antarctic for another winter in order to continue and complete my work.'[54] The telegram initiated an uncertain ten months, during which Amundsen was fêted, while mystery surrounded Scott's fate.

While Amundsen celebrated, images of Scott and his companions flickered across screens throughout Britain. The Gaumont Company released the second series of Ponting's *With Captain Scott* in two parts, on 30 September and 14 October 1912. Part one concentrated on the Antarctic landscape, natural history, and scientific work, but part two focused on the assault on the Pole, devoting considerable attention to the ponies, dogs, and motor-sledges (**Fig. 2.3**).

Amundsen's success certainly dented Ponting's hopes for an Edwardian blockbuster like the Milano Company's *Dante's Inferno*. But the second series of *With Captain Scott* appears to have been

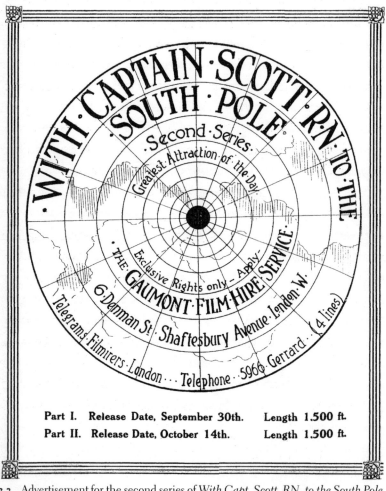

2.3 Advertisement for the second series of *With Capt. Scott, RN, to the South Pole.*

both a commercial and critical success, playing in cities throughout Britain. *Encore* declared *With Captain Scott* 'the best film yet presented to the British public'.[55] The Gaumont Company exploited the rise of the new exclusive system of film distribution, in which exhibitors paid the hiring company to act as the exclusive outlet for a film in a particular city, and a number of exhibitors hired *With Captain Scott* as their first ever exclusive.

Roland Huntford has condemned the British response to Amundsen's success: the 'most astonishing manipulations of facts were performed in order to prove that the British had not been worsted and, but for a little bad luck, all would have been well . . . Shackleton was almost alone to give Amundsen ungrudging public recognition'.[56] His account exaggerates the bitterness of the British reaction. Both the *Illustrated London News* and the *Daily Chronicle*, for example, had a financial interest in promoting Amundsen's achievement, having paid substantial sums for exclusive coverage of the expedition. The *Illustrated London News* published over ten pages of photographs, pictures, and maps illustrating the Norwegian triumph. The *Manchester Guardian* published a fair-minded assessment of Amundsen's alleged duplicity: 'Amundsen has been reproached for concealing his intention to attack the Pole until the last minute, and then springing it on his rivals. If there be any cause for reproach we may fairly take it as wiped out by the courage of the choice in taking the route he did.'[57]

An article in *Young England*, while lamenting that the Pole had not been won by an Englishman, celebrated Amundsen's triumph:

> let none of us grudge to the brave Norseman – worthy descendant of those redoubtable sea-rovers to whom the stormy sea was a highway, a thousand years ago – the honour which has fallen to him. He deserved it to the full. It is true he had 'better luck' than

> our own Shackleton had, but a good deal of the difficulties which
> beset other competitors were absent from his path because he had
> planned differently his 'ways and means'.

The *Boy's Own Paper* recommended that Amundsen's two-volume *The South Pole* 'should be read by every British boy'.[58]

British admiration, though, was certainly tempered by three aspects of the Norwegian triumph. First, Amundsen's concealment of his decision to mount an Antarctic expedition. Second, the absence of a detailed scientific programme. And, finally, the Norwegians' use of dogs.

In his memoirs, Amundsen accused Curzon of proposing a sneering toast of three cheers for the dogs when he spoke at the RGS.[59] Kathleen Scott did indeed have to persuade Clements Markham to remove a sentence from an article, which declared: 'In the long run Britons can beat dogs.' But the extent of the criticism of Amundsen's use of dogs should not be exaggerated. Manhauling was largely Markham's personal obsession. The *Terra Nova* expedition's fund-raising pamphlet of September 1909 proposed utilizing a combination of dogs, ponies, and motor sledges to reach the Pole, concluding that 'a picked party of men and dogs will make the final dash across the inland ice sheet'.[60] Neither the pamphlet, nor Scott's speech to the RGS in 1910, asserted the moral superiority of manhauling.

Criticism centred more frequently on the absence of a scientific programme in the Norwegian's plans. 'Captain Scott had important scientific work to do,' reported the *Pall Mall Gazette*, 'and he may well bring back with him results of value far beyond the fillip to national pride to be gained from being first at the Pole.' The RGS in particular emphasized the distinction between Scott's scientific expedition and Amundsen's 'mere dash for the Pole'. Clements Markham wrote a letter to *The Times*, published under the headline

'No "Race" to the Pole', arguing that Scott's 'grand object . . . was valuable research in every branch of science'. A leader confirmed that Scott would 'not grudge to another his victory in a "race" for which the English sailor never entered'.[61]

When Amundsen visited England in the autumn of 1912, Herbert Ponting wrote to *The Times* announcing: 'Captain Scott has not been racing, nor has he been engaged in a mere dash to the Pole. He is leading a great scientific expedition.' Curzon introduced Amundsen's lecture by declaring that Scott's expedition was gathering 'a harvest of scientific spoils which, when he returns, will be found to render his expedition the most notable of modern times'. Even Amundsen himself distinguished between the aims of the Norwegian and British expeditions in *The South Pole*, published towards the end of 1912. 'The British expedition was designed entirely for scientific research', wrote Amundsen diplomatically. 'The Pole was only a side-issue, whereas in my extended plan it was the main object.'[62]

Scott's commitment to science was clear, but the claim that Scott would not care whether Amundsen was first was highly disingenuous.[63] Scott's fund-raising pamphlet had opened by declaring that 'The main object of this Expedition is to reach the South Pole, and to secure for the British Empire the honour of that achievement', an object which he repeated in his speech to the RGS. Moreover, while Amundsen's entry was unexpected, rumours of foreign competition, most notably from the American Robert Peary, had circulated widely before the departure of the *Terra Nova*.

The most serious smear on Amundsen's reputation, though, concerned his bad sportsmanship in concealing his decision to mount an assault on the South Pole. He failed to notify the RGS, which had provided a grant of £100 for his proposed Arctic expedition. The Society's qualified response to Amundsen's achievement resulted more from disapproval of the Norwegian's conduct than hurt national pride. Deception over the aims of an expedition was simply unacceptable. Amundsen's sin was compounded as his deceit brought him into direct competition with one of the Society's favoured sons.

The RGS had little option but to honour the first man to set foot on the South Pole. But by hiring the Queen's Hall for Amundsen rather than the Royal Albert Hall where Peary had recently spoken, and declining to mint a special gold medal, the Society's officers expressed their disapproval of the Norwegian's methods. After a considerable amount of thought, Darwin agreed to dine with Amundsen before he addressed the Society. Clements Markham resigned from the council in protest.

'I do not think quite as badly of Amundsen as you do,' Darwin explained to another senior councillor, Admiral Sir Lewis Beaumont.

> He did not behave like a gentleman, but then we must remember that codes of honour differ in different countries. He is at all events not so unclean in the hands as many a millionaire in the heights of Society. We can never convince him that he is in the wrong, and I don't know that it is our business to try. He has, in truth done a big feat from certain points of view, and I think we ought to be very careful to ensure that our actions do not appear to be, and are not, dictated by any petty national jealousies, and in this, we are sure of Scott's sympathy. On the other hand we must not encourage any such tricks in the future. We therefore have a difficult course to steer.

Darwin summarized his attitude more succinctly in a letter to Kathleen Scott, writing simply Amundsen 'has not played the game'.[64]

While Darwin agonized over etiquette, Captain Scott had been dead for many months. Scott, Bowers, Evans, Oates, and Wilson had all perished on their return from the South Pole. 'Tell Sir Clements I thought much of him', Scott wrote to his wife, 'and never regretted his putting me in command of the *Discovery*.' Scott penned many letters in the tent before he died, but none to Clements Markham, the man who had done most to shape his fate. Perhaps he thought of the dog tracks at the Pole, and what might have been. He had marched 1,600 miles in five months.

Surgeon Edward Atkinson, who had assumed command after Scott failed to return, faced a more pressing dilemma than the officers of the RGS. Should he send a search party south, to look for the dead? Or should they head north, in an attempt to reach the six men led by Victor Campbell, who had been stranded after ice prevented the *Terra Nova* collecting them from the coast of Victoria land, and who might still be alive? Nine men had left the Antarctic with the *Terra Nova* the previous summer, leaving thirteen at Cape Evans. Atkinson convened a meeting. They voted twelve to one to head south. 'It is impossible to express and almost impossible to imagine how difficult it was to make this decision', Cherry-Garrard later wrote. 'Then we knew nothing: now we know all.'[65]

The RGS was not preoccupied with polar matters alone, while Cherry-Garrard spent his third dark winter in the hut at Cape Evans. The RGS's expansion, which owed so much to the exploits of Shackleton and Scott, had made the acquisition of new premises an urgent priority. A solution was found through the endeavours of Lord Curzon, who succeeded Darwin as President. At the Eton versus Harrow cricket match in 1912, Curzon learnt that Lowther Lodge in South Kensington was for sale and, in typically decisive fashion, the grand house was purchased before the summer was out for £100,000.

The move to Lowther Lodge sealed Curzon's conversion regarding the admission of women as RGS fellows. With the support of his former adversary Douglas Freshfield, Curzon wrote to the entire fellowship arguing the case for women's eligibility. In addition to working as students and teachers, women, he declared, 'have read some of the ablest papers before our society; they have conducted explorations not inferior in adventurous courage or in scientific results to those achieved by men; they have made valuable additions to the literature of travel.'[66]

Atkinson's search party could well have found no sign of Scott and the world might have been left to speculate endlessly over the fate of the polar party. Perhaps a crevasse had claimed them during the descent of the Beardmore? Or had scurvy added five new victims to its long list of polar casualties? But, then, on 12 November, the party found a tent and a story covered in snow. And when the searchers returned to Cape Evans, they also found relief: Campbell's party had got back safely, marching 230 miles along the coast from the ice-cave in which they had sheltered during the winter.

On 15 January 1913, three days before the *Terra Nova* picked up the remaining members of the expedition, a special general meeting ratified an overwhelming ballot in favour of the admission of women as RGS fellows. The election of women would generate record receipts and the first group of sixteen were to join the fellowship on the evening of Monday, 10 February.[67] Early that morning, the *Terra Nova* steamed quietly into the harbour at Oamaru on the eastern coast of New Zealand's South Island. The story carried in a battered Dundee whaling ship shook the world that afternoon.

· CHAPTER THREE ·

DISASTER IN
THE ANTARCTIC

'These rough notes and our dead bodies must tell the tale'

EXCITEMENT mounted on the morning of Monday, 10 February 1913, as billboards announced the sighting of the *Terra Nova* off the coast of New Zealand. But a brief report printed in the London evening papers shocked the nation.

> CHRISTCHURCH (N. Z.) – Monday – Captain Scott reached the South Pole on January 18 of last year, and there found the Norwegian tent, and records. On their return (a word here is indecipherable), the southern party perished. Scott, Wilson and Bowers, died from exposure and want during a blizzard about March 29, when eleven miles from 'One Ton Depot,' or 155 miles from the base at Cape Evans. Oates died from exposure on March 17. Seaman Edgar Evans died from concussion of the brain on February 17. The health of the remaining members of the expedition is excellent.[1]

Film of the explorers merrily setting out for the Pole had been exhibited throughout the country only a few weeks earlier, and most people assumed Scott would return safely after Amundsen's success. The press instantly hailed five new martyrs in the ancient struggle between Man and Nature, frequently drawing comparisons with the death of Sir John Franklin. 'The secret was wrested from the Antarctic,' reported the *Daily Express*, 'but the revengeful forces of the cold white ends of the earth did to death the great adventurers.'[2] Lyrical descriptions of pitiless blizzards, ghastly crevasses, and glittering glaciers abounded in the absence of hard information.

The lips of the crew of the *Terra Nova* had been tightly sealed when the ship steamed into Oamaru harbour. The business of exploration demanded absolute secrecy. The network of trans-continental cables would transmit any leak around the globe in a matter of hours, instantly rendering thousands of pounds of investment worthless. The sanctity of the story had to be preserved at all costs.

So the *Terra Nova* remained offshore, while Thomas Crean rowed Atkinson and Lieutenant Harry Pennell into the harbour in a small dinghy. A lighthouse-keeper had spotted the ship and a reporter was waiting. ' "We was attacked on the wharf by a man, sorr!",' Crean breathlessly recalled, ' "But we came away quick, & I told him nothing, sorr!" '[3] The night-watchman of the Oamaru harbour board rang Captain Jack Ramsay, who gave Pennell and Atkinson a bed for the night. The *Terra Nova*, though, sailed north towards Lyttelton without docking. Many of the crew had been away for twenty-seven months and yearned for civilization, but they would have to wile away another fourty-eight hours with the same old faces, conversations, and distractions. The story had to be protected. Absolute secrecy was maintained and in the excitement which followed the sighting of the *Terra Nova*, some New Zealand newspapers even reported that Scott himself had come ashore at Oamaru.

The exact timetable of the transmission of news to London is obscure.[4] First, Pennell and Atkinson appear to have sent a brief message from Oamaru Post Office after breakfast on Monday, declaring simply that 'Captain Scott reached the South Pole on January 18 last year. The party was overwhelmed in a blizzard on the return journey, and Captain Scott and the entire Southern party perished.'[5] The cable operator later claimed to have been confined to his room to prevent any leakage of news.

Pennell and Atkinson then boarded a train to Christchurch. Reporters again harassed them during the journey. One recognized Pennell and enquired if his companion was Captain Scott, but the two men refused either to identify themselves or to divulge any information. After arriving at Christchurch, they passed an official report to the expedition's experienced New Zealand agent, J. J. Kinsey, who had administered the affairs of many Antarctic expeditions. Before sending this report, however, Kinsey wired a short dispatch to London to notify the bereaved, so that they would not learn of the deaths of their loved ones through the newspapers.

The British press were the first narrators of the story of Scott of the Antarctic. The Central News Agency had paid £2,500 for the right to act as sole agents for the worldwide distribution of the expedition's official reports. Founded in 1870, the now defunct Central News was a fierce rival to the Press Association and Reuters: the agency had delivered news of the death of General Gordon twelve hours ahead of its competitors in 1885. One early press historian judged the coverage of Scott's last expedition 'one of the greatest "exclusives" ever achieved by a news agency'.[6]

The two fateful dispatches from Oamaru and Christchurch arrived around lunch-time and the Council of the RGS received a telephone call from Central News just after 3.00 p.m. The agency could not sit on such an explosive story and wait for the official report to arrive, while their rivals swarmed over New Zealand hoping to steal an exclusive. So Central News issued the cables and the world learned that Captain Scott was dead.

The brevity of the initial reports caused much confusion. Winston Churchill, First Lord of the Admiralty, had to explain to

MPs that the government had no information concerning the disaster.[7] Many hoped there had been some mistake, inspired by the comments of Shackleton, Amundsen, and Nansen, who questioned whether an experienced traveller like Scott could have been killed by a blizzard, as the report claimed.

The news operation proved so successful that the people of New Zealand only learned of the disaster the following day, when the story was cabled back from London. The centre of Christchurch ground to a halt, as people rushed to grab the first editions from the newsboys' bundles.

The official 2,487-word report was received in London in the early hours of Tuesday morning. Teddy Evans had returned to the Antarctic to take command of the expedition, after recovering from the scurvy which had almost killed him the previous year. Evans assembled a committee of six of the expedition's officers, who composed the report while the *Terra Nova* sailed to Oamaru.[8]

The official report was the founding text of the story of Scott of the Antarctic, and its reception dramatically intensified the public response to the disaster. The report described the expedition's activities over the previous year, with an account of the fate of the polar party drawn from the records found with Scott. Two passages from Scott's sledging journal were quoted verbatim: Scott's account of Captain Oates's death, and a 'Message to the Public', written at the end of his journal.

Concerning the death of Captain Oates the report stated:

> Captain Scott writes: 'He was a brave soul. He slept through the night hoping not to wake, but he awoke in the morning. It was blowing a blizzard. Oates said "I am just going outside and I may be some time." He went out into the blizzard and we have not seen him since'.

Captain Scott adds: 'We knew that Oates was walking to his death, but though we tried to dissuade him, we knew it was the act of a brave man and an English gentleman'.

The report described how, after Oates's death, Scott, Bowers, and Wilson pushed on until 21 March. 'They were then eleven miles south of the big depot at One Ton Camp, but this they never reached, owing to a blizzard which is known from the records to have lasted nine days. When the blizzard overtook them their food and their fuel gave out.' The report then reproduced Scott's 'Message to the Public' in full. Composed by a starving, exhausted man who knows he is about to die, amidst temperatures dipping below −40°F, Scott's 'Message to the Public' remains one of the most remarkable documents in British history: part apologia, part heroic testament, part anguished plea for the bereaved.

The 'Message' listed the causes of the disaster which, Scott claimed, was 'not due to faulty organisation, but to misfortune in all risks which had to be undertaken', singling out the failure of the expedition's ponies, and the unusually bad weather and poor sledging conditions encountered on the Beardmore Glacier. It concluded:

We are weak, writing is difficult, but for my own sake, I do not regret this journey, which has shown that Englishmen can endure hardship, help one another and meet death with as great a fortitude as ever in the past.

We took risks – we know we took them.

Things have come out against us, and therefore we have no cause for complaint, but bow to the will of Providence, determined still to do our best till the last.

But if we have been willing to give our lives to this enterprise, which is for the honour of our country, I appeal to our country-men to see that those who depend on us are properly provided for.

Had we lived I should have had a tale to tell of the hardihood, endurance, and courage of my companions which would have stirred the heart of every Englishman.

These rough notes and our dead bodies must tell the tale; but surely, surely, a great rich country like ours will see that those who are dependent on us are properly provided for.

(Signed) R. Scott. 25th March, 1912

Scott's 'Message to the Public' would be the cornerstone of his heroic reputation.

The report went on to note the erection of memorials by the search party, and added: 'It should here most certainly be noted that the southern party nobly stood by their sick companions to the end, and in spite of their distressing condition they had retained every record and thirty-five pounds of geological specimens, which prove to be of the greatest scientific value. This emphasises the nature of their journey.' The report concluded with the arrival of the *Terra Nova* at Cape Evans on 18 January and the erection of 'a large cross on Observation Hill, overlooking the Great Ice Barrier, where our gallant leader and his brave comrades sacrificed their lives for the honour of their country after the achievement of the great object of their expedition'.[9]

The first official report thus emphasized both the scientific and patriotic aims of the expedition, the comradeship and courage shown by the dead explorers, and the need to provide for the bereaved. The central elements of the story of Scott of the Antarctic were in place from the very beginning.

This report was the sole source of information on the disaster for nearly three days. Press and public clamoured for additional details, while Central News complained that the dispatch failed to honour their contract with Scott, which promised an account of 8,000–10,000 words. But the contract also directed the expedition to remain at sea after the first dispatch to safeguard confidentiality, and the *Terra Nova* thus delayed its arrival in Lyttelton until Wednesday, 12 February. 'There is evidently a tremendous feeling of admiration for the Polar Party everywhere,' wrote Cherry-Garrard after disembarking, 'quite beyond anything I have ever imagined – I suppose we have been out of the world too long.'[10]

Kinsey swiftly arranged meetings with the officers and scientific staff at his home on consecutive evenings, composing two further official reports, cabled to London on Thursday, 13 and Friday, 14 February.[11] The cable of 13 February carried further details of the memorials which the expedition had erected, including the epitaph chosen by Atkinson and Cherry-Garrard for Captain Oates: 'Hereabouts died a very gallant gentleman.' The cable of 14 February contained an extended account of the scientific achievements of the expedition's northern party, under the command of Victor Campbell, and the western party, led by the geologist Thomas Griffith Taylor.

The dispatches from New Zealand caused a sensation, not only in Britain but around the world. The Antarctic disaster dominated national and local newspapers from the Tory *Pall Mall Gazette*, through the popular pictorial *Daily Mirror* and moderate *Daily Chronicle*, to the socialist *Daily Herald*. 'Many times in our history there have been done deeds of heroism that have thrilled the nation to its heart', marvelled the popular *Daily Graphic*, 'but in all our records there is nothing to surpass the prolonged struggle and the courageous death of Captain Scott and his comrades.' In an open letter to the press, Lord Curzon wrote that public sentiment had been 'quickened by this tale of mingled heroism and disaster as by no other event in my time'.[12]

Scott's 'Message to the Public' and the death of Captain Oates were singled out for praise. The *Aberdeen Express* declared 'the pages of romance, the classic days of Greece and Rome, present nothing more spirit stirring, nothing more glorious, than the passing of Captain Oates', while the *Newport Advertiser* claimed that Scott's message told 'a story of heroism in the face of which the classic deeds of the Gods of the ancients paled into insignificance'. An advertisement for the *Strand Magazine*'s serialization of Scott's diaries, even described his message as 'the most impressive document ever read by man'.[13]

The press fed a voracious public appetite for news of the expedition. The issue of the *Daily Chronicle* announcing the disaster sold more copies than any other edition of the newspaper that year. The *Daily Mirror*'s special 'Captain Scott Number' of 21 May was the first to publish the photographs taken by the explorers at the Pole and sold 1,342,000 copies, the highest circulation of any *Daily Mirror* in 1912 or 1913, and one of the best-selling editions of any daily newspaper published before the war.[14]

The unexpected disaster echoed around the world. The international press feasted on a sensational story of romance and tragedy, while foreign governments and societies queued up to pay tribute to the dead explorers. Messages of sympathy from Norway and Italy were read out in the House of Commons. The American President William Taft, and President-Elect Woodrow Wilson, sent telegrams to King George V. Fridtjof Nansen announced that 'the heart of the nation has been deeply stirred', while in France the *Excelsior* declared 'the civilised world will salute the memory of the explorer, who died in his desire to increase the sum of human knowledge'. The RGS listed 119 individuals and institutions from which it received messages of condolence, including the Royal Yacht Club of Belgium and the Johannesburg stock exchange. The *Evening News* declared simply: 'People think of nothing else, talk of nothing else, read nothing else.'[15]

Memorial services were held throughout the country, 'as numerous and as crowded', reported the *British Weekly*, 'as those which followed the *Titanic* disaster'. A special service at St Paul's in London attracted an unprecedented clamour for tickets, while St John's church, Cardiff, and St Giles' cathedral, Edinburgh, drew an 'immense crowd of mourners'. Services were also held throughout the empire, including one at St Andrew's cathedral in Sydney attended by the Australian premier, the Lord Mayor, and many leading citizens.[16] The scale of the tragedy proved too much for some. The Revd E. T. Griffiths, Vicar of Cam and Rural Dean of Dursley, Gloucestershire, referred to the death of Captain Scott and his party at the post of duty while preaching on the first Sunday following the announcement of the disaster, at which his own voice failed and he fell down the steps of his pulpit and died.[17]

'How Much Are You Sorry?'

Scott's dying plea for the bereaved dominated early reports of the disaster. Newspapers implored the government to intervene, describing the 'Debt of Honour' which Scott had bequeathed to the nation. Kathleen Scott was sailing to New Zealand when the story broke, and the papers were filled with speculation over whether or not she had heard the news. 'That was a glorious courageous note & a great inspiration to me,' she wrote after learning of her husband's death. 'If He in his weak agony-wracked condition, could face it with such sublime fortitude, how dare I possibly whine.'[18]

The leading Conservative politician Austen Chamberlain enquired in the House of Commons whether the government would meet Scott's last request. Prime Minister Asquith replied by praising Scott's last message as 'one of the most moving and pathetic utterances in the annals of discovery', and promising that 'his appeal will not fall on deaf ears'. The Admiralty announced that the two naval representatives, Scott and Evans, would be treated as if they had been 'killed in action', which, the press reported, mistakenly in Evans's case, would entitle their relatives to higher pensions.[19]

But the government response remained uncertain and in the absence of a clear lead, the initial reaction to Scott's dying request was chaotic.[20] The disaster triggered a frenzy of commemorative activity, with the publication of a bewildering array of special newspaper editions, pictures, postcards, poems, songs, and books. By the morning of Thursday, 13 February no less than four separate national memorial funds had been opened: by the British Antarctic Expedition (BAE) committee, by the Lord Mayor at London's Mansion House, by the *Daily Chronicle*, and by the *Daily Telegraph*.[21] Local funds were also announced throughout the country, by many councils, churches, and newspapers, including the *Scotsman*, *Yorkshire Post*, and *Western Morning News*. The *Daily Express* published an 8-page pamphlet, 'The People's Tribute to the Heroes of the Antarctic'; 26,000 pamphlets, costing a penny each, were ordered in less than a week, with the department store Selfridges taking 5,000 to complement a special window display. The *Express* reminded the public that 'almost everyone can spare a penny'.[22]

Although the public were primarily motivated by concern for the bereaved, the various funds solicited money to pay off the expedition's debts, finance the publication of scientific results, and raise memorials. The *Daily Telegraph* fund, for example, focused on the erection of a national monument. 'Scott is dead, but his fame will never die', the newspaper proclaimed. 'Our gratitude – our vindication of our claim to be the fellow-citizens of Captain Scott and his comrades – must be set forth in concrete form before the eyes of the generations which come after us.'[23]

The initial public response was disappointing, however, and a week after news of the disaster reached London the combined takings of the four national funds had not even reached £10,000.

The King himself refused to contribute until the campaign was properly co-ordinated. 'The whole situation has been grossly mis-managed,' complained the *Daily Express*, 'and the appearance has been given of a slur on heroic memories of a national reluctance to respond to the most stirring appeal that ever a dying hand has penned.' The government's failure to follow up Asquith's initial declaration fostered uncertainty. J. M. Barrie highlighted the confusion in a an open letter to the *Daily News and Leader*, published on the front page, which asked 'How Much Are You Sorry?' and blamed the government for sowing confusion.[24]

The Lord Mayor hurriedly convened a meeting at which it was agreed to amalgamate the four national appeals into a single Mansion House Scott memorial fund, administered by the mayor's experienced private secretary, Sir William Soulsby. Asquith then publicly committed the government 'to provide out of national funds for all relatives dependent on Captain Scott and his four companions, so as to secure that they shall be in as good a pecuniary position as they would have been had the disaster not taken place'. A few days later it was further announced that Kathleen Scott would be granted a title as if her husband had been awarded a knighthood, 'as he would have been had he survived'.[25] The widow of the British hero of the Indian Mutiny, Henry Havelock, had been granted a similar title, and the award met with widespread approval.

The announcement of the amalgamation of the funds prompted a surge in donations, led by £200 from the King. The amount collected rose rapidly and the Mansion House fund was officially closed in June 1913 after £75,000 had been raised; £34,000 was directed to the families of the deceased through a series of trust funds, and in addition, the fund allocated £5,100 to pay the expedition's debts, £17,500 to publish the scientific results, and £18,000 to erect suitable memorials.[26]

The government had delayed making an announcement about pensions until Kathleen Scott returned to England at the beginning of April. She delivered Scott's final letters to three prominent naval officers, Admiral Sir Lewis Beaumont, Vice-Admiral Sir Francis Charles Bridgeman, and Vice-Admiral Sir George Egerton, asking them to petition the Admiralty on his family's behalf. Egerton wrote directly to Winston Churchill to use his 'influence with the Prime Minister to obtain as large a Govt Grant as possible'.[27]

The government announced the level of pensions at the end of April. The bereaved were thus provided for through a combination of public and private finance: government pensions, and trust funds from the Mansion House appeal (see **Fig. 3.1**). Both the Treasury and Mansion House made strenuous efforts to guarantee Asquith's promise, by compiling detailed tables of the past and projected incomes of the relatives of the dead.[28]

The provision appears generous, but the distribution of funds reflected the steep social hierarchy and class prejudices of Edwardian society In total, Kathleen and Peter Scott received a lump sum of £2,676, Admiralty and government pensions worth £325 p.a., and the income from a combined trust fund of £12,000. Lois Evans and her three children, Norman, Muriel, and Ralph, on the other hand, received a lump sum of £96, Admiralty and government pensions worth approximately £91 p.a., and the income from a trust fund of £1,250. Mrs Evans also had to prove her children were alive each year in order to receive the government pension.

Given that only five men had died, the £75,000 raised by the Mansion House was a huge sum, equivalent to the purchasing power of £4,500,000 today. One recent appeal had raised only £45,000 for relatives of the 440 victims of the Sengenhydd mining disaster. The *Scotsman* alone raised £4,700, from over 2,500 separate donations.[29] The lists of subscribers published in the press expose

	ADMIRALTY PENSIONS	GOVERNMENT PENSIONS	MANSION HOUSE TRUST FUNDS	OTHER INCOME
Kathleen Scott	£200 p.a. £693 gratuity £86 back-pay	£100 p.a.	£8,500	BAE salary: £1,666 Also £10,000 estimated income from book/articles
Peter Scott	£25 p.a. until age 18 £231 gratuity	—	£3,500	—
Hannah Scott and her two daughters	—	£300 p.a.	£6,000	£230 p.a.
Oriana Wilson	—	£300 p.a.	£8,500	BAE salary: £636
Emily Bowers (mother) and her two daughters	—	£100 p.a. (from India Office)	£4,500	BAE salary: £116 £220 p.a. £200 captial
Lois Evans (wife) and Norman, Muriel, and Ralph Evans	7s. 6d. a week, plus 2s. a week for each child, until boys' age 14 and girl's age 16 (£35 p.a.) £52 back-pay	12s. 6d. a week, plus 3s. a week for each child, until age 18 (£56 p.a.)	£1,250	BAE salary: £44
Mrs Evans (mother)	—	—	£250	—
Mrs Brissenden and one child	—	—	£750	—
Mrs Abbot	—	—	£750	—

3.1. Pensions awarded to the relatives of the deceased of the BAE

Sources: 'The Captain Scott Fund – Report of the Committee', July 1913, MS 1464/5, SPRI, 'Exhibit C – Circumstances of Dependents', uncatalogued folder of papers titled 'History of SPRI. Captain Scott's Antarctic fund', SPRI; Table of Incomes, 'British Antarctic Expedition, 1910–12', T164/404, PRO.

the vibrant associational culture of Edwardian Britain, with schools, churches, the armed forces, youth groups, Masonic lodges (Scott had been a freemason), and businesses appearing frequently. Evelyn Noble, daughter of a friend of one of Scott's sisters, raised over £225 from 4,000 English girls through a chain letter scheme. The periodical *Truth*, however, criticized the 'English Girls' Fund' for wasting money on stamps.[30]

The appeal exposed the global impact of the disaster. The Prime Minister of Nepal sent £200, while the boys of La Martiniere school in Calcutta collected donations for a special memorial hall. Scott's mother, Hannah, received a letter of sympathy signed by over seventy students of the Girls' College of Sant'Agostino, Piacenza in Italy, 'on whose imagination the daring exploits and tragic end of Captain Scott have made a profound impression'. Kathleen Scott received letters from a bizarre range of organizations, including the Christchurch bowling association, representing the bowlers of North Canterbury, New Zealand, and the dental board of New South Wales, which passed 'the Motion unanimously in silence, standing'. And, buried in the archives of the Scott Polar Research Institute, are two 5-peso notes, the subscription of Mexican schoolboys towards a memorial for Captain Scott, which were never exchanged.[31]

Blame and Accusations

Speculation swiftly mounted about the causes of the disaster after 10 February. Reports generally followed Scott's 'Message to the Public' by blaming the tragedy on misfortune rather than poor planning. Paeans to the exemplary organization of the expedition were commonplace, in part reflex expressions of respect for the dead. On the day news reached London, Douglas Freshfield announced to the RGS that 'no Arctic or Antarctic party was, I suppose, ever sent out better equipped', while Clements Markham declared that 'all the arrangements were perfect'.[32]

But the causes of the disaster were also widely debated. In private Freshfield feared that 'we may hear their means and mode of transport were inadequate'. The 'brevity, and in some cases the peculiar wording of the first dispatch which we received attracted immediate attention here,' commented the general manager of the Central News Agency, John Gennings, 'and gave rise to an almost universal belief that something had occurred which it was sought to hide.' Atkinson and Cherry-Garrard both agreed that news had been held back too much, creating the impression of a cover-up.[33]

The press initially identified four factors in need of further investigation: the breakdown of Petty Officer Edgar Evans; the failure of the relief party led by Cherry-Garrard to reach Scott; fuel shortages at the supply depots; and the incidence of scurvy among the polar party. The first three issues deflected attention away from Scott, but the discussion of scurvy called his preparations into question. Some early reports made Petty Officer Edgar Evans a scapegoat for the disaster. The first official dispatch had quoted Scott's 'Message' in which he pointed an accusing finger at Evans: 'The advance party would have returned to the glacier in fine form and with surplus of food, but for the astonishing failure of the man whom we had least expected to fail. Seaman Edgar Evans was thought the strong man of the party.'[34] The second official report, composed at Kinsey's instigation, also emphasized how Evans's 'condition delayed the party, and their surplus food was gradually diminished'. Speculation mounted that the description of Evans's concussion of the brain concealed the fact that he had gone mad.

Teddy Evans denied the accusations against his namesake, but several commentators took their cue from the official reports and blamed Evans for the disaster. 'The sudden breakdown of Seaman Evans, who appeared to be the strongest of the party,' observed the *Daily Mail*, 'was a disastrous blow and was probably fatal.' A sonnet, dedicated to Evans, by the renowned cleric and poet Canon Rawnsley lamented:

> Ah, well for him he died, nor ever knew
> How his o'er-wearied stumbling forward drew
> Death's snare about his friends to hold them fast . . .

And, in his first speech following the news, Lord Curzon observed that Evans's 'unaccountable breakdown was the first symptom, and possibly the initial cause, of the ultimate disaster'.[35]

Evans's collapse engaged with a range of Edwardian concerns about the relationship between physical strength, mental capacity, and social status. The description of Evans as the 'strong man' of the party was frequently repeated, to emphasize how physical strength did not equate to good character. The front page of the *Daily Express* carried the headline: 'The Problem Of Seaman Evans – Why He "Failed" The Expedition – Was He Handicapped By His Strength?' The *Express* interviewed a specialist, who stated that polar exploration imposed particular strains on an uneducated man, who, without a storehouse of information to contemplate during long marches, might fall into a state of 'self-mesmerism, followed by mania'. 'All experience proves that in crises where moral factors react upon the physical,' noted the *Observer*, 'hard, intellectual fortitude is more than bodily strength.'[36]

The scapegoating of Evans reached its apogee in J.E. Hodder Williams's children's book, *Like English Gentlemen*, published anonymously in March 1913 to raise money for the Mansion House fund. *Like English Gentlemen* presents Scott's story as a simple morality tale, conveying messages about comradeship, class, and character. The contrasting responses of Petty Officer Evans and Captain Oates to adversity lie at the heart of the book. The book describes how, on the way back from the Pole, 'the man of mighty muscles seemed to have lost his strength. He was always a little behind the others'. Evans's deterioration is depicted as a decisive and ultimately fatal burden. 'It was their life blood the heroes gave for this simple seaman . . . they were English gentlemen, these four, the hero, and Dr. Wilson and Captain Oates and Lieutenant Bowers, and so such a thing as leaving Evans behind never came into their heads'. Oates, on the other hand, begs his companions to save themselves when he can go no further, eventually walking out into the snow and dying, in contrast to Evans, 'as an English gentleman, – a very gallant gentleman'.[37] The highest character displayed through sacrifice was the preserve of the officer class.

The extent of the criticism of Edgar Evans should not, however, be exaggerated. Most commentators did not single out Evans as especially culpable but rather noted his collapse as one among a catalogue of factors which contributed to the disaster. *Like English Gentlemen* was exceptional, by far the most explicit contrast between the burden imposed by Evans and the noble sacrifice of Captain Oates.

Indeed, reports more frequently treated the two explorers together, noting the drag on the party imposed by the need to care for sick companions. The *Daily News and Leader* even singled out the collapse of Oates, not Evans, as the final cause of the disaster, noting that 'the party would have survived even this fearful month had not Captain Oates also been taken ill'.[38]

And Evans's courage was also widely praised. After *John Bull* launched a campaign to raise money for a replica of the *Terra Nova* to be presented to Peter Scott, readers called for a similar ship to be presented to Petty Officer Evans's sons containing 'the full story of his father's heroism and sacrifice'.[39] Evans thus occupied an ambiguous status in narratives of the disaster, capable of representation as both a valiant blue-jacket or simple-minded seaman, whose great physical strength offered no protection against the peculiar mental strains of polar exploration.

Apsley Cherry-Garrard offered a second target for criticism. With the Russian dog-driver Dimitri Gerof, Cherry-Garrard had left the expedition's base camp and sledged south with two dog-teams at the end of February 1912 carrying additional supplies. The first official report recorded that they reached One Ton Depot on 3 March, but were compelled to return a week later because of bad weather and the deteriorating condition of the dogs. After returning to Cape Evans, 'Mr. Cherry Garrard collapsed as the result of having overstrained his heart, and his companion was also sick'.

The primary purpose of the dog-teams was not to relieve the polar party, but to speed their return and help Scott reach the *Terra Nova* with news of his triumph, before the onset of winter ice drove the ship back to New Zealand. Cherry-Garrard simply followed orders by not pushing on past One Ton Depot: Scott had left instructions that the dog-teams should be protected for a second assault on the Pole in November 1912, in case the first attempt failed.

Some commentators, however, criticized Cherry-Garrard, suggesting greater efforts might have been made to reach the polar party. The New Zealand press even reported that Dimitri Gerof wanted to press on, but was prevented from doing so by his companion – a report which infuriated Cherry-Garrard. Teddy Evans emphatically denied the accusations and Central News issued a statement that Scott's family felt assured that every possible effort had been made to assist the southern party. Cherry-Garrard had braced himself for criticism, but was dismayed at the allegations: 'What a rotten end it is to a good expedition.'[40]

Several newspapers also picked up on the reference to fuel shortages in Scott's last message. 'Out of his diary leaps a phrase which demands elucidation insistently,' observed the *Daily Express*, ' "We should have got through in spite of the weather . . . but for a shortage of fuel in our depots for which I cannot account." The words are ominous. Will they ever be explained?' Scott's comment implied that the supporting parties had taken more than their fair share of fuel on their return. The leading *Daily Chronicle* correspondent John Drummond interviewed Teddy Evans shortly after the *Terra Nova* reached Lyttelton, and reported that Evans became very reticent when asked about the fuel shortages, replying 'I think you had better not touch upon it'.[41]

In fact, the fuel shortages resulted not from the greed of the supporting parties but from inadequate equipment. Leather washers on Scott's fuel containers perished in the extreme conditions, allowing paraffin to leak or evaporate. The same problem had occurred on the *Discovery* expedition, but Scott had done little to remedy it. The meticulous Amundsen, by contrast, had observed the phenomenon on his North-West Passage expedition a few years earlier, and soldered the spouts of his own customized containers to prevent leakage.

Fuel shortages, Cherry-Garrard's command of the dog-teams, and the collapse of Evans and Oates, shifted responsibility for the disaster away from Scott. The possible incidence of scurvy, however, was more controversial, implying that inadequate preparations might have been to blame for the disaster.

Edwardian perceptions of scurvy were complex. The disease had largely been eradicated in the Royal Navy through the nineteenth century by the use of lime juice. But, while doctors recognized that fresh food prevented scurvy, they didn't understand why. In the first decade of the new century, Axel Holst and Theodor Frølich published new research, arguing that scurvy was caused by a deficiency in some as yet undiscovered dietary substance found in fresh food, which was broken down by prolonged cooking. In 1910, however, many (including Atkinson, the expedition's naval surgeon) still believed that scurvy was caused by tainted food leading to acid intoxication, contamination rather than deficiency. Scott appears to have been influenced by Fridtjof Nansen's forceful rejection of Holst's arguments.[42] The Polish scientist Casimir Funk did not give vitamins their name until a year after Scott's assault on the Pole, and the precise mechanisms of scurvy were not identified until the 1930s.

Yet, in spite of the mystery shrouding the origins of the disease, the presence of scurvy was still widely perceived as a taint on expeditions, evidence of organizational failure. Shackleton's men had not suffered from scurvy on their recent southern march. Both Teddy Evans and Atkinson, who led the search party which found Scott's body, strongly denied the presence of scurvy among the polar party. But Evans had himself been struck down by scurvy during the return of the final supporting party, and Amundsen, Nansen, and Shackleton all suggested in the press that scurvy was the most likely cause of the disaster.[43]

A number of historians have speculated that the presence of scurvy was covered up by the crew. There is evidence of tacit agreement to avoid discussion of the disease. Canon Rawnsley amended a poem describing the explorers as 'Worn down by scurvy or by blizzard slain', substituting 'hunger' for 'scurvy' when the poem was published a second time.[44] Neither Apsley Cherry-Garrard nor Teddy Evans devoted much attention to scurvy in their published accounts of the expedition, even though Evans had suffered from the disease and Cherry-Garrard identified inadequate diet as a primary cause of the disaster. Atkinson reportedly admitted that the polar party might well have been suffering from scurvy in 1921, but 'felt it would be disloyal to Scott to say so . . . it was a reflection on his ability as an organiser to say that scurvy had developed'.[45]

The polar party's sledging diet contained no vitamin C and was also deficient in other vitamins, thiamin, riboflavin, and nicotinic acid. But Susan Solomon's recent account has argued that scurvy was not a central factor in the failure of the polar party. In modern tests, subjects first develop scurvy when deprived of vitamin C for between nineteen and thirty weeks.[46] On the return from the Pole, the explorers consumed a large quantity of pony meat after seventeen weeks on sledging rations, greatly reducing the likelihood of scurvy. Furthermore, the death of Edgar Evans (because of a high-altitude cerebral edema, brought on by dehydration, she suggests) would have raised the polar party's rations to an adequate level. Teddy Evans alone developed scurvy because he had been on sledging rations longer than any other member of the southern party.

Solomon argues instead that unseasonably adverse weather conditions were the primary cause of the disaster. Meteorological data gathered on the Great Ice Barrier since 1983 suggest that Scott's assault on the Pole was fatally hampered by atypical weather conditions on two occasions: first, at the foot of the Beardmore Glacier, and second, in the period from late February to mid-March, when temperatures on the Barrier were 38°F lower than temperatures at the expedition's coastal base camp, almost double the usual differential. This unseasonable cold proved fatal in two ways: first, below −20°F sledging conditions become increasingly difficult, as ice takes on the characteristics of sandpaper. Secondly, below −20°F, the possibility of frostbite is massively increased; frostbitten feet crippled first Oates and then Scott in this critical period. Temperatures as cold as those Scott experienced in 1912 have been recorded only once on the Barrier since 1965. Scott's emphasis on unexpectedly extreme weather as the primary cause of the disaster may after all have been correct.

Solomon does, however, dismiss the possibility of the nine-day blizzard, which Scott claimed had kept the explorers tent-bound before their deaths. Antarctic blizzards caused by cold air rushing down from the Pole to the coast simply never last that long. Bowers and Wilson could have made a last, desperate attempt to reach One Ton Depot, but chose to die with Scott in the tent.

Of Dogs and Men

With many questions still unanswered two months after the announcement of Scott's death, Lord Curzon considered whether the RGS should convene 'an informal enquiry, semi-confidential in character'. After meeting with Kathleen Scott on 16 April, Curzon privately speculated that Edgar Evans had suffered from scurvy, and that Oates had taken opium to ease his death. Admiral Beaumont, however, advised Curzon against an inquiry as no one could predict where it might lead.[47]

Some historians have argued that the characteristics on display in Scott's last expedition – the straitjacket of tradition, class prejudice, the glorification of sacrifice over achievement – indicated a nation well past its sell-by date. The failure to confront the real causes of the disaster marked Scott as 'a suitable hero for a nation in decline'.[48] The reliance on manhauling to conquer the Pole encapsulated the bankruptcy of Edwardian society. A recent biographer of Scott, Michael de-la-Noy, agrees that the 'whole expedition had been founded upon a blind, and very British, belief in the moral superiority of human muscle power ... Scott thought it far more manly for men to haul the sledges themselves. Five of them died as a result.'[49]

Yet the suggestion that the British revelled in the moral superiority of manhauling, usually based on quotations from Clements Markham and one passage in Scott's *Voyage of the Discovery*, is highly misleading. Praise of manhauling was largely absent from British tributes in 1913. The journalist Henry Leach did report that his friend Scott had told him that, 'while modern inventions and resources must be utilised to the full, he wished, if he could go near to the Pole, to go there in something like the simple manner of the great explorers of old, depending so much, like the handy sailor-man, on their own fine strength and grand resource'. And the most ardent champion of Victorian methods, Clements Markham, hailed Scott for accomplishing 'this deed of derring-do, without the aid of dogs to be slaughtered afterwards, but by their own unaided efforts'.[50]

But such comments were exceptional, and certainly not a prominent feature in reports of the disaster. Neither the expedition's fund-raising prospectus nor Scott's RGS speech had made any reference to the moral superiority of manhauling. Scott had, instead, proposed to utilize a combination of ponies, dogs, and motor sledges to reach the Pole. Scott did remain squeamish about cruelty to animals, a grave hindrance in the unforgiving Antarctic environment. But neither Scott's 'Message to the Public' nor the official reports cabled from New Zealand emphasized the nobility of manhauling. Moreover, not one of forty-one leaders published in thirteen national and regional newspapers in the week following the announcement of the disaster which I have examined makes any comment about the moral superiority of manhauling.[51]

Indeed, more commentators drew the obvious lesson about the superiority of Amundsen's methods from the disaster. The polar expert R. N. Rudmose Brown declared in the *Manchester Guardian* that a combination of Amundsen's proficiency with skis, and Scott's inadequate complement of ponies and dogs, accounted for the Norwegian's success. The one lesson to be drawn from recent polar expeditions, observed the *Westminster Gazette*, was that 'the dog is by far the most efficient means of transport, for in the last resort the dogs provide food for each other & for the human members of the party'.[52]

Some directly criticized Scott. A correspondent in the *Scotsman* stated bluntly that 'the number of dogs was totally insufficient for the work they were called to do', inspiring a vitriolic exchange with Herbert Ponting.[53] At a meeting of the Association of Public Schools Science Masters, Professor Armstrong offered a similar assessment of the Norwegian and British expeditions. 'Every action [of Amundsen's] was carefully thought out. There was not a word of evidence that Scott's party did anything of the kind.'[54]

The most scathing attack was mounted by the polar commentator Alfred Harrison. After Amundsen's victory, Harrison had criticized the outdated Victorian methods of the RGS, which saw naval officers appointed to polar commands ahead of more experienced captains, such as Ernest Shackleton, William Bruce, and David Hanbury.

> If the methods of the Royal Geographical Society are continued, the chance of Great Britain ever recovering her leading position in the world of exploration will be lost. There will be talk, advertisement, the collection of funds, and all the outward appearance of energy and effort, but the man at the helm, the

pilot who is to put the British ship first in the International race, will always be the wrong man, who was not chosen by nature for the post, but by the Royal Geographical Society.[55]

Harrison sustained his critique after the announcement of Scott's death. He initially conceded that the disaster was primarily down to 'persistent and accumulated ill-fortune', but went on to condemn Scott's methods, contrasting the British attitude towards dogs with the practice of Peary, Amundsen, and Nansen. 'Is it so certain that proper provision was made and that the result was due to circumstances which could not be foreseen', Harrison concluded. 'I do not think so, and this opinion is shared by others.'[56]

Many of his criticisms were justified and the central point about the imperative of using dogs on polar expeditions was irrefutable. Harrison's citation of Shackleton alongside Bruce and Hanbury as a more accomplished polar explorer than Scott is more dubious. As a charismatic leader Shackleton reigned supreme, but his recent expedition had displayed many of Scott's failings, most notably his preference for ponies over dogs, and lack of proficiency with skis.

It is clear, then, that the organization of Scott's last expedition was hotly debated in 1913. Amundsen's success was widely acknowledged as decisive proof of superior Norwegian methods. Some still cherished the nobility of manhauling. After arriving at the Pole, Bowers himself noted: 'It is sad that we have been forestalled by the Norwegians, but I am glad that we have done it by good British manhaulage.'[57] But such proclamations were rare, and played little role in the establishment of Scott's heroic reputation in 1913. The resonance of Markham's eulogies to manhauling had diminished considerably since the launch of the *Discovery* in 1901. Curzon may have mocked Amundsen in the Queen's Hall, but he wrote to Keltie a year later that Shackleton's new Antarctic expedition 'ought to have more dogs'.[58]

Scott's Journals

The causes of the Antarctic disaster were thus widely debated, and the superiority of Amundsen's methods acknowledged by many. But it is now commonly believed that an establishment conspiracy covered up Scott's failings, creating a hero by the careful editing of his sledging journals, with the assistance of the playwright J. M. Barrie. 'For publication,' wrote the polar historian Roland Huntford, principal proponent of the conspiracy theory, 'his diaries were purged of all passages detracting from a perfect image'.[59] 'The aim was to prettify Scott's image, conceal blunders and project the myth of a perfect martyred hero.'[60]

This interpretation cannot be sustained. Scott's reputation was certainly guarded by many, and his journals were edited prior to their publication, first in four monthly instalments of the *Strand Magazine* from July to October 1913, and then in the first volume of *Scott's Last Expedition*, published by Smith, Elder in November. But the censorship was far less extensive than has been alleged.

Kathleen Scott arrived in Wellington, New Zealand, on 28 February 1913. Atkinson presented her with her husband's journals, which she stayed up all night reading. 'Any more magnificent, invigorating document I never read, & one would be a poor creature indeed if one could not face one's world with such words to inspire one.' A few days later Kathleen wired a dispatch to London announcing that Scott's journal was excellent and complete, and would be published towards the end of the year, with some preliminary articles appearing in the *Strand Magazine*.[61]

The *Strand* had paid £2,000 for serialization rights and, after returning to England in April, Kathleen met with the editor, H. G. Smith, who persuaded her to allow both the publication of a facsimile of the 'Message to the Public', and the insertion of quotation marks around extracts taken directly from Scott's journal.[62] Leonard Huxley, son of the eminent Victorian scientist Thomas Huxley, was engaged to prepare the journals for publication

In the magazine coup of 1913, the *Strand Magazine* elaborated on the story told in the initial reports from New Zealand, illustrated with a number of previously unseen photographs. Part one described the voyage south and the establishment of a base camp at Cape Evans; part two outlined the expedition's first year in the Antarctic and included the first account of the unprecedented winter journey to the emperor penguin rookery at Cape Crozier undertaken by Wilson, Bowers, and Cherry-Garrard; finally, parts three and four told the story of the assault on the Pole. The editor of *Outlook* recalled the almost 'painful eagerness with which one looked forward to the monthly instalments'. But the accounts of the deaths of the explorers and the finding of their bodies actually added little to the information already published. Curzon had advised Kathleen Scott to retain the full description of the return march for the book.[63]

Having agreed the content of the *Strand Magazine*, Kathleen met with Lewis Beaumont, Clements Markham, and Reginald Smith at the end of May to settle the form of the book. In spite of Beaumont's presence, the Admiralty appears to have played no role in the preparation of Scott's journals for publication. Beaumont himself did not even see Scott's original before publication, in spite of offers from Kathleen Scott.[64]

Two men were primarily responsible for editing the journals: Leonard Huxley arranged the narrative, while Cherry-Garrard supplied first-hand information about such matters as the precise geomorphology of the gateway to the Beardmore Glacier. Smith, Markham, and Barrie also contributed, but Huxley and Cherry-

Garrard were the principal editors and the book's title page clearly acknowledged Huxley's contribution.[65]

A systematic comparison of the published journal with Scott's original exposes relatively few examples of direct censorship. Interventions reflect the conventions of popular biography, not an establishment conspiracy. The following list shows the seventeen substantial alterations made to Scott's account of the march back from the South Pole, notably the alteration of some temperature readings and the omission of critical comments about Petty Officer Evans and the returning support parties. The reduction of temperatures exaggerated the difficulties faced by the explorers, although the rationale behind the changes is unclear, as most were so small as to be of little significance, while on at least one occasion (19 December 1911) the temperature published was actually increased.

30 January 1912	Cut criticism of Edgar Evans: 'which makes me much disappointed in him'
4 February 1912	Change description of Edgar Evans: from 'stupid' to 'dull'
5 February 1912	Cut criticism of Edgar Evans: 'and very stupid about himself'
7 February 1912	Cut implied criticism of amount of fuel taken by supporting party from supply depot: 'They have taken on their full allowance of food'
11 February 1912	Change temperature reading from '+6.5 and +3.5' to '−6.5 and −3.5'
11 February 1912	Cut self-criticism: 'We ought to have kept the bearings of our outward compass that is where we have failed'
13 February 1912	Change temperature reading from '+10' to '−10'
13 February 1912	Cut criticism of Edgar Evans: 'is a great nuisance and very clumsy'
14 February 1912	Change temperature reading from '+1' to '−1'
15 February 1912	Change temperature reading from '+10 and +4' to '−10 and −4'

16 February 1912	Change temperature reading from '+6.1 and + 7' to '−6.1 and −7'
16 February 1912	Cut criticism of Edgar Evans: 'and has become impossible'
21 February 1912	Change temperature reading from '+9.5 and −11' to '−9.5 and −11'
2 March 1912	Change reference to fuel shortages from: 'we found a shortage of oil' to: 'we found a ½ gallon of oil instead of full'
5 March 1912	Cut criticism of condition of supply depot after visit of supporting party: 'a poor one'
10 March 1912	Cut criticism of amount of fuel taken by supporting party: 'but generosity and thoughtfulness have not been abundant'
10 March 1912	Cut criticism of condition of supply depot after visit of supporting party: 'it is a miserable jumble'

This editing undoubtedly enhanced Scott's reputation by concealing his lack of generosity towards colleagues and competitors. Asides about Shackleton's 'exaggerated' (8 November and 9 January) and 'overdrawn' (18 January) account of the conditions encountered were cut from the published version. Critical comments about Teddy Evans's leadership of his sledge team on the outward journey, including his 'terrible lack of judgement' (11 December), were also omitted. Kathleen Scott decided Evans should never be allowed to handle the original manuscript.[66]

But, the alteration or excision of only sixty-eight words in a 60-page account of the march back from the Pole cannot explain the appeal of Scott's story. Most importantly, the two most significant passages, the account of Oates's death and 'Message to the Public' were published *exactly* as Scott had written them. Moreover, many unattractive passages were left untouched. On 10 December, for example, Scott bemoaned the 'extraordinary difference in fortune' between his and Shackleton's expeditions, remarking that 'at every step S.'s luck becomes more evident'. A series of critical comments about Oates were also left intact. On 6 March Scott described Oates as a 'terrible hindrance', and again on 10 March as 'the greatest handicap'. Then, on 11 March 1912, Scott wrote

> Titus Oates is very near the end, one feels. What we or he will do, God only knows. We discuss the matter after breakfast; he is a brave fine fellow and understands the situation, but he practically asked for advice. Nothing could be said but to urge him to march as long as he could. One satisfactory result to the discussion; I practically ordered Wilson to hand over the means of ending our troubles to us, so that any one of us may know how to do so. Wilson had no choice between doing so and our ransacking the medicine case. We have 30 opium tablets apiece and he is left with a tube of morphine.

The suggestion that Scott pressured Oates to take his own life caused outrage in the 1970s, but the implication had been in print since 1913. The moodiness, anxiety, and fatalism of the expedition's leader was clearly apparent in the published journals.

Much has been made of J. M. Barrie's involvement in the preparation of Scott's journals. It was decided to include a description of 'The Last Scene' in the book, placed immediately after Scott's final journal entry, and before extracts from his last letters and the 'Message to the Public'. The staging of an appropriate death scene was a staple element of heroic myth-making: Dr Livingstone on his knees with his hands clasped at prayer, General Gordon lowering his revolver at Khartoum. Barrie, a close family friend, was an obvious choice to compose the passage:

> Wilson and Bowers were found in the attitude of sleep, their sleeping-bags closed over their heads as they would naturally close them.
>
> Scott died later. He had thrown back the flaps of his sleeping-bag and opened his coat. The little wallet containing his three notebooks was under his shoulders and his arm flung across Wilson. So they were found eight months later.

By opening his coat Scott indicates his defiance in the face of death, while his gesture towards Wilson emphasizes their friendship. Both the illustrator of the *Sphere* and the artist R. Caton Woodville combined the idea that Scott was the last to die, with the delivery of the 'Message to the Public' in theatrical images of the disaster.

It was fitting for the leading actor to leave the stage last, providing a suitable finale to the Antarctic drama. Huntford has suggested that a note indicating Bowers was the last to die has been suppressed by the Scott Polar Research Institute.[67] Whatever the truth of his accusation, the belief that Scott died last was certainly not invented by Barrie. On 27 November 1912, two days after the return of the search party which discovered the explorers' bodies, Raymond Priestley wrote in his diary that 'Uncle Bill [Wilson] and Birdie [Bowers] were lying quietly in their bags and looked as if they had fallen asleep but the Owner [Scott] was half out of his bag with one arm stretched out towards Uncle Bill. Evidently he had tried to keep awake until the last minute in case of help arriving.' After the *Terra Nova* relieved the shore party on 18 January, Wilfrid Bruce recorded in his diary that 'Scott himself apparently the last to die'.[68]

Unofficial reports declared that Scott was the last to die immediately after the announcement of the disaster. The Christchurch correspondent of the *Daily Mail* reported that Scott was found half-sitting up, with his diary propped between his head and the tent-pole on Friday, 14 February, and an interview with Teddy Evans confirming that Scott died last, was widely distributed by Reuters. When interviewed sixty years later, Tryggve Gran revealed one detail omitted from the reports: that in order to retrieve his journal, the search party had to break Scott's arm, which snapped with the sound of a pistol crack.[69]

Scott's Last Expedition, arranged by Leonard Huxley and with a preface by Clements Markham, was published by Smith, Elder on 6 November 1913. Volume one contained 'The journals of Captain R. F. Scott', while volume two described 'The reports of the journeys and the scientific work undertaken by Dr. E. A. Wilson and the surviving members of the expedition'. The most significant revelations in the book were the inclusion of Scott's final journal entry, 'For God's sake look after our people', which had been omitted from the dispatches sent from New Zealand in February, and extracts from his last letters, which reiterated the principal themes of the 'Message to the Public': that the disaster was caused by misfortune not inadequate preparation, the burden of caring for sick companions, the display of courage and comradeship in the face of death, and the need to provide for the bereaved.

The book was a spectacular success, running through four editions in four months and rapidly selling 13,000 copies. 'It is a great book, perhaps the greatest ever written', exclaimed the *Daily Graphic*, while the *Bookseller* agreed that 'no book issued within our time . . . has carried with it so sure a promise of immortality'.[70]

Scott's story had already been widely disseminated by November 1913, however, through newspapers, magazines, and film. Priced at 42s. the book was extremely expensive and beyond the reach of most readers. A cheap edition was not published until after the war. The significance of *Scott's Last Expedition* resided more in its iconic function than as a vehicle for the transmission of information about the expedition. With its striking cream dust-jacket, two photogravure frontispieces, six original sketches by Wilson, 18 coloured plates, 260 black and white illustrations, panoramas, and maps, and a facsimile of Scott's 'Message to the Public', *Scott's Last Expedition* was a lavish monument to the victims of the Antarctic disaster.

The arrangement of the book served a dual purpose. The

devotion of a second volume to the broader research programme foregrounded the expedition's scientific aims. But the narration of the story through Scott's journal cast the expedition as a journey into the self: the exploration of Antarctica was as much about the delineation of Scott's heroic character as the attainment of the South Pole.

Clements Markham's preface for once made no mention of the nobility of manhauling, and the superiority of dogs was widely acknowledged after the appearance of *Scott's Last Expedition*. A review in the *British Weekly* noted 'some good teams of dogs might have saved the situation'. Another in the *Westminster Gazette* agreed that 'good dog teams would have saved the situation. Amundsen had extraordinarily good fortune in the matter of weather, but the simple secret of his success and his safety was the dogs.' The *Nation* went further, criticizing Scott's prejudices, and hailing Amundsen's superior arrangements: marking his course more accurately, soldering his fuel containers, and greater proficiency with dogs and skis.[71]

Arguably the most significant cover-up of the expedition's affairs in 1913 concerned the actions not of Scott, but of his second-in-command. Teddy Evans's exuberant personality had won him many friends, when he captained the *Terra Nova* from Cardiff to New Zealand. But Scott gradually lost faith and regretted appointing Evans his deputy. Others followed, particularly Cherry-Garrard who condemned Evans's weak sledging performance, self-aggrandizement, and disloyalty to Scott. 'I should like to see that man branded the traitor and liar he is,' Cherry Garrard wrote. 'It would be an everlasting shame, if the story of this Expedition were told by the one big failure in it.'[72]

After the *Terra Nova* docked at Lyttelton, Kinsey also complained about Evans, writing 'that swelled-head, over-burdened conceit, and a desire to accentuate self were very prominent'.[73]

Tragically, Evans's wife Hilda died suddenly during the voyage back from New Zealand. Grief, though, appeared to concentrate his efforts to make his name out of the expedition. He was made a Commander of the Order of the Bath, met with the King at Buckingham Palace, and was promoted to the rank of Captain. He lectured throughout Britain, Europe, and America, and received medals on behalf of the expedition from the most prestigious international geographical societies.

But his self-promotion exasperated many. He came into conflict with both the expedition's organizing committee and the Mansion House fund committee, as they attempted to wind up the expedition's affairs. Lewis Beaumont complained to Kathleen Scott that Evans intended 'to magnify himself in the eyes of the Public – at any cost – even at the sacrifice of his loyalty to his former chief'. Reginald Smith and Herbert Ponting both objected to Evans's lecture tour, far more extensive, they argued, than any Scott had planned, severely damaging their own commercial arrangements. After the war, Ponting too described Evans as 'the one great failure on the Expedition'.[74]

Ten days after news of Scott's death reached London, John Scott Keltie confessed to the French polar explorer Jean Charcot that he did 'not know that any event ever made such a wide-spread impression all over the world'.[75] The magnitude of the response was not surprising. The fate of only the second party to set foot on the South Pole was destined to be headline news. But the first official report cabled from New Zealand dramatically intensified the public reaction. Scott's account of Captain Oates's self-sacrifice and his 'Message to the Public' – this remarkable testament in the face of death – struck a resonant chord in a society beset with anxieties about national decline and the materialism of modern life. Films and photographs imprinted the story on the public consciousness, while Scott's anguished plea for the bereaved denoted an accessible human tragedy.

After the announcement, the surviving crew members guarded Scott's reputation, motivated by a combination of friendship, loyalty, respect for the dead, and a sense of duty to the expedition. Taking their cue from the 'Message to the Public', debates about fuel shortages, relief parties, and the collapse of Evans and Oates deflected attention away from Scott's mistakes, although speculation about the presence of scurvy did call his leadership into question. 'One cannot state facts plainly when they reflect on the organisation,' Teddy Evans wrote to Oates's mother, Caroline.[76] Oates's letters home had been highly critical of Scott; the wealthy cavalry officer, accustomed to the casual authority of those born to lead, had no patience with his frequently indecisive and capricious commander.

But there was no concerted establishment cover-up. The trials of polar life generated the usual animosities on Scott's last expedition, but they were not exceptional. The causes of the disaster were widely debated beneath the hyperbole and Amundsen's superiority, particularly regarding the use of dogs, was acknowledged. Neither, was Scott transformed into a heroic figure by the skilful excisions and embellishments of Huxley or Barrie. He needed no editor to inspire the nation. Yet, even if there was no establishment cover-up, was this outpouring of sentiment orchestrated by the British government? National martyrs had many uses in a society challenged by socialists, suffragettes, and Irish nationalists, an imperial nation struggling to maintain its status in an increasingly unstable international arena. The extent to which the British government exploited public sympathy for Captain Scott will be the subject of our next chapter.

· CHAPTER FOUR ·

REMEMBERING THE DEAD

Friday, 14 February 1913, St Paul's Cathedral

So great were the crowds around St Paul's on the foggy morning of Friday, 14 February 1913 that Captain Oates's sister could not gain entry to the memorial service. Eventually the wife of the organist, Lady Martin, escorted her up to the organ loft.[1]

The day after news of Scott's death reached London, Dean William Inge had announced that a special service would be held in St Paul's. The whole of the cathedral was opened to the public, except for 200 seats in the choir for officials and relatives of the dead. 'St. Paul's is the Cathedral Church, the mother church, indeed, of the British Empire,' observed one newspaper, 'and when a great disaster occurs which stirs the heart of the nation to its depths, it is within its historic walls that the people assemble to pay their tribute to the great and brave dead.' Thirty seats were reserved for the RGS, but one disappointed fellow still complained: 'why those M. P.'s – who are no use to anyone – should demand special accommodation for themselves I fail to see.'[2]

St Paul's was indeed the natural venue for a national memorial service. Governments had paid to erect statues of military and naval officers in the cathedral since the 1790s and, with Wellington and Nelson buried in the crypt, St Paul's was particularly associated with the armed forces. 'While Westminster holds the bones of those who have lived for us,' observed the *Daily Telegraph*, 'St. Paul's has become the garner of the fame of those who have gone to their deaths in our service.'[3] Westminster Abbey housed Poets' Corner and was more frequently used for royal occasions, but St Paul's increasingly provided a focus for national mourning before 1914, hosting services for the victims of the South African War and the *Titanic* disaster. Paintings such as Niels M. Lund's *The Heart of the Empire* (1904) had raised the cathedral as arguably the most iconic of all London landmarks, long before the smoke of the Blitz encircled the dome.

Speculation about the retrieval of the bodies of the dead appeared almost immediately after news of the disaster reached London. Reuters reported that the high commissioner of New Zealand had offered the steamer *Hinemoa* for use in recovering the bodies. The members of the expedition, however, swiftly opposed the proposal. Edward Wilson's father wrote first to Reginald Smith and then to *The Times* pleading that the dead be left 'to sleep on, with the eternal snows around them and their great achievement their most fitting monument. I should feel as if it were a desecration to move them'.[4]

The contrast with the treatment of David Livingstone forty years earlier is striking. Livingstone's followers, Abdullah Susi and James Chuma, had overseen the transport of the Scottish explorer's body from the southern shore of Lake Bangweulu to the African coast. The P&O steamer *Malwa* then carried the body from Zanzibar to Southampton free of charge; but Susi and Chuma did not accompany the coffin, as a colonial official declined to pay their passage without specific orders from Whitehall. The body was eventually taken to the map room of the RGS, where an autopsy confirmed the identity of the corpse by its fractured left humerus, an injury sustained during Livingstone's famous encounter with an African lion. Livingstone's remains were 'transferred from the rough coffin of Zanzibar wood', reported *The Times*, 'to a coffin of English

oak, very simply decorated'.[5] Speaking in Glasgow a few days before
the announcement of Livingstone's death, the RGS President, Sir
Henry Bartle-Frere, had referred to 'questionings as to the degree
in which I suppose he has naturalised himself and become like
one of the Africans'.[6] The transfer of Livingstone's body to a coffin of
English oak and burial in Westminster Abbey insulated the explorer
from the enervating African environment.

But if Africa threatened contamination, Antarctica offered
purification, and a fitting resting-place for Captain Scott and his
companions. Lord Curzon declared his hope that 'their bodies may
be left where they lie, with the snow as their winding sheet, the
eternal ice as their tomb, and the solemn Antarctic wastes as the
graveyard in which it has pleased God that they should sleep'.[7]

The absence of bodies precluded a funeral procession, so
the Scott memorial service followed the model established for
the *Titanic* ten months earlier, with psalms, hymns, and biblical
readings, but no sermon. The service was attended by a host of
dignitaries, including Prime Minister Asquith, the Conservative
leader Andrew Bonar Law, Home Secretary Reginald McKenna,
Lord Curzon, the Lord Mayor, the Archbishop of Canterbury, and
the Bishop of London.

The most prominent mourner, though, was King George V.
It was unprecedented for a British monarch to attend either a
funeral or memorial service for someone who was not a member
of a royal family, and the King's attendance was widely commented on. In the absence of the bodies of the explorers the King,
dressed in the uniform of the Admiral of the Fleet, offered a focal
point for the ceremony. Neither the King nor Asquith had attended
the *Titanic* service, and their presence transformed the Scott
memorial service into a majestic display of the power and unity of
the nation-state.

The cathedral doors opened at 9.30 a.m. and 'Church Full' signs appeared within an hour. The king arrived as Beethoven's 'Funeral March' was drawing to a close. The ceremony built to a climax with the lesson from 1 Corinthians 15, read by Dean Inge: 'Death has been swallowed up in victory. Where, O death, is your victory? Where, O Death, is your sting?' As the echo of the Dean's words faded away, a single drummer from the Coldstream Guards stood beneath the cathedral dome to perform a steadily rising drum roll, which introduced the 'Dead March' in *Saul*. The names of the five dead men were then intoned in the Prayer of Committal. The service lasted just over an hour and concluded with the National Anthem.

Scott's sister Grace wrote she 'never imagined anything so wonderful and uplifting'. Clergymen, too, enthused over the service and Canon Alexander expressed his delight that the public turned to their cathedral in moments of national sorrow or rejoicing. The proceedings were extensively reported on Saturday, allowing individuals throughout the country to participate in the ceremony and providing a climax to the week's coverage of the disaster. The Topical Film Company's newsreel footage of the service generated an exceptionally large demand.[8]

The service was predominantly represented as a display of national unity. 'It was above all a citizens' tribute,' declared the *Daily Chronicle*:

> all classes, rich and poor, wives and mothers from the suburbs, town folk and country folk, aged invalids and strapping young schoolboys, clergymen, nurses – some on ambulance duty, though there was, happily, little need – with a very noticeable proportion of old Service men. These knew best of all the inner meaning of this tribute to courage and to sacrifice. They knew that it is sweet and beautiful to die for one's country's honour.

They knew that there is nothing greater than this, 'that a man should lay down his life for his friend'.

The unprecedented attendance of the King secured the disaster as a sacrifice in the name of the nation. 'The presence of the KING', wrote C. W. Brodribb in *The Times*, 'conveyed a symbolism without which any ceremony expressive of national sentiment would have been inadequate.' One poem concluded with a dramatic image of the King at the service, and asked the dead explorers: 'Can you see the Dome of the Golden Cross | And our King upon his knees?'[9]

At the end of the service, the National Anthem was sung in its entirety at St Paul's for the first time in many years.[10] The *Daily Mirror* reported that, as the King left the cathedral, a solitary voice began to sing 'God Save our Gracious King';

> 'Long Live our noble King,' joined in a hundred voices.
>
> 'Send him victorious,' came from a thousand throats, and as the words 'Happy and glorious' were reached the vast concourse of people were singing as one man sings . . .
>
> People on the hill joined in and workers in the warehouses and the shops heard the sound and sang the final words 'Long to reign over us, God save the King!'
>
> It was the unrehearsed expression of a people's sorrow, and they were singing the only thing that sprang half-thought of from their minds.
>
> For even in the sorrow of the scene – aye, even in the tragedy that robbed our country of five of its noblest sons – was there not that triumphant note of a people's love and of a nation's loyalty that in England can never be dissociated from the person of the monarch.
>
> Who knows? Perhaps it was the last song the explorers sang before the snow conquered them. It was certainly the most fitting end to a service of sorrow.

For out of that sorrow and out of that anguish will be born a new patriotism, and from it will spring even a new desire for service to the nation and its head.

Of that patriotism, which made Scott die as bravely as he and his fellow-heroes died, the King was doubtless thinking as he drove home to his palace.

For because of such patriotism does a nation remain really great.[11]

King, ministers, and people, joined in mourning within the cathedral church of empire. The energy generated by the service — by the crowds gathered outside, by the voices raised in communal song, by the roll of the kettledrum rising in a crescendo, by the rich biblical language of sacrifice and solemn intonation of the names of the dead – was harnessed beneath the dome of St Paul's and channelled into the mute body of the King. In such moments the mystique of the monarchy was renewed.

The RGS and Lord Curzon's Frustration

The service at St Paul's offered a powerful display of the majesty of the British nation-state, but central government played a minimal role in the organization of the event. The service was arranged by the Dean and Chapter of St Paul's, not the government; Prime Minister Asquith's Cabinet letters to the King make no mention of the Antarctic disaster. The private secretary of the Chancellor of the Exchequer, Lloyd George, even wrote to the RGS requesting tickets, only to be informed that applications should be directed to St Paul's.[12]

One politician, though, did strive to exploit the Antarctic disaster for his own ends, but he was out of office in 1913. Lord Curzon was by now a Conservative heavyweight destined, many believed (himself included) for the party leadership. Curzon was fascinated by public ceremonial. While Viceroy of India he had masterminded the spectacular Delhi Coronation Durbar in 1903, and subsequently organized pageants to mark his installation as Lord Warden of the Cinque Ports (1904) and Chancellor of Oxford University (1907). The Antarctic disaster presented the sort of occasion he relished, choreographing the presentation of the past to transmit a message to the future. The RGS had changed dramatically under his presidency, with the move to Lowther Lodge and admission of women as fellows. Curzon saw an opportunity to harness Scott's memory for the benefit of the Society and consolidate the recent reforms. But his many schemes would end in frustration.

Curzon was lying ill at his home in Basingstoke when news of the disaster reached England. The announcement appears to have roused him, prompting a flurry of correspondence, a telephone call to chastise the Lord Mayor for acting prematurely, and a visit to St Paul's to attend the memorial service. Ever mindful of public theatre, Curzon suggested the RGS council should enter the cathedral together.

His first attempt to orchestrate the response to Scott's death for the benefit of the RGS came in an open letter to the press published the day after the St Paul's service. Curzon argued that a Scott memorial hall adjacent to the Society's new Kensington home would prove the most appropriate monument to the dead.

> Would not a building so erected and named, so decorated and employed, do as much to keep alive the memory and service of these heroes as a score of beds in a hospital or a monumental pile of smoke-begrimed bronze. It would be a hall of meeting dedicated to the propagation of that science to which Scott and his

companions yielded up their lives. But it would be also a Temple
of Fame dedicated to themselves.

The *Daily Express*, however, criticized Curzon's letter, declaring
his argument faulty and proposal wrongheaded. The *Express*
asserted that the essence of any memorial should be 'its public
and national character . . . This cannot be done by perpetuating a
great memory in the private grounds of an exclusive and scientific
society.' Even some RGS fellows opposed the proposal, and in his
first speech on the disaster ten days later, Curzon backed down,
calling only for the erection of 'some visible monument'.[13]

The RGS officially commemorated Scott's death with two
events in May. In lieu of one of the Society's gold medals, Lady
Scott was presented with a silver casket to hold the awards Scott
had received following the *Discovery* expedition. The Society's
other gold medal was awarded posthumously to Dr Wilson, and
accepted by his widow, Oriana. Curzon had claimed Wilson as an
RGS fellow in February, but Oriana informed Keltie that her late
husband had not been able to afford the subscription fee.[14]

The climax of the Society's commemorations came on 21 May,
when Teddy Evans followed Stanley, Nansen, Scott, Shackleton,
and Peary as only the sixth explorer to deliver an RGS lecture in the
Royal Albert Hall. Curzon and Keltie had corresponded about the
possibility of such a lecture barely twenty-four hours after news of
Scott's death reached London. Around 9,000 people attended the
lecture, including Sir Robert Baden-Powell, Admiral Prince Louis
of Battenburg, General Sir Douglas Haig, the Duke of Somerset,
and the bishops of Bangor and Newcastle. Keltie wrote to one
disappointed fellow that 'the demand for tickets for the present
meeting in the Albert Hall is unprecedented. We could have filled
it three times over.' Evans offered a plain account of the progress of

the expedition, concluding with a tribute to the 'seamen and stokers of the *Terra Nova* – worthy fellows, whose bye-word has been, "Play the game".' Evans's lecture was published in the *Geographical Journal*, but without illustrations, which Reginald Smith feared would damage the sales of the *Strand Magazine* serialization and the forthcoming book.[15]

Responsibility for the erection of a national memorial had by now passed to the Mansion House Scott memorial fund committee, on which Curzon played a leading role. The committee secretary, William Soulsby, reported that he had received hundreds of suggestions regarding the form of a memorial.

> Some are of a useful and some are of a ludicrous and grotesque character. Among the former may be mentioned the endowment of orphanages for seamen, provision for further Antarctic research, erection of a Church at Devonport (Captain Scott's birthplace), a cottage home for non-commissioned officers (as a memorial to Captain Oates), the purchase of the *Terra Nova* etc. Included in the grotesque category may be mentioned an Eiffel Tower on Parliament Hill, helping the victims of the Charing-Cross Bank, raising an Aerial Fleet, a sanctuary for outcasts, housing old age pensioners, and the restoration of St. Paul's cathedral.[16]

The tension between functional and symbolic memorials, whether to found a hospital or erect a statue in honour of the dead, foreshadowed the debates which would surround commemorations of the First World War.

The committee eventually resolved to divide the £18,000 allocated for the commemoration of the disaster between three projects: first, a bronze memorial tablet in St Paul's Cathedral, for which the Dean and Chapter had already given permission; second, 'a sculptured monument in bronze in a public place in London (preferably the space immediately behind the railings in Hyde Park, fronting Lowther Lodge, the new home of the Royal Geographical Society) to contain the figures of the five dead men, by a sculptor of approved eminence'; and, third, the balance, estimated at around £10,000, to be 'devoted to an Endowment Fund in aid of future Polar Research. . . . This is an object which it is believed would have commended itself greatly to the late Captain Scott.'[17] A subcommittee was appointed to administer the erection of these memorials, comprised of Soulsby, Harry Lawson (the Editor of the *Daily Telegraph*), Sir Edgar Speyer, and, inevitably, Curzon. With Lawson's support, Curzon argued that a further £3,000 should be diverted from the publication of scientific results to the provision of memorials, but his request was overruled.[18]

It seems likely that Kathleen Scott strongly influenced the choice of memorials. Curzon's papers contain a handwritten sheet with comments on possible memorials under the heading 'Lady Scott'. A 'Bas Relief' in St Paul's, a 'Possible memorial outside L. L. in Kensington', and a 'Fund for endowment of Antarctic Research' are all marked favourably. But Lady Scott is described as being 'dead agst.' the provision of cheap hospital beds, while the proposal to establish a church in Plymouth is dismissed with the observation that 'Scott never went into a church'.[19]

With his earlier opposition to a 'monumental pile of smoke-begrimed bronze' quietly forgotten, Curzon turned his attention to securing a site opposite Lowther Lodge for the national memorial statue. On 6 August he called the attention of the first Commissioner of Works, Earl Beauchamp, to the Mansion House committee's proposal for an imposing London monument. The use of London parks was a controversial topic in 1913, however. So many statues had been erected in the nineteenth century that both politicians and the people were increasingly protective of public space in the crowded city. The placement of a statue of J. M. Barrie's 'Peter Pan' in Kensington Gardens had aroused considerable controversy the previous year, while even the identification of a site for a memorial to King Edward VII had proved difficult. Curzon, however, argued that 'in the present case the sacrifice of space inside the Park would be so infinitesimal as scarcely to deserve the name of sacrifice. . . . the Captain Scott tragedy touched the public heart more than anything in recent times, and the public . . . would be disappointed' if a visible memorial was not erected in London.[20]

Sir Lionel Earle, the secretary to the Commissioner of Works, believed Parliament would resist any attempt to lose even 'a blade of grass for statues' in the royal parks, and telegraphed the royal yacht at Cowes, to secure the King's consent for a rejection of Curzon's request.[21] Beauchamp explained in the House of Lords that while the Board of Works 'did not lag behind anyone else in our admiration of Captain Scott and his comrades . . . we find ourselves barred by the jealous dislike which had been shown on more than one occasion by the public to any addition being made to the memorials in the Park'.[22]

The debate spilled over onto the letters pages of *The Times* when Percy Harris, Liberal London County Councillor for Bethnal Green, complained that the capital had been singularly unsuccessful in commemorating its heroes. But Captain Arthur Murray, MP, responded that, in a large city like London, 'every tree, every leaf and every blade of grass is worth untold gold', while another correspondent urged Mr Harris to stop spoiling London parks and devote his energy to improving East End slums.[23] Publications such as the *Sphere* and the *Daily Telegraph* supported the clamour for a prominent London memorial, but the Board of Works remained firm. Curzon appears to have lost interest after the rejection of a site in Hyde Park and resigned from the memorial subcommittee in November.

Soulsby confessed his desire to close the fund after Curzon's resignation:

> Personally, I think a modest memorial in St. Paul's would be quite ample, without any further statue or commemorative group else-where. If you were to take a census of London statues, you would find that nine-tenths of the subjects are quite forgotten & their achievements obsolete. At Guildhall we have busts and statues of politicians &c. – such as Stafford Northcote & W. H. Smith – who are out of all recollection nowadays, and I conclude from this that the Public have a very short memory & that in a few years Capt. Scott and his companions will have drifted into the same obscurity as many more distinguished men.

Soulsby quickly retracted his suggestion after Curzon reminded him, in typically brusque fashion, that the erection of a prominent national memorial had been one of the declared aims of the Mansion House appeal. 'It was stupid of me to forget the large sum "earmarked" for a tangible memorial,' replied Soulsby. 'Of course, we cannot over-ride donors' wishes without infinite trouble & probably getting into Chancery!'[24]

Curzon's other significant scheme for harnessing Scott's memory to the RGS was his attempt to acquire Scott's journals as the prize exhibit for a new museum of exploration in Lowther Lodge. At the Society's anniversary meeting on 26 May, Curzon had reported that, after using the journal for the forthcoming book, Lady Scott 'will place the original on loan with us, where she may be sure that we will cherish it as a treasure beyond price'. Three days later, however, Curzon wrote to ask Kathleen Scott if, as 'soon as his things come back, perhaps you will let me know what personal relics you would like to let us have for the museum', suggesting that no definite commitment had yet been made.[25]

In October, Curzon wrote again to ask Kathleen Scott if she remembered 'promising me for Museum at RGS loan of your husband's priceless diary and also gift of some personal effects to put in glass case in Museum?' Kathleen Scott replied, however, that while she appreciated his 'wish to have some further momento [sic] of my husband at the R. G. S. . . . I really made no promise as to his journals, and after very careful reflection think I want them (if out of my own keeping) to be in the British Museum'.[26]

Curzon angrily reminded Kathleen Scott of their meeting in her house last May, when he had suggested she deposit the journals in the new RGS museum. 'You said that you could not do this at once because you wanted the diary for purposes of the book, and that you would not like to part with it altogether and would prefer therefore to place it on a sort of permanent loan. I entirely agreed. I reported this conversation at once to Keltie and mentioned it at the next meeting of the Council.' Curzon quoted from his speech at the Society's anniversary meeting and concluded 'But really, I did not think there was any doubt about it'.[27]

Curzon was more successful in persuading Scott's family to commission a new portrait of the dead explorer, intended for a prominent position in Lowther Lodge. Harrington Mann, an established painter who would build a global reputation from New York after the war, produced perhaps the most innovative artistic composition inspired by the Antarctic disaster. The intense stare, crossed arms, and square shoulders challenge the viewer to imagine the suffering behind Scott's inscrutable expression. Curzon, however, took an instant dislike to the painting, and sent it back for alterations.[28]

14. Edgar Evans, Bowers, Wilson, and Scott (l. to r.) in still from *With Capt. Scott, R.N., to the South Pole*. The climax of the second series of Ponting's films was a sequence in which the four explorers pitched their tent, made dinner, and settled down to sleep. Scott, Bowers, Evans, and Wilson had already been dead for six months when this footage was first released in October 1912. (LEFT)

TRIUMPH BEFORE DEATH: THE FIVE HEROES AT THE SOUTH POLE.

15. Oates, Bowers, Scott, Wilson, and Evans (l. to r.) at the South Pole, 18 January 1912. The photographs taken by the explorers at the Pole remain the most enduring icons of the disaster. The circulation of the *Daily Mirror* increased overnight by an unprecedented half a million copies with the publication of the images. Bowers operates the camera here using a piece of string. *Hello! Magazine* featured this photograph on the front cover of its photographic history of the twentieth century.

16. The St Paul's Memorial Service. Clockwise from top left-hand corner: Kathleen Scott, Captain Scott, Peter Scott, Wilson, Evans, Oates, Bowers. Large crowds surrounded St Paul's before the national memorial service on Friday, 14 February 1913. (LEFT)

17. *Britannia Consolatrix.*
    The relatives of the dead featured prominently in the first reports of the disaster, prompted by Scott's dying plea for the bereaved to be provided for. (BELOW)

"It shall now be *my* part to care for you."

"Had we lived I should have had a tale to tell of the hardihood, endurance, and courage of my companions which would have stirred the heart of every Englishman. These rough notes and our dead bodies must tell the tale; but surely, surely, a great, rich country like ours will see that those who are dependent upon us are properly provided for."
—(Captain Scott's last words.)

18. 'Armchair Explorers'. The disaster dominated conversation following the announcement of Scott's death.

"Our sons will die like English Gentlemen"
Wendy

"LIKE ENGLISH GENTLEMEN"
TO PETER SCOTT
FROM THE AUTHOR OF
WHERE'S MASTER?

(*7):91(08)
[1910–13]

19. *Like English Gentlemen*. The title refers to a passage in J. M. Barrie's *Peter Pan*: 'At this moment Wendy was grand. "These are my last words, dear boys," she said firmly. "I feel that I have a message to you from your real mothers, and it is this: 'We hope our sons will die like English gentlemen.'" (LEFT)

20. 'A Tale To Tell'. Henry Graves & Co. commissioned the well-known illustrator Richard Caton Woodville to compose a print to raise money for the Mansion House Scott memorial fund. The drawing was taken to Buckingham Palace to receive the King's approval. A small portrait of Peter Scott was included in the bottom right-hand corner of the print. (BELOW)

"HAD WE LIVED I SHOULD HAVE HAD A TALE TO TELL OF THE HARDIHOOD, ENDURANCE AND COURAGE OF MY COMPANIONS WHICH WOULD HAVE STIRRED THE HEART OF EVERY ENGLISHMAN."

21. 'The Last Message'. The popular illustrated weekly *Sphere*, published a special memorial edition in May 1913, which included the photographs taken by the explorers at the Pole. The illustrator followed Caton Woodville in fixing on the delivery of Scott's last message as the definitive image of the disaster.

(a)

(b)

(c)

22. (a) The death of Captain Oates. Some commentators have suggested Scott invented Oates's last words. But Scott's own style tended to be more lyrical. The dry announcement recorded by Scott certainly fitted the character of the taciturn cavalry officer.

(b) Last entry. Scott's famous last journal entry, 'For God's sake look after our people', was omitted from initial reports of the disaster in February 1913, and only made public with the publication of *Scott's Last Expedition* in November.

(c) 'Message to the Public'. A special facsimile of the 'Message to the Public' which Scott wrote at the end of his sledging journal was included in the two-volume *Scott's Last Expedition*. One advertisement described the 'Message' as 'the most impressive document ever read by man'.

THE SPHERE

AN ILLUSTRATED NEWSPAPER FOR THE HOME

With which is incorporated
"BLACK & WHITE"

Volume LII. No. 683. | REGISTERED AT THE GENERAL POST OFFICE AS A NEWSPAPER | London, February 22, 1913. | Price Sixpence.

"DEATH IS SWALLOWED UP IN VICTORY"—THE IMPRESSIVE MEMORIAL SERVICE TO THE POLAR HEROES AT ST. PAUL'S

DRAWN BY F. MATANIA

St. Paul's Cathedral has been the scene of many impressive memorial services but no one, least of all those fortunate members of the public who gained admittance, will question that the service held there last week in memory of Captain Scott and his gallant companions will bear comparison with the greatest of them. The King was present; the Prime Minister and several members of the Cabinet and ambassadors and ministers of foreign states were among the congregation. The cathedral was filled to its utmost capacity, and it is computed that about 10,000 persons were unable to gain admission

23. The King at St Paul's. With the bodies of the explorers left in the Antarctic, King George V provided a focal point for the National Memorial Service at St Paul's cathedral.

SITE OF PROPOSED MEMORIAL TO BE ERECTED IN WHITE MARBLE AND BRONZE

Drawn by F. Matania

The smaller view shows the effect of the monument when silhouetted against an evening sky

A PROPOSED MONUMENT TO CAPTAIN SCOTT.

"WHEN YOUR CHILDREN SHALL ASK THEIR FATHERS IN TIME TO COME, SAYING, WHAT MEAN THESE STONES?"—Joshua, iv, 21

THE SPHERE here puts before its readers a suggestion for a monument to Captain Scott. The question will soon become a practical one. Various ideas have already been put forward but none has yet taken a form which appears to us to be desirable. We feel that the monument should take a form which would appeal in some bold—and yet not overbold—manner to the passerby. For this purpose a mere portrait statue would seem inadequate. A mural tablet in St. Paul's must also fall short from what is desirable in the present circumstances. The death of Captain Scott and his companions stirred this nation very deeply, and it is greatly to be desired that the monument should reflect in some way both the deed and the emotions which it created in the minds and hearts of Englishmen.

We have ventured, therefore, to design a monument, and Mr. F. Matania has carried out our suggestion in an elevation view, which shows the general structure of the proposed monument. One of the basic ideas is that the main portion of the design should consist of white marble and bronze. A rough mass of white marble would represent the snow and ice of the Antarctic. Over this sloping mass would be seen a bronze

group of Captain Scott and his two companions struggling with their sledge to their final camp. It is proposed that the lower portion of the monument should be of classic design, in the walls of which could be let high-relief bronze panels showing other striking incidents of the expedition. The main block of the monument would be oblong in form with an apse at each end. A figure of Britannia with a globe would face the steps at one end. A classic prow together with a portrait bust of Captain Scott would project from the other apse. Around the central portion of the monument would extend a marble platform, to be reached by four flights of marble steps. Bronze penguins would be placed at various intervals round the base of the monument.

The question of a site for such a memorial is, of course, a matter of importance. The position which will readily suggest itself as solving most of the essential requirements is Waterloo Place at the foot of Regent Street. Here already there is a large space in which such a memorial could be easily erected. Statues of Franklin and other great men are in the immediate vicinity. Passers-by would be able to approach the memorial and study its panels without danger from passing traffic.

A Suggested Site for the Above Memorial

The position at the bottom of Regent Street has much to recommend it. There is already a statue to another polar explorer there, and the surrounding area would enable the passer-by to study the memorial in safety

24. 'A Proposed Monument to Captain Scott'. The *Sphere* proposed an imposing London memorial at the end of Regent Street, with three bronze figures of Scott, Bowers, and Wilson striding across an expanse of white marble. Both the absence of Captain Oates and the presence of penguins on the balustrade are worthy of note.

National Memorials

By the end of 1913 Scott's legacy had transcended the RGS. Scott, Bowers, Evans, Oates, and Wilson had not sacrificed their lives in the name of a private scientific society. The RGS would continue to honour Scott's memory, but the immense public reaction to the disaster demanded national recognition.

Ignoring (and possibly inspired by) Curzon's exasperated appeals, Kathleen Scott decided to loan her late husband's sledging journals to the British Museum. With nearly a million visitors in 1913, the museum was one of London's most popular attractions. The trustees formally accepted the loan at a meeting on 10 January 1914. Sir Frederick Kenyon, the Museum's director, wrote that the trustees believed the journals 'may do much to enforce the lesson which was often in Captain Scott's mind during the latter days of his great march, the lesson that men of English race can face death without flinching for the honour of their nation'.[29] The journals were placed on display in the manuscripts saloon a week later.

Individual initiative also secured Scott's place in the capital's other principal hall of fame, the National Portrait Gallery. The Gallery did not attract the crowds drawn to the British Museum (around 135,000 visits were recorded in 1913), but it still offered a significant barometer of national taste. The addition of a portrait of Scott to the collection had been discussed in the immediate aftermath of the disaster, but no action appears to have been taken until December, when Charles Percival Small approached the trustees. Small had painted a posthumous portrait from two photographs he had taken of his friend Scott before the departure of the *Terra Nova*. After a long discussion, the trustees agreed that, while they would 'infinitely prefer' a sketch by Kathleen Scott to a posthumous portrait by another person, they would waive the Gallery's rule of not considering portraits until ten years after the death of the sitter providing, first, that the portrait was offered as a gift, and second, that the portrait met with Lady Scott's approval.[30] Kathleen Scott considered the portrait good and the trustees accepted the gift from Sir Courtauld Thompson.

The acquisition of Small's portrait offers insights into both the rationale of the National Portrait Gallery and Scott's fame in 1914. The portrait was insipid, and Small an insignificant artist; the Gallery catalogue does not even record his date of death. From its foundation in 1856, however, the Gallery had acquired portraits based on the celebrity of the subject, rather than artistic merit. Historical eminence remains the primary criterion for admission to the collection. Waivers of the ten-year rule were uncommon, although not exceptional. But the Gallery rules forbade the admission of modern copies. The acquisition of authentic portraits, drawn from life, furnished the Gallery with its distinctive *raison d'être*. Earl Stanhope, among others, had believed that by exhibiting authentic likenesses of the nation's greatest figures, the Gallery would offer a source of moral inspiration to the public. For this reason, the trustees rarely acquired posthumous works, and the acceptance of Small's portrait offers a notable indication of Scott's celebrity.

The Mansion House Scott memorial fund subcommittee, however, was to oversee the centrepiece of the nation's commemoration of the Antarctic disaster. Curzon was replaced on the subcommittee by the civil servant Lionel Earle, and Sir Thomas Brock, who had designed the Victoria memorial outside Buckingham Palace. Six leading sculptors were invited to submit designs for a statue: Stanley Nicholson Babb, Charles Hartwell, Albert Hodge, Thomas Stirling Lee, A. G. Walker, and Francis Derwent Wood. On 8 July 1914 the committee unanimously chose Albert Hodge's design, 'Pro

Patria'. The *Builder*, an influential commentator on British art and architecture, declared itself in hearty agreement with the decision, condemning the other entries for 'the one unforgivable fault of being unrelievedly dull'.[31]

Hodge, who had trained at the Glasgow School of Art in the 1890s, was best known for his decorative work on a number of public buildings, including the Royal Academy of Music and the Royal Exchange. He was praised for bringing his architectural training to bear on his work, which showed a 'perfect adaptation and correlation of architectural and sculptured form'.[32]

> A granite pylon is surmounted by a bronze group representing Courage sustained by Patriotism, spurning Fear, Despair and Death, the figure Courage being crowned by Immortality. Below the group the words 'For King,' 'For Country,' 'For Brotherly Love,' and 'For Knowledge' are inscribed. The front of the pylon bears the names of the five men, whose portrait medallions in bronze occupy the most prominent positions on the monument.

The pylon stands on a podium with four bronze panels depicting the expedition:

> 'To strive' (showing the difficulties surmounted on the journey); 'To seek' (showing the start for the Pole); 'To find' (showing the party at the Pole); 'And not to yield' (showing the tent covered with snow – the last resting place of the heroes).

Hodge estimated the total height of the monument would be around 37 feet. He had attempted 'to teach the great lesson of heroism of the expedition, not by merely representing any incident but by telling the story for future generations'.[33]

The Mansion House committee had originally called for a statue representing all five dead explorers. Kathleen Scott favoured a naturalist approach to sculpture, and met with Derwent

Wood a number of times before the subcommittee's decision was announced. But Hodge's success, ahead of more naturalist tableaux proposed by Derwent Wood and Nicholson Babb, reflected the influence of continental ideas about public monuments. The *Builder* had been critical of London statuary in recent years, and advised British sculptors to follow the 'practice of the Continent and make our monuments symbolic of the personality and life-work of the person commemorated, and educate the public to be satisfied with a portrait in the form of a medallion or bust as part of a monument, which should be allegorical rather than photographic'.[34] The placing of a statuary group on a pedestal decorated with bas-reliefs echoed William Hamo Thornycroft's influential statue of General Gordon, then in Trafalgar Square. But Hodge's statuary group, with the central figure representing not Captain Scott but 'Courage', was certainly more allegorical than photographic.

Hodge's design, with a winged 'Immortality' recalling a triumphant Britannia and the defiant posture and military costume of 'Courage', was the most forceful example of nationalist propaganda generated by the Antarctic disaster. Here was the British government, working through Sir Lionel Earle, secretary of the Board of Works, and Sir Thomas Brock, designer of Queen Victoria's official monument, exploiting Scott's memory to glorify the idea of sacrifice in the name of king and country.

Yet this statue was never built. Kathleen Scott and a number of senior RGS fellows strongly objected to Hodge's design. Douglas Freshfield, who had succeeded Curzon as RGS President in May, complained directly to Brock:

> we feel that its general character is out of keeping with the occasion to be commemorated. We consider that a record of quiet protracted and heroic endurance calls for a design more reserved

and less allegorical in conception. In particular the strained and somewhat theatrical attitude given to the figure grasping a military banner and apparently trampling underfoot nude bodies strikes Captain Scott's friends as singularly out of all connection both with polar exploration and the man it is designed to honour and to represent.

Brock replied, surprisingly, that he agreed 'with what you say in the advantage of introducing a somewhat more personal and restrained element in the group surmounting the pedestal'. It was the reply, Freshfield considered, of an artist and a gentleman. By the end of September, Brock was able to inform Freshfield that Hodge was 'quite ready and anxious to reconsider the design . . . and to do what he can to meet your views'.[35]

Hodge made substantial revisions. In particular, the central figure was transformed. The defiant posture, uniform, and spear were replaced with a more contemplative pose, sledging gear and ski-stick, in a direct representation of Scott himself. The nude figures representing 'Fear, Despair and Death', which the *Builder* had praised for reaching 'a level of excellence rarely attained by monumental sculpture in this country', were completely removed, along with the helmet and triumphant salute of the winged 'Immortality'.[36]

Yet in spite of the resolution of the conflict over Hodge's design, the memorial subcommittee was unable to secure a suitable London site for the statue. Locations outside the National Portrait Gallery, in Battersea Park, on Chelsea Embankment, and between the India Office and Foreign Office buildings were considered, but no firm offer was made. The Admiralty offered a site beside Greenwich Hospital, but the committee preferred to hold out in the hope of finding somewhere in London which was more accessible to the public. During the war, Hodge, with

Kathleen Scott's support, lobbied for a site in Victoria Tower Gardens beside the House of Lords. Lionel Earle, however, simply reiterated Parliament's opposition to the erection of statues in royal parks.[37]

The other principal commemorative project initiated by the Mansion House committee, the placement of a tablet in the crypt of St Paul's, proceeded much more smoothly. The selection of a design by Nicholson Babb attracted little comment in May 1914, and Prime Minister Asquith unveiled the memorial at a special service in the cathedral two years later.

But Hodge's statue, intended as the centrepiece of national remembrance, continued to be dogged by problems. First, Hodge died suddenly on 31 December 1917, before he had completed the statue.[38] Then the Admiralty withdrew the offer of a site in Greenwich, and Sir Thomas Brock died, prompting Earle and Soulsby to consider abandoning the entire project. Earle, though, finally secured from the War Office a site on Mount Wise in Devonport, the town where Scott had been born.[39] The national memorial statue for the victims of the Antarctic disaster was finally unveiled on 10 August 1925, more than twelve years after the closure of the Mansion House Scott memorial fund.

Local Memorials

When Hodge's statue was finally unveiled in 1925, more than thirty other memorials had been erected in Britain alone. While the Mansion House committee's efforts to commemorate the Antarctic disaster on behalf of the nation were disrupted by internal disputes and a lack of political will, the endeavours of local communities proved much more successful. Schools,

Map of British memorials commemorating the Antarctic disaster, 1913–1925.

churches, councils, societies, newspapers, the armed forces, and individual philanthropists were the principal agents of the public commemoration of Captain Scott and his companions.

Local councils and schools had provided essential finance for the *Terra Nova* expedition, and both proved active in commemorating the Antarctic disaster. Outside London, councils could act swiftly on behalf of their citizens. The Mayor of Cheltenham called for subscriptions to erect a statue of the city's former resident, Edward Wilson, on the Promenade. Kathleen Scott sculpted a simple statue of Wilson in sledging gear, which was unveiled by Clements Markham on 8 July 1914. A brass plate included Scott's description of Wilson: 'He died as he lived, a brave true man, the best of comrades and staunchest of friends.'[40]

In recognition of the city's contribution to the expedition, the *Terra Nova* both commenced and finished her voyage to the Antarctic from Cardiff docks. With a population of 1,870 in 1801, Cardiff had been only the twenty-first largest town in Wales, but grew rapidly in the second half of the nineteenth century with the expansion of the coal industry. By 1901, with a population of 164,333, Cardiff had risen to the status of the world's premier coal port, and the Antarctic expedition served as an impressive advertisement for the civic achievements and commercial prowess of the city.

Special trains carried an estimated 60,000 sightseers to Cardiff after the return of the *Terra Nova* on 14 June. Four separate memorials were erected in the city within four years of the announcement of the disaster. Public subscriptions paid for a memorial bed in the Royal Hamadryad hospital and a bronze tablet in the city hall. The shipping company Bowring Brothers exercised their option to repurchase the *Terra Nova* for £5,000 and the company's chairman, F. C. Bowring, then paid for the erection of both the figurehead of the *Terra Nova* and a clocktower in Cardiff's Roath Park. Bowring's status as a prospective Liberal party candidate for the city may explain his generosity.[41]

Schools and churches also expressed their associations with Scott's last expedition, able both to raise money and allocate appropriate memorial sites with relative ease. Cheltenham College honoured their old boy, Edward Wilson, with a life-size portrait in the library, a window representing 'Fortitude' in the chapel, and a tablet in the old boys' stalls. The captain of Stubbington House, which Scott had attended before joining the training ship *Britannia*, wrote to inform Scott's mother that a large framed photograph of her son had been hung in the school library. 'So many of us go into the services from Stubbington that we shall have many chances of copying, in some way, his splendid example of duty and courage.'[42]

Parishes associated with the expedition proved particularly generous. A local appeal raised money to place a tablet in Meanwood church, Leeds, where Oates had often visited relatives as a child. The tablet was unveiled on 6 November to coincide with the publication of *Scott's Last Expedition*, in the presence of the Lord Mayor, the Vice-Chancellor of Leeds University, and representatives of both the Inniskilling Dragoons and the Leeds Rifles. The tablet read simply: 'This monument is placed here by fellow citizens as a record of the brave act of a very gallant gentleman.' 'Leeds youths will remember this great act,' promised the Vicar of Leeds. 'It will live in them, become a living force within them, for the powers of the strong saint-men are stronger than those of evil.'[43]

Finally, officers in the army, navy, and Royal Indian Marine initiated a wide range of schemes to honour their dead comrades. In February 1914, Bowers's mother wrote to Lady Ellison-Macartney that the Royal Indian Marine had arranged for the erection of identical memorial tablets in both St Ninian's church, Rothesay on the Isle of Bute near her home, and in Bombay cathedral. The inscription on the tablet included Scott's description of Bowers: 'As the troubles have thickened about us his dauntless spirit ever shone brighter, and he has remained cheerful, hopeful, and indomitable to the end.'[44]

Officers in the Inniskilling Dragoons erected a memorial brass in St Mary's church, Gestingthorpe, near Oates's family home. The inscription proclaimed that when 'all were beset by hardship he being gravely injured went out into the blizzard to die in the hope that by so doing he might enable his comrades to reach safety'. Major-General E. H. H. Allenby unveiled the tablet in a special service on 8 November 1913. The Regiment also commissioned a painting from J. C. Dollman, *A Very Gallant Gentleman*, which still hangs in the Cavalry Club, and began a long-standing tradition by holding an annual service in Oates's honour on the Sunday nearest the day of his death, 16 March.[45]

The Royal Navy erected a number of memorials, including tablets in the chapel at Chatham Barracks, and on the training ship *Britannia*. But the navy made no effort to commemorate the efforts of Petty Officer Edgar Evans. Indeed, the only memorial dedicated solely to the working-class seaman was a tablet placed by his wife Lois in St Mary's church, Rhosili, Glamorgan.

Naval officers did, by contrast, erect a statue of Captain Scott in London. Scott's old friend Admiral Sir George Egerton, recently appointed as Commander-in-Chief at Devonport dockyard, raised £1,000 from naval officers for a special Fleet memorial. His committee approached Winston Churchill to procure a suitable site in London, pointing out that there were, surprisingly, only two well-known statues of naval officers in the capital: Nelson's column and a statue of Sir John Franklin. Lionel Earle suggested the committee approach the Office of Woods, which offered a site in the gardens at the back of the United Service Club, facing the Franklin statue.[46]

Having heard rumours that the committee had approached the dead explorer's widow, Earle advised that 'it would be the greatest mistake to entrust such a work to Lady Scott's hands. From all I hear, she may be an admirable woman, but is absolutely devoid of all real artistic sense.'[47] Egerton ignored this advice and commissioned Kathleen Scott to produce the statue. Admiral Beaumont, among others, however, objected to her decision to represent Scott in sledging gear:

> I do not think that the statue in Waterloo Place will best honour Con [Scott] and his memory to future generations if it represents him in his rough sledging dress – I think it is necessary to give up something of the verisimilitude which might be given in other circumstances in order to raise the statue in dignity and importance, or rather, that it should not *lose* in dignity and importance by contrast with the other statues near . . . so it should be, not working clothes, but a dress suitable to the greatness of the character.[48]

But Kathleen Scott refused to modify her design, and the Fleet memorial statue was unveiled in November 1915.

One commemorative scheme caused both Kathleen and Scott's family considerable irritation. Both navy and army collaborated on the Imperial Services Exhibition, which showcased the latest technology of the armed forces at Earl's Court from May to October 1913. Exhibits included reconstructions of both an army camp on the North-West Frontier, and an engagement off the coast of a seaboard town on a flooded stage in the Empress Hall, complete with model aeroplanes, crumbling fort walls, and explosions.

Albert Markham initially approached Kathleen Scott in the spring about the exhibition and, after the return of the *Terra Nova* in June, Teddy Evans and Cecil Meares swiftly arranged an Antarctic section at Earl's Court. The inner lining of the tent in which Scott, Wilson, and Bowers died, was set up at the entrance to the section. Exhibits included Scott's sledge, skis, and theodolite, the camera used at the Pole, empty provision bags, a thermometer, and a book, *By Order of Country*, alongside a sign: 'The book they were reading.' The Antarctic section was highlighted in advertisements for the exhibition and one periodical commented that 'remarkable interest is sure to be taken . . . in the Relics of the Scott Expedition to the South Pole'.[49]

Kathleen Scott, however, was appalled when Oriana Wilson informed her that there was an exhibit 'in very bad taste' at Earl's Court. She immediately telephoned Teddy Evans, and then complained in writing that

> the exhibition of the Tent, wherein the Explorers died, their skis, and a novelette purporting to have been ready [*sic*] by them, is singularly out of place and in very bad taste, exhibited as they are side by side with mannequins dressed in Wolseley underwear, advertising the firm. I hope you will be kind enough to see that the above named articles (Tent, skis, book) be removed today from the exhibition.
>
> Notices were put up to say the exhibition had been given with my consent. My consent was neither asked nor given and I had no knowledge of it whatsoever.[50]

Evans removed some of the offending articles the following day, but Scott's sister Grace still found the display distasteful, and returned with Evans to remove further items. The managing director of the exhibition complained to Kathleen Scott that the public would now be deceived, as all the items of greatest interest had been removed. A compromise was eventually reached, with the relics of the polar party screened off from the rest of the section and exhibited without labels.

A chorus of voices joined in the song of the dead after the announcement of the Antarctic disaster in February 1913. Yet this chorus was conducted neither by central government, nor by Lord Curzon, in spite of his attempts to exploit the disaster for the benefit of the RGS. The death of the explorers had inspired so many, that no single individual could control their story (see **Fig. 4.1**).

Schoolteachers, clergymen, councillors, journalists, presidents of scientific societies, military officers, and philanthropists told the story of Scott of the Antarctic, representatives of the distinctive combination of a vibrant civil society and active local government which characterized Edwardian Britain. The successful efforts of Cardiff councillors and Yorkshire vicars stood in stark contrast to the government's refusal to sacrifice a single blade of grass in a royal park for a statue of Captain Scott.[51]

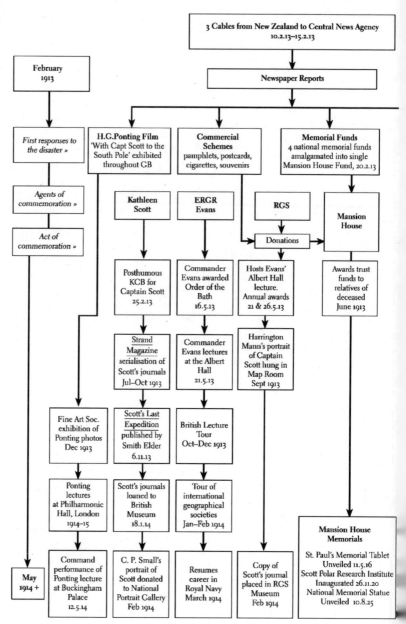

4.1 The public commemoration of the Antarctic disaster in Britain.

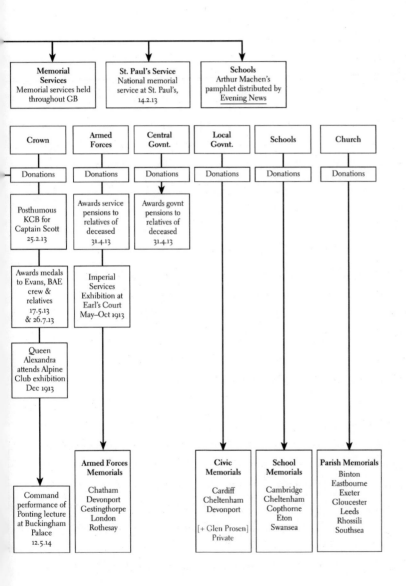

Memorial Services — Memorial services held throughout GB

St. Paul's Service — National memorial service at St. Paul's, 14.2.13

Schools — Arthur Machen's pamphlet distributed by Evening News

Crown	Armed Forces	Central Govnt.	Local Govnt.	Schools	Church
Donations	Donations	Donations	Donations	Donations	Donations

- **Crown**
  - Posthumous KCB for Captain Scott 25.2.13
  - Awards medals to Evans, BAE crew & relatives 17.5.13 & 26.7.13
  - Queen Alexandra attends Alpine Club exhibition Dec 1913
  - Command performance of Ponting lecture at Buckingham Palace 12.5.14

- **Armed Forces**
  - Awards service pensions to relatives of deceased 31.4.13
  - Imperial Services Exhibition at Earl's Court May–Oct 1913
  - **Armed Forces Memorials** — Chatham, Devonport, Gestingthorpe, London, Rothesay

- **Central Govnt.**
  - Awards govnt pensions to relatives of deceased 31.4.13

- **Local Govnt.**
  - **Civic Memorials** — Cardiff, Cheltenham, Devonport [+ Glen Prosen] Private

- **Schools**
  - **School Memorials** — Cambridge, Cheltenham, Copthorne, Eton, Swansea

- **Church**
  - **Parish Memorials** — Binton, Eastbourne, Exeter, Gloucester, Leeds, Rhossili, Southsea

· CHAPTER FIVE ·

'MARTYRS OF SCIENCE'

KING GEORGE V may have inherited the largest empire the world had ever seen, but uncertainty pervaded British society and culture in 1913. An array of Victorian shibboleths had been called into question over the previous decade. An increasingly bellicose Germany threatened British naval supremacy. A section of the Conservative party mounted the most significant challenge for over half a century to free trade, ideological emblem of national greatness. The crisis of local government finance compelled central government intervention in social policy for the first time, prompting Asquith's pioneering Liberal administration to lay the foundations of the modern welfare state with the introduction of old age pensions and national insurance. The wealthy railed against the redistributive taxation necessitated by rearmament and social expenditure, fearful of the seemingly inevitable rise of organized labour. The threat of civil war in Ireland was tangible. Sexual scandals, scientific investigations, and the campaign for women's suffrage questioned established norms of gender, morality, and sexuality. Intellectuals lamented the spiritual vacuum of mass urban society, while artists sought new forms to express the discontents of modernity.

The anxieties generated by these challenges to old orthodoxies were amplified by rapid technological advance, including the first London appearance of a motorbus in 1899, the first purpose-built cinema in 1907, and the first electric escalator in 1911. The rhythms of everyday life were in flux, the pace rapidly accelerated.

These developments touched the crew of the *Terra Nova*. The expedition had to decline offers of an aeroplane and wireless system to take to the Antarctic: the tired old ship was already bursting at the seams. As a landowner, Apsley Cherry-Garrard moaned about the government's new wealth taxes. Kathleen Scott may have been only the second woman in Britain to fly an aeroplane. And Scott himself feared his absence in the Antarctic might preclude his involvement in a future conflict with Germany.

It would be misleading, of course, to characterize these years as a period of progressively worsening, unmitigated anxiety. Recent academic research has emphasized the vigour of the British economy before the First World War. Technological advance created optimism and opportunity as well as uncertainty. But the symphony of geopolitical, social, economic, and moral challenges was resounding.

The song of the dead pierced this anxious cacophony, a hymn of traditional manliness. Captain Scott and his companions offered a reassuring example of heroic character and idealism, to counter anxieties about national decline and the materialism of the modern world. Many versions of Scott's story rang out through Britain before the First World War, as different communities invested the disaster with different meanings. Albert Hodge's statue strove to encompass these differences, representing the explorers' sacrifice 'For King', 'For Country', 'For Brotherly Love', 'For Knowledge'. But the different versions could be dissonant, as we have seen, leading to conflicts over the memory of the dead. The following three chapters will chart these variations, as Captain Scott and his companions were hailed as icons of manliness, national saviours, and martyrs of science.

Idealism and Materialism

At 7.30 p.m. on Monday, 10 February 1913, Lord Curzon received a telegram from the King, who expressed his grief at the sad news of the death of Captain Scott and his party. 'I heartily sympathise with the Royal Geographical Society', the telegram continued, 'in the loss to science and discovery through the death of these gallant explorers. Please send me any further particulars. George R.'[1]

The King's decision to send his first message of condolence to the President of the RGS is telling. Although Scott's last expedition was an independent venture, the Society was the spiritual home of British exploration. The press besieged Lowther Lodge after the announcement of the disaster. 'Evidently we are expected to take the lead in this matter,' wrote the RGS secretary John Scott Keltie, 'and I suppose it is natural that we should.'[2]

The five men had not died in a military engagement, or on imperial assignment, but while returning from the South Pole. The selflessness of their endeavour sanctified their sacrifice. 'They died on no mere quest of gold,' explained the *Daily Mail*.

> To reach the Pole is an aim of pure idealism ... It is not besmirched by the dusty finger of politics. The explorers who have lost their lives in the pursuit of this ideal had no hopes of planting prosperous colonies upon the frozen surface of the Pole. There is no wealth to beckon them thither ... The sacrifice of our heroes is unsullied and unstained.[3]

The distinctive character of Antarctic exploration thus moulded the explorers' heroic reputation. But the nature of their endeavour was also hotly debated. In particular, the significance afforded the expedition's programme of scientific research varied widely. All agreed that the disaster marked a triumph over materialism. But science generated conflicting associations in Edwardian Britain, representing idealism to some, soulless materialism to others.

Many commentators followed the official line, by emphasizing Scott's intent to gather the greatest possible scientific harvest which the circumstances would permit. Initial reports frequently reiterated the contrast between the Norwegian and British expeditions, which had featured so prominently after Amundsen's success. The *Scotsman* compared Norwegian 'athletes' with British 'explorers', while *The Times* agreed that Scott 'never headed "a mere dash to the Pole." He went steadily forward with his scientific exploration.'[4]

Here, science was presented as a noble and romantic cause. Clements Markham proclaimed Scott a 'martyr in the cause of science', while the *Morning Post* wrote of the 'martyrs, like so many of their race, in the thirst of knowledge'. Even *Nature*, so critical of Scott's command of the *Discovery*, paid tribute to the explorers who had 'laid down their lives in the pursuit of geographical knowledge'.[5] Such emphasis was not confined to the highbrow press. The *Daily Mirror* published a double-page spread of Ponting's photographs and Wilson's watercolours, under the headline 'Heroes Who Laid Down Their Lives In The Cause Of Science'.[6]

The description of the polar party as martyrs of science was, however, misleading. In his speech to the RGS, Scott had made clear that the assault on the Pole was motivated less by science than by the symbolic resonance which the completion of such an ancient quest would hold for the nation. Although meteorological and topographical observations were taken, Scott's decision to follow Shackleton's route ensured the polar party contributed little to the mapping of Antarctica. H. R. Mill publicly criticized Scott's choice of route, arguing that an attempt to circumnavigate the continent would have produced more valuable results.[7] The assault on the Pole was the least scientific aspect of the expedition.

Scott himself remained consistent. His 'Message to the Public' made no mention of the scientific results of the assault on the Pole. But the official dispatches cabled from New Zealand blurred the distinction Scott had drawn in 1910. The first dispatch announced that 'in spite of their distressing condition they had retained every record and thirty-five pounds of geological specimens, which prove to be of the greatest scientific value', while the second claimed that 'these fossils should finally settle the age of the latest sedimentary deposits yet found in Victoria Land'. Many took their cue from these reports. The veteran *Times* leader writer John Ross felt that by clinging to their records, 'they snatched victory out of the jaws of death'.[8] This emphasis on the geological specimens facilitated the representation of the assault on the Pole as a scientific quest, reinforced by the contrast between the Norwegian and British expeditions. A pile of rocks secured the disaster as a sacrifice for knowledge.

Some commentators, however, dismissed the expedition's scientific pretensions entirely, declaring that the results were simply not worth the deaths of five men. Such attacks, though, did not proceed to denigrate Scott and his companions, but to highlight their idealism. The explorers' deaths were redeemed not by an insignificant collection of rocks, but by the heroism they had shown in adversity. Here science indicated not idealism, but materialism, the dismal technological advance crushing the spirit of humanity.

The Nonconformist preacher Ernest Rattenbury, for example, asked if the explorers had died in vain:

> In one daily paper I see this answer given: 'No; because they have made certain additions to science'; but I say that, even if they had gained no knowledge, their deaths would not have been in vain. They have given us by their sacrifice something far higher

than material gains; they have left the world a splendid vision of human nature in its highest endowments. Their death will create life, their sacrifice will create sacrifice, their courage will inspire courage for many years to come.

The scientific achievements of the explorers were frequently acknowledged, only to be dismissed as insignificant in comparison with their inspirational legacy. 'The value of the scientific knowledge gained by those who have perished was doubtless great,' asserted the *Evening News*, 'but the example which they have set, not only to their countrymen, but to all the world, is a thing beyond price.'[9]

The journalist Filson Young wrote that people had heard a great deal about the splendid scientific results of the expedition, but that from this point of view the tragedy simply was not worth the price in lives or money. Such a judgement revealed 'the worthless-ness and untruth of the utilitarian standard . . . For there is no question that the world thinks that the lives of Captain Scott and his three comrades well lost, lost in a worthy and glorious cause. Not in the cause of science, not in the cause of material advance-ment, but in the cause of courage and heroism.' In answer to the question 'Is it worth it?', Young concluded: 'It is a thousand times worth it.'[10]

Exploration and Sacrifice

Nearly a year after the departure of the *Terra Nova* from Cardiff, Major Leonard Darwin delivered his final Presidential Address to the RGS. He repeated the familiar lament that the days of pioneer exploration were drawing to a close:

for some years to come large areas are likely to exist our knowledge of which can only be increased at the risk of the traveller's life. But although the available topographical information concerning many regions will for long remain imperfect, yet it is inevitable that the day will come when the whole world will be mapped with fair accuracy, and to that condition of things this Society will have to adapt itself.

The traveller of the future would have to be a trained topographer, whose objective was 'not the gathering of more crops, but rather the tedious task of systematising, collating, and indexing what is already at hand'.[11]

Two years later, Lord Curzon struck a different note at the first anniversary meeting following the announcement of Scott's death.

The shrinkage of the Earth and the control of the forces of nature by the organised skill of man has not, since the days of the Tudors, made a greater advance in a single decade than during the last ten years, which have witnessed the conquest of the two Poles of the Earth by human explorers and the discovery of the art of aerial navigation by bodies heavier than air

Curzon noted that this rapid progress had prompted some

arm-chair geographers . . . to complain that the days of adventure and risk in exploration are over. The past year gives the melancholy lie to such fireside fallacies. The toll of human life is still demanded and is still cheerfully paid. Should the day ever arise when it is not, then indeed may geographical societies shut their doors and hand over their work to an educational bureau of the State.[12]

Curzon celebrated the heroic example set by the explorers, who had shown that sacrifice was still required in the cause of geographical progress.

While the press debated the significance of the research programme, the network of international geographical societies
consistently emphasized the expedition's scientific aims. The RGS
received letters of condolence from scores of international scientific
societies, including the geographical societies of Adelaide and
Lima, the Society of Naturalists of Odessa, and the Zoological
Society of France.[13] This international network, bound together
through awards, correspondence, and congresses, firmly represented Scott and his companions as martyrs of science.

Differences between national cultures have been accorded
considerable explanatory power in accounts of the heroic age of
polar exploration. Scandinavian proficiency with skis was obviously
founded on experience accumulated since childhood. But other
generalizations about national cultures are less persuasive. Roland
Huntford has contrasted a Norwegian concern for efficient polar
travel, with a British veneration of heroic deeds. Norwegians de-
mythologized the polar environment, while the British romanticized
exploration and glorified sacrifice.[14]

This interpretation underestimates the extent to which the
network of geographical societies sustained a heroic language of
exploration across national boundaries, in which explorers battled
against the forces of nature to secure the spoils of scientific knowledge. The fellows of the Turkestan Section of the Imperial
Russian Geographical Society, for example, unanimously honoured
'the memory of science's heroes and martyrs'. The Geographical
Institute of Argentina expressed condolences 'por la trájica muerte
del explorador Capitan Roberto Scott y parte de su comitiva,
desgracia que ha tenido profunda repercusión en esta República,
siendo especialmente sentida en sus asociaciones científicas'.
And the Geographical Society of Geneva declared 'Scott et ses
compagnons, par les terribles épreuves qu'ils ont endurées, laissent

le souvenir d'hommes exceptionnellement héroiques. Ils ont montré, une fois de plus, que la vaillance humaine peut aussi se dépenser pour des œuvres scientifiques.'[15]

Many prominent foreign explorers sent their condolences to the RGS, including Guido Cora, Erich von Drygalski, and Adrien de Gerlache. The German explorer Wilhelm Filchener argued that 'Scott was a real hero because he died in the cause of science. He was not merely a sportsman. His methods and purposes were scientific and the results of his expedition should be valuable'. Jean Charcot proposed to circulate his tribute to Scott to 'all the public schools in France as a great example to men of all nations'.[16] Monuments to the dead would be erected in France, Norway, and Belgium.[17]

Teddy Evans's lecture tour consolidated this emphasis on the expedition's scientific aims, binding the network of geographical societies together. When introducing Evans's Royal Albert Hall lecture, Lord Curzon had declared that the publication of the scientific results of the expedition would be the real monument to Scott and his men. Five days later, at the Society's annual awards ceremony, Major Darwin also sought consolation for the disaster in the 'splendid harvest of scientific results which they have brought . . . the great white spaces round the poles on our maps have been covered with a network of recorded fact'.[18]

Gerald Christy of the lecture agency Christy & Moore commissioned Evans to carry out the tour he had planned for Scott, and the naval officer spent much of the summer of 1913 lecturing in the United States and Canada. Evans returned to Britain after the publication of the final *Strand Magazine* instalment, to undertake an extensive national tour, speaking in over fifty towns and cities in the last three months of 1913 (**Fig. 5.1**). In the new year Evans embarked on a further tour through the geographical societies of

Commander EVANS' LECTURE TOUR, 1913.

The whole of the arrangements for this Tour have been made by
GERALD CHRISTY,
of THE LECTURE AGENCY, Ltd., The Outer Temple,
Strand, London, W.C.

GERALD CHRISTY also arranged the Lecture Tours of Dr. Fridtjof Nansen,
Captain Robert F. Scott, Sir Ernest Shackleton, Admiral R. E. Peary, and
Captain Roald Amundsen.

Mon.,	Oct. 13,	**Harrow School**
Wed.,	,, 15,	**Bournemouth**
Wed.,	,, 15,	**Southampton**
Thurs.,	,, 16,	**Portsmouth**
Fri.,	,, 17,	**Ryde**
Sat.,	,, 18,	**Brighton**
Mon.,	,, 20,	**Oxford**
Tues.,	,, 21,	**Eton College**
Wed.,	,, 22,	**Reading**
Fri.,	,, 24,	**Tunbridge Wells**
Sat.,	,, 25,	**Eastbourne**
Mon.,	,, 27,	**Hull**
Tues.,	,, 28,	**Sheffield**
Wed.,	,, 29,	**Chester**
Wed.,	,, 29,	**Liverpool**
Thurs.,	,, 30,	**Leeds**
Fri.,	,, 31,	**Manchester**
Mon.,	Nov. 3,	**Leicester**
Tues.,	,, 4,	**Birmingham**
Thurs.,	,, 6,	**Southport**
Fri.,	,, 7,	**Harrogate**
Mon.,	,, 10,	**Cambridge**
Tues.,	,, 11,	**Nottingham**
Wed.,	,, 12,	**Shrewsbury**
Thurs.,	,, 13,	**Bradford**
Fri.,	,, 14,	**Hanley**
Sat.,	Nov. 15,	**Cheltenham**
Mon.,	,, 17,	**Aberdeen**
Tues.,	,, 18,	**Dundee**
Wed.,	,, 19,	**Edinburgh**
Thurs.,	,, 20,	**Edinburgh**
Fri.,	,, 21,	**Glasgow**
Mon.,	,, 24,	**Greenock**
Tues.,	,, 25,	**Newcastle**
Wed.,	,, 26,	**Sunderland**
Thurs.,	,, 27,	**Middlesbrough**
Sat.,	,, 29,	**St. Albans**
Tues.,	Dec. 2,	**Leamington**
Wed.,	,, 3,	**Bath**
Wed.,	,, 3,	**Bristol**
Thurs.,	,, 4,	**Plymouth**
Fri.,	,, 5,	**Exeter**
Mon.,	,, 8,	**Cardiff**
Tues.,	,, 9,	**Chatham**
Thurs.,	,, 11,	**Coventry**
Fri.,	,, 12,	**Bolton**
Mon.,	,, 15,	**Dublin**
Tues.,	,, 16,	**Belfast**
Thurs.,	,, 18,	**Preston**
Fri.,	,, 19,	**Kendal**
Sat.,	,, 20,	**Lancaster**

ANTARCTIC STAMPS.
VICTORIA LAND ISSUE.

The Stamps issued by the New Zealand Government, overprinted
"Victoria Land," for use in the Post Office established at the base of
the Southern Party, at Cape Evans, can be obtained at the Lecture
Ticket Office, or from

F. HUGH VALLANCEY,
89, Farringdon Street,
London, E.C.

5.1 E. R. G. R. Evans's British lecture tour, October to December 1913. The
expedition issued special Antarctic stamps to raise funds. The Mansion House
Committee objected to the issue of the stamps after the closure of the Mansion House Scott memorial fund in June, as it had pledged to pay off the
expedition's debts. The dispute caused further tensions with Teddy Evans.

Europe. He received diplomas of honour from the societies of Antwerp, Berlin, Budapest, Christiania, Copenhagen, Gothenburg, Rome, Stockholm, and Vienna, gold medals from the societies of Brussels, Budapest, Edinburgh, Marseilles, Newcastle, and Paris, and the Hauer Silver Medal, the highest award of the Vienna Geographical Society.[19]

The tour was a great success. Evans's lecture was heard by Archduke Joseph Francis and Archduchess Augusta in Budapest, and the King of Italy in Rome. The diploma issued by the Hungarian Geographical Society praised 'one of the most memorable, complete and successful expeditions that ever started in any scientific quest' and hoped that 'the admiration and gratitude of the whole civilised world may have let you forget your privations and sufferings in the Antarctic in the sacred cause of science'.[20]

The highest acclaim came in France. First, on the afternoon of 26 January, Evans received the gold medal of the city of Paris at a reception at the Hôtel de Ville. The following evening, he lectured to an audience of over 5,000 at the Sorbonne, before being awarded the Légion d'honneur by the President of the Republic. Evans himself considered this lecture his greatest success. Charcot declared that Evans had

> conquered Paris. Poor Scott was not forgotten. For the first time I think the President of the Republic was present and before the whole Sorbonne gave himself the Legion of Honour to Evans. Generally when he gives the Legion of Honour he says 'In the name of the French Republic I give you etc. . . .' This time he said 'In the name of France etc . . .' and this was much noticed by everyone.

The *Bioscope* reported that two further lectures in Paris were 'packed on each occasion . . . the ticket agents besieged for seats many days in advance'.[21]

Evans followed a well-trodden path. Both Nansen and Shackleton had lectured to a host of geographical societies after returning from their record-breaking polar expeditions. The international network of geographical societies requires further examination. National differences undoubtedly conditioned the representation of explorers as heroes and the pattern I have traced reflects, in part, a formal language of condolence, which obscures national peculiarities. Nevertheless, the global tributes to Captain Scott demonstrate that the heroic language of exploration transcended national boundaries. The British were not alone in glorifying sacrifice.

Scott's Last Expedition and the Strand Magazine

Alongside this international network of geographical societies, the official narratives composed by members of the expedition also consistently foregrounded the explorers' scientific aims.

In July 1913 the Strand Magazine published the first detailed account of the expedition's progress since the initial dispatches from New Zealand. The second paragraph of the first instalment emphasized that

> the expedition was no mere dash to the Pole to snatch priority from rival explorers, though the hope of this laurel-leaf in the crown of adventure was an added spur to ambition. The whole was organised on such a scale and with such a wide range of talent that it should reap a rich harvest of scientific results, whether the Southern party attained its goal or not.[22]

The contrast with Amundsen's expedition was clear.

The second instalment described the winter journey to the

emperor penguin rookery at Cape Crozier, which had been undertaken by Wilson, Bowers, and Cherry-Garrard between 27 June
and 1 August 1911. In his report on the zoology of the *Discovery*
expedition, Wilson had conceived a plan to travel to Cape Crozier,
in order to obtain penguin eggs at such a stage of development
to furnish a series of embryos. The emperor penguin was at this time
believed to be the most primitive bird on earth. Influenced by the
German biologist Ernst Haeckel, Wilson hoped that a study of the
penguin's embryology would reveal the origin of birds and their
relationship to other vertebrates. The plan required the first significant sledge-journey undertaken during the Antarctic winter. The
explorers marched for two weeks to reach the rookery, travelling in
continual darkness through a succession of blizzards, experiencing
temperatures as low as −77°F.

Instead of the 2,000–3,000 emperor penguins expected, however, only 100 were found nesting at Cape Crozier. Wilson,
Bowers, and Cherry-Garrard collected five eggs and set off back
to Cape Evans The return journey through terrible conditions
almost ended in disaster when their tent was blown away. For
forty-eight hours they lay in an open igloo in darkness, without
food or drink, covered in snow. Without a tent, they would
certainly have died. But they were saved by a miracle. During a
lull in the blizzard, Bowers found their tent on a slope in perfect
condition barely a quarter of a mile away. Scott described the
bedraggled party which returned at the beginning of August as
'more weather worn than anyone I have yet seen'. Three eggs
survived.

The account of the winter journey to Cape Crozier was the
dramatic highlight of the second instalment of the *Strand*
serialization. Scott's own tribute to Wilson, Bowers, and Cherry-
Garrard was published for the first time:

> Wilson is disappointed at seeing so little of the penguins, but to
> me and to everyone who has remained here the result of this effort
> is the appeal it makes to our imagination as one of the most gallant
> stories in Polar History. That men should wander forth in the
> depth of a Polar night, to face the most dismal cold and fiercest
> gales in darkness, is something new; that they should have per-
> sisted in spite of every adversity for full five weeks is heroic. It
> makes a tale for one generation which I trust will not be lost in the
> telling.

The winter journey was raised as an emblem of the expedition's
devotion to scientific research. The *Alpine Journal* declared the
journey 'a tale of endurance in the cause of pure knowledge hardly
to be surpassed in the history of science'.[23]

The publication of *Scott's Last Expedition* in November
consolidated the representation of the expedition as a scientific
quest. Clements Markham's preface emphasized that 'the object
of Captain Scott's second expedition was mainly scientific, to complete and extend his former work in all branches of science . . .
Captain Scott's objects were strictly scientific . . . The principal aim
of this great man . . . was the advancement of knowledge.'[24]

Most importantly, the two-volume structure of the book
encapsulated the combination of scientific research and heroic
adventure at the heart of the expedition. The first volume, with
Harrington Mann's portrait of Scott as its frontispiece, told the
story of the expedition through Scott's journals. Exploration of the
Antarctic becomes an exploration of character, as the reader follows
Scott's responses to the challenges of the polar environment.

As the expedition settled into the Antarctic, Scott complied an
evocative list of his impressions of polar life:

> The seductive folds of the sleeping bag.
> The hiss of the primus and the fragrant steam of the cooker
> issuing from the tent ventilator . . .

> The crunch of footsteps which break the surface crust . . .
>
> The crisp ring of the ponies' hoofs and the swish of the following sledge . . .
>
> The gentle flutter of our canvas shelter . . .
>
> The drift snow like finest flour penetrating every hole and corner – flickering up beneath one's head covering, pricking sharply as a sand blast . . .
>
> The eternal silence of the great white desert . . .
>
> The blizzard, Nature's protest – the crevasse, Nature's pitfall – that grim trap for the unwary – no hunter could conceal his snare so perfectly. (2 February 1911)

Within three months, the sun had set on the long Antarctic winter, and Scott witnessed that most magnificent of Antarctic spectacles the *Aurora Australis*, the dancing lights of the southern skies.

> It is the language of mystic signs and portents – the inspiration of the gods – wholly spiritual – divine signalling. Remindful of superstition, provocative of imagination. Might not the inhabitants of some other world (Mars) controlling mighty forces thus surround our globe with fiery symbols, a golden writing which we have not the key to decipher. (21 May 1911)

The breathtaking vision touched the soul of a poet.

But exploration also measured manliness, and the reader follows Scott as he struggles against weather, terrain, animals, competitors, comrades, and his own helplessness. 'Miserable, utterly miserable,' he wrote, barely a month after setting out for the Pole.

> We have camped in the 'Slough of Despond'. The tempest rages with unabashed violence. . . . The snow is steadily climbing higher about walls, ponies, tents, sledges. The ponies look utterly desolate. Oh! but this is too crushing, and we are only 12 miles from the Glacier. A hopeless feeling descends and is hard to

fight off. What immense patience is needed for such occasions!
(6 December 1911)

Scott's anguish as the party struggles to return from the Pole is
intensified by the reader's awareness of the impending tragedy.
'God help us, we can't keep up this pulling that is certain. Amongst
ourselves we are unendingly cheerful, but what each man feels in
his heart I can only guess' (3 March 1912). 'We have two days' food
but barely a day's fuel. All our feet are getting bad' (19 March). And
then the final entry, on 29 March: 'outside the door of the tent it
remains a scene of whirling drift. I do not think we can hope for any
better things now. We shall stick it out to the end, but we are getting
weaker, of course, and the end cannot be far. It seems a pity but I do
not think I can write more.'

While the first volume thus measured the man, the second
volume described the expedition's efforts to measure the world.
Subtitled 'The reports of the journeys and the scientific work
undertaken by Dr. E. A. Wilson and the surviving members of
the expedition', with a photograph of Wilson as its frontispiece, the
second volume opened with Cherry-Garrard's own account of
the winter journey to Cape Crozier, and then published the first
detailed narrative of the exploits of the northern party, led by
Commander Victor Campbell, RN.

Campbell's northern party spent their first year in the Antarctic
working from a second camp at Cape Adare, around 450 miles north
of the base at Cape Evans. In January 1912 the party were picked
up by the *Terra Nova* and transported south, where they landed
with the intention of exploring Victoria Land for a month before
returning to the ship. Ice conditions, however, prevented the *Terra
Nova* from reaching the party, leaving them stranded. The terrible
realization slowly dawned on Campbell, the Royal Naval surgeon

George Murray Levick, the geologist Raymond Priestley, and three Royal Naval seamen, George Abbott, Frank Browning, and Harry Dickason, that they would have to shelter in Terra Nova Bay through the Antarctic winter.

After much discussion, the six men chose to construct an underground igloo, 12 feet by 9 feet, insulated with blocks of snow and seaweed, on a small island which they christened Inexpressible. The igloo would be their home for six months. The appalling weather which fatally delayed the polar party lashed the coast with hurricanes and freezing temperatures. The party laid in a store of penguin and seal meat, and Levick worked hard to vary their diet, keeping a close watch for scurvy. But the blubber essential to their survival caused incessant bowel problems. Frank Browning suffered from almost continuous bouts of diarrhoea, exacerbating the cramped conditions. And the burning of lamps and stoves threatened either to asphyxiate them when the vents became blocked, or melt the ceiling of their precious shelter. Small supplies of biscuits, cocoa, and chocolate were carefully rationed, providing some respite from the monotonous diet. The discovery of thirty-six fish in the stomach of a seal triggered joyous celebration.

Campbell maintained naval discipline, drawing a line down the centre of the cave with the sole of his shoe to separate the men's mess deck from the officers' quarterdeck. 'As on board ship,' Priestley later reported, 'everything that is said and done on the messdeck will be the responsibility of the men and it shall not be heard or paid attention to or interfered with by any of the officers.'[25] Such rituals seem macabre today, but the pretence of normality may have helped the party survive the winter. Charles Dickens certainly provided sustenance. The sixty-four chapters of *David Copperfield* brought entertainment for two months. Finally, as the weather improved and sun returned, the party left the igloo on

30 September and sledged for 230 miles, before reaching safety at Cape Evans in early November.

The accounts of the winter journey to Cape Crozier and of Campbell's northern party occupy the first 180 pages of the second volume, vivid narratives of endurance in the cause of scientific research. The volume then published accounts of the efforts of the western geological party and the final year of the expedition, before concluding with a series of essays summarizing the preliminary findings in different fields. The presentation of the expedition's work in ice physics, physiography, meteorology, marine biology, and geology was an essential accompaniment to Scott's personal journal, proof that the expedition was a serious scientific endeavour. Clements Markham described the polar party's geological specimens as 'a magnificent addition to knowledge, a contribution to geological science made, as it were, with their life's blood'.[26] But Frank Debenham offered a more measured assessment in the second volume. The samples, he wrote, 'contain impressions of fossil plants of the late Palaeozoic age, some of which a cursory inspection identifies as occurring in other parts of the world. When fully examined, they will assuredly prove to be of the highest geological importance.'[27]

Reviews of *Scott's Last Expedition* again exposed the ambiguous status of scientific research in narratives of the Antarctic disaster. Some took their cue from Markham. *The Times* devoted a leading article to the book, which quoted from the preface and observed that 'the scientific chapters demonstrate the true object of the expedition . . . Scott's last expedition aimed pre-eminently at the acquisition of knowledge'.[28] But, repeating the pattern which emerged after the announcement of the disaster, other reviewers played down the expedition's scientific programme. Scott's friend Henry Leach observed in *Chambers's Journal* that

Some good scientific work was done in the meantime; but it is not
that which counts so much in the reckoning of the value of *Scott's
Last Expedition* . . . What does count is the manner of life and
death, the thoughts and the deeds, the greatness and grandeur of
the soul, the magnificent inspiration that they must yield to every
man whose own soul is still alive.[29]

Here, again, the scientific claims of the expedition were dismissed,
in order to highlight the spiritual inspiration bequeathed by the
explorers.

Henry Leach exemplified those commentators who equated
science with materialism, the curse of modernity. He later blamed
the outbreak of the First World War on modern science:

Science, and science alone, with its servant, engineering, has
brought us to such an awful pass of over-civilisation, over-
development, and fearfully organised and elaborated war-system
. . . the price of discovery has been too great . . . Science
stands for materialism, and the modern Germans are the most
utterly materialistic people in the world, as they are greatest in the
laboratories and the philosophical schools. . . . As it [Germany]
has abandoned itself to the plague of science, its inner culture,
its soul refinement, has been weakened . . . and now, in a mad
fury, it has leapt to an attempted murder of the world.[30]

Both the structure and content of *Scott's Last Expedition*
foregrounded the scientific character of the expedition. Reviews of
the book, however, offered a more complex picture, as different
versions of Scott's story articulated misgivings about scientific
progress in Britain on the eve of the First World War.

The Films, Photographs, and Lectures of Herbert Ponting

Herbert Ponting was a forgotten casualty of the Antarctic disaster. A superb photographer and true innovator of the early cinema, the images he captured in the south were touched by genius. Yet he died in 1935 frustrated and bitter, his later career marred by misguided business ventures and commercial failure. His photographs and lectures, however, stand alongside the *Strand Magazine* serialization and *Scott's Last Expedition* as the most significant accounts of Scott's story published before the outbreak of the First World War.

Born in England in 1870, Ponting worked briefly as a banker before emigrating to the United States. He soon married and had a daughter, but financial problems forced the family to return to London, where a son was born. After nine months Ponting returned to California and began to study photography. His passion for photography destroyed his marriage. Ponting took photographs throughout Europe and Asia, serving as the accredited photographer to the first Japanese Army in Manchuria during the Russo-Japanese war. His work was displayed in a variety of exhibitions, pamphlets, and periodicals including *Harper's Weekly* and *Country Life*. In 1906 Ponting abandoned his wife and children, declaring that they interfered with his art. Many years later he observed with sadness that he 'could be walking down Oxford Street, with my son passing me, and with me not knowing that it was him'.[31]

Ponting became interested in polar exploration after meeting Cecil Meares on a steamer sailing from Yokohama to Shanghai in 1905. The son of an army officer, Meares was also widely travelled, and infected Ponting with his enthusiasm for polar exploration. When crossing Russia on the Trans-Siberian railway in 1907, Ponting took along Scott's *Voyage of the Discovery*, 'appropriate reading for a journey in the frigid conditions of climate which prevail in Siberia at that time of year'.[32] After Scott announced his second Antarctic expedition, Meares applied and was appointed transport officer. At this time Ponting was preparing for a two-year photographic tour of the empire for the Northcliffe Press, but he was impressed by Scott and changed his plans to join the crew of the *Terra Nova*.

The 'camera-artist', as he preferred to be known, exposed around 25,000 feet of film and 2,000 photographic negatives during the expedition. The two series of Ponting's *With Captain Scott, RN, to the South Pole* released by the Gaumont Company in November 1911 and October 1912 were highly successful. Amundsen's victory reduced the appeal of the second series, but news of Scott's death rejuvenated interest in Ponting's pictures. The *Daily Mirror* urged that *With Captain Scott* be shown in every picture palace in the kingdom.[33] The second series was again exhibited throughout the country, with many venues arranging collections for the Mansion House memorial fund. Some histories have suggested that a third series of Ponting's films was released after the announcement of the disaster, but the Gaumont Company simply had no new footage of the polar party to distribute.

The Fine Art Society (FAS) mounted the first public exhibition of Ponting's photographs at their gallery in New Bond Street, London on 4 December 1913. The exhibition displayed 146 of Ponting's photographs. The Society also printed postcards and two special sets: the first containing Ponting's portraits of the polar party; the second containing four photographs of the explorers at the Pole and a photograph of the memorial cairn. The FAS received around 680 orders for over 1,400 prints, eventually receiving over £2,350 from sales and framing fees. One of the most enthusiastic purchasers was the future Conservative Prime

Minister Stanley Baldwin, who ordered fifteen prints.[34] The exhibition was later mounted in Glasgow, Cambridge, Portsmouth, and Paris.

Although a central screen was devoted to Scott, Bowers, Evans, Oates, and Wilson, the exhibition presented a much broader picture of the range of activities pursued in the Antarctic than had yet appeared. The 146 photographs can be classified into 6 categories: (1) 49 of the Antarctic landscape; (2) 32 portraits of members of the expedition; (3) 25 of native animal-life (12 of penguins; 8 of weddel seals; 3 of skua gulls; 1 of a killer whale; 1 of an albatross); (4) 14 of scientific research; (5) 13 of daily life on board the *Terra Nova* and at Cape Evans; and (6) 13 of the expedition's ponies and dogs. The order books reveal that photographs of the Antarctic landscape proved as popular as portraits of the explorers. Only thirteen copies of the special set devoted to the polar party were ordered, one by Stanley Baldwin.

Ponting's work consistently emphasized the scientific aims of the expedition. His first public pronouncement on the disaster was that Scott and his companions 'have given their lives for science'.[35] After the opening of the FAS exhibition, Ponting told Cherry-Garrard he was making 'every possible effort to carry out the promises I made to Capt. Scott, which were to show by the films and my photographs that this was not a mere Pole Hunt, but the greatest enterprise of the kind ever sent out from any land. My show in New Bond Street proves it.'[36]

In the exhibition catalogue, Marcus Huish quoted Scott's RGS speech of 1910, noting that

> the interests of science demanded that he [Scott] must not rest content with bringing back a bare record of the endeavour, but must garner complete data of every phase encountered . . . In no more popular way, perhaps, can this be accomplished than by

placing before the public a serious display of the work of one of
the several departments organised by him, especially as it largely
records the thoroughness of the endeavours and the zeal displayed
by those engaged in other branches of the work.

Huish claimed the exhibition made 'a liberal contribution to the
sum of human knowledge', which 'has a value both personal,
historic, artistic, and scientific'.[37] Such comments reveal the
seriousness of Ponting's intentions. His work was not merely an
amusing diversion; he believed his visual records should be considered alongside geological or meteorological observations, as a
contribution to knowledge of Antarctica.

While the exhibition was an undoubted success, the crowning
achievement of Ponting's association with Scott was the lectures he
delivered from Friday, 23 January 1914 at the Philharmonic Hall in
London, 'With Captain Scott in the Antarctic, and Animal and Bird
Life in the South Polar Regions'. The lectures proved tremendously
popular. Lecturing for over two hours twice a day, by the end of
March Ponting had given over 100 performances to an estimated
audience of 120,000 people. As he approached 200 performances,
the *Bioscope* noted that the lectures continued to attract a remarkable amount of interest. The lectures proved so popular that Cecil
Meares embarked on a provincial tour while Ponting was at the
Philharmonic Hall. A Parisian season was inaugurated in May 1914,
with Victor Marcel delivering a French translation of Ponting's
script.[38]

One commentator observed that Ponting drew all fashionable
London to the Philharmonic Hall.[39] The former American
President, Theodore Roosevelt, attended Ponting's lecture with
Arthur Lee, Conservative MP for Fareham. Roosevelt wrote person-
ally to Ponting: 'I do not know when I have seen an exhibition
which impressed me more than yours did. The pictures were

wonderful, and I would not on any account have missed seeing them.'[40]

The pinnacle of Ponting's fame arrived with an invitation to lecture at Buckingham Palace. After dinner on Tuesday, 12 May, a sparkling audience drawn from the royal families of Europe assembled in the palace ballroom, including King George V and Queen Mary, the King and Queen of Denmark, Queen Alexandra, and the Prince of Wales. The *Daily News* reported that 'for the first time in the brief history of living pictures, one film, already famous, has received the Royal command . . . Mr. Ponting has now succeeded in obtaining for photography all the acknowledgements which were reserved for the drama, painting and literature.' Ponting recorded that King George 'told me that he hoped I should be able to deliver my Lecture throughout the provinces, as he thought that everyone, and more especially every British boy, should have an intimate knowledge of the Expedition'. The King presented Ponting with a diamond scarf-pin as a memento.[41]

The programme published to accompany his lectures echoed the FAS catalogue, by declaring that the expedition was no mere 'Pole Hunt', but was the best equipped scientific enterprise ever sent out from any land. Ponting later wrote that Scott had hoped Wilson would 'not only *tell* about the zoology of the Far South, but, by means of photographs and films he would be able to *show* the nature of the animal life there'.[42]

While the FAS exhibition was dominated by the Antarctic landscape, the animals were the leading actors in Ponting's lectures, with sections devoted to seals, skua gulls, and penguins. Ponting believed he had made his performances 'popular among the masses, who will not be educated unless they can be amused, by introducing numerous animal scenes, without which the "show" would be a total failure'.[43] Although the climax of the performance, the assault on the Pole actually occupied only a small part of the lecture. Adélie penguins held far more screen-time in the Philharmonic Hall than Captain Oates.

Indeed, penguins were the stars of Ponting's lectures, featuring prominently in its promotional material. Ponting had filmed a history of the life of the Adélie penguin, which occupied almost a quarter of the lecture. Ponting's penguins were anthropomorphized, their antics compared with an array of human stereotypes. The *Daily Telegraph* noted that 'the tragedy of the story is relieved by Mr. Ponting's entrancing slides of nature in the southern seas, and on the frozen continent . . . above all, the Adélie penguins, providing scene after scene of inimitable comedy'.[44] The comic interlude heightened the subsequent drama of the assault on the Pole.

Yet the widespread appeal of Ponting's work also caused concern. Curzon introduced Teddy Evans's Royal Albert Hall lecture with the sole complaint that it gave

> an inadequate idea of the privations and sufferings endured by his companions and himself. When you see the magnificent slides and films taken by the talented photographer of the party, Mr. Ponting, and see the glories of the Polar ice and snow, you must not forget the other side of the picture, the risks incurred, the strain involved, the appalling hardships experienced, the constant battle with the pitiless elements, and that which was even worse, viz. disappointment, accident, and misfortune.[45]

While capturing the grandeur of the polar environment, Curzon feared Ponting's work failed to convey the perilous nature of Antarctic exploration.

As a result, Ponting's images were consistently displayed alongside text describing the harsh Antarctic environment. Marcus Huish emphasized that Ponting's photographs 'were, in most cases, obtained under circumstances and difficulties seldom paralleled in the history of Photography'. Ponting had been attacked by killer whales, braved temperatures as low as 40 degrees below zero, and endured 'weeks of patient watching . . . and hours of waiting, almost motionless, beside the camera to secure records of curious habits, never before illustrated', of Antarctic animal-life. Freezing temperatures were particularly highlighted. The Philharmonic Hall programme also emphasized that 'these results were in many cases obtained under circumstances and difficulties seldom paralleled in the history of Photography'.[46]

It is easy to forget the sense of wonder which Ponting's Antarctic visions must have generated among Edwardian audiences. The southern continent had offered a distinctive imaginative landscape, a mysterious stage for Victorian fantasies: both Jules Verne and Edgar Allan Poe wrote stories set around the South Pole. A recent bibliography of Antarctic fiction includes a number of novels which explored the related premises that the Antarctic was either a temperate zone with native inhabitants, or a gateway to a land inside the earth. In Godfrey Sweven's *Riallaro*, published in 1901, for example, a young Briton sails his steam yacht *Daydream* into a mysterious ring of fog circled by an Antarctic current and explores the inhabited islands within the ring.[47]

Ponting's images offered a remarkable window to a continent on which no recorded landing had been made less than twenty years before. The *Bioscope* declared that

> in spite of the paramount importance of the films as a pictorial history of a splendid adventure, it would be a mistake to lose sight of their scientific, educational and even aesthetic values in one's enthusiasm for their deep sentimental interest. They are a record without a parallel in art or in literature, and their fascination can never stale.

This judgement was endorsed forty years later, when the official historian of British cinema, described Ponting's work as 'one of the really great achievements, if not the greatest, of British cinematography during this unhappy period'.[48]

The Sketches and Watercolours of Edward Wilson

Although much less widely exhibited than Ponting's work, Edward Wilson's evocative sketches and watercolours offered an alternative vision of the Antarctic. From the age of 3, Wilson's parents noted, their young son was always drawing and at seven he began to make his own Christmas cards. After graduating from Cambridge, he studied medicine at St George's Hospital in London, hoping to attend evening classes to improve his skills. He never found the time, spending any spare hours in the countryside or in the galleries and museums of London.

Like Ruskin before the geologists' hammers shattered his faith, Wilson worshipped God by observing the natural world. His pictures of birds, he wrote, were 'just visible proofs of my love for them, and attempts to praise God and bring others to love Him through His works'. He could not bring himself to go to church on one glorious spring morning, 'when the whole creation calls me to worship God in such infinitely more beautiful and inspiring light and colour and form and sound . . . it *is* better than the best Church service, there *can* be no doubt about it'.

While some, Wilson argued, might perceive an Antarctic expedition as

> rather more 'worldly' and 'scientific' than 'spiritual,' yet there *is* a spiritual work to be done here. And as for its main object, the acquisition of knowledge pure and simple, surely God means us to

find out all we can of his works, and to work out our own salvation, realizing that all things that have to do with our spiritual development 'are understood and clearly seen in things created,' and if it is right to search out his works in one corner of his Creation, it is right for some of us to go to the ends of the earth to search out others.[49]

For Wilson, painting Antarctica was an act of worship, of homage to the beauty and wonder of God's creation, science and religion in harmony.

On the *Discovery* expedition Wilson completed a portfolio of 200 coloured sketches of the Antarctic landscape and animal life, a number of which were exhibited at the exhibition devoted to the NAE at the Bruton Galleries. The eminent naturalist Sir Joseph Hooker battled illness to visit the exhibition and described Wilson's sketches as 'marvellous in number, interest, and execution. No naval expedition ever did the like. The heads and bodies of the birds by Dr. Wilson are the perfection of ornithological drawing and colouring. They are absolutely alive.'[50] Wilson presented one of his watercolours to Edward VII when he received the Antarctic Medal from the king at Buckingham Palace. He also edited an *Album of Photographs and Sketches* from the NAE, published by the Royal Society.

Following an address to the British Ornithologists Union in March 1905, Wilson was invited to become the field observer for the Agricultural Commission on the Investigation of Grouse Disease. The post utilized Wilson's talents both as a scientist-surgeon and as a first-rate artist. Wilson also received offers to illustrate a new edition of *Bell's British Mammals* and Yarrell's standard work on *British Birds*. He travelled south with Scott a second time in 1910 as an illustrator of considerable renown.

After news of her husband's death reached London, Wilson's

widow Oriana approached the Alpine Club to ask if she could hold an exhibition of her husband's work in the Club hall. Wilson had been the only member of the Alpine Club elected on a 'purely Arctic, or Antarctic, qualification; and he was, further, the only prominent Polar explorer who has valued Alpine experience and attainment sufficiently to seek our membership'.[51] His interest in Alpinism came through his association with keen climbers such as Walter Larden, his first form-master at Cheltenham College.

The Alpine Club council agreed to postpone a planned photographic exhibition, and allow the use of the hall to exhibit Wilson's work between 8 and 29 December 1913. Speaking at the annual winter meeting on 15 December, the President, Sir Edward Davidson, announced that for the rest of the month an exhibition of Wilson's work would be exhibited in the Club, a 'living testimony to the rare and remarkable talent of our deceased fellow-member'. Over 1,300 Club members and their guests viewed Wilson's work at the winter meeting.[52]

The exhibition was very well received, and visitors included Queen Alexandra, her daughter Princess Victoria, and Queen Amelie of Portugal. Reviews argued that, by combining his artistic talent with scientific knowledge, Wilson offered profound insights into the Antarctic world. 'These pictures and sketches are authentic documents,' emphasized *The Times*. 'They tell us more than words could, and tell it just as accurately. They are not to be judged as works of art, but as records of fact.' The *Evening Standard* compared Wilson's watercolours to the work of William Blake, 'an instance of how fidelity to the facts may rise to the heights of imaginative art ... Literal accuracy, however, is an understatement of the impression conveyed by the exhibition ... there is present the feeling of human beings penetrating for the first time into the secret places of Nature.' Wilson was a rare combination of poet and scientist, a 'Seer among the Snows'.[53]

The similarity of these assessments is striking. Through his absolute fidelity to the facts, made possible by his understanding of the physical processes which influenced the genesis and mutation of ice formations or of atmospheric phenomena, Wilson's work penetrated surface appearances to illuminate the essence of the strange and magnificent Antarctic world.

The central article in the Sphere's special Scott memorial edition asked 'Cui Bono?' Was an Antarctic expedition worth the deaths of five men? Man's historic desire for knowledge of the earth drove Scott and his companions south, a desire channelled through the stuffy congress-room of the RGS.

> That the real inception of so-called 'races to the Pole' is really to be found in the cloistered realms of science can readily be proved. One speaks of the first or second 'Scott expedition,' but this is merely a popular symbol to express something which really had its origin in a dry-as-dust International Geographical Congress held as far back as 1895. This white-headed congress came to the conclusion that the exploration of the Antarctic regions was the greatest piece of geographical exploration remaining to be undertaken, and that it should be resumed before the close of the nineteenth century. It was resumed under the personal leadership of Captain Robert Falcon Scott, but we can see that all the deeds of heroism, the walking of a young lieutenant to his death, and the persistent gathering of scientific data in the face of swirling blizzards, spread out as the branches of a tree, the roots of which were nourished in this, doubtless stuffy, congress-room, in which the dominating idea was a desire for knowledge.[54]

Exploration is represented here, to use Cherry-Garrard's evocative phrase, as 'the physical expression of the Intellectual Passion'.[55]

The scientific aims of Scott's last expedition may have been debated in 1913, but they could not be ignored. Every official account of the disaster – from the first New Zealand dispatches, through Teddy Evans's lectures, the *Strand Magazine* serialization, and Smith, Elder's *Scott's Last Expedition*, to exhibitions of Ponting and Wilson's powerful images – consistently stated that the expedition was no mere Pole Hunt. Led by the RGS, the network of international geographical societies reinforced this message by commemorating the martyrs of science who had given up their lives in their desire for knowledge.

Elsewhere, however, the place of scientific research in the meaning of the disaster was contested. All emphasized the selfless idealism of the dead, but, while the geographical societies represented the pursuit of scientific knowledge as a romantic quest, others equated science with the crushing materialism of modernity.

The co-ordinates upon which such assessments turned were not fixed. Teddy Evans, for example, may have emphasized the expedition's scientific achievements to the fellows of the RGS, but, when unveiling a tablet in memory of Captain Oates, highlighted 'a lesson that is far more valuable than any scientific results, the lesson to young English men and women to do their duty'.[56] It is to such evocations of the nation that we shall turn next.

25. *Captain Scott* (1913). Harrington Mann's posthumous work for the Royal Geographical Society is the most intriguing portrait of Captain Scott. Scott's eyes draw the viewer into the painting, to contemplate the suffering he endured before his death. (LEFT)

26. Captain Scott writing his diary. Scott had his own small compartment in the hut at Cape Evans, decorated with photographs of his wife Kathleen and son Peter. Some of these photographs are in the archives of the Scott Polar Research Institute, identifiable by tears where they had been pinned to the wall. (BELOW)

27. Albert Hodge's successful design for a National Monument. Hodge's winning design included a pair of snow shoes on the back. Cherry-Garrard informed Hodge that the expedition had not used snow shoes and they were subsequently changed to skis.

28. National Monument at Mount Wise, Devonport. Hodge modified his design after protests from Kathleen Scott and various RGS officials. After a series of delays, the statue was finally unveiled on Mount Wise in Devonport on 10 August 1925.

29. The Cape Crozier party - departure. Henry Bowers, Edward Wilson, and Apsley Cherry-Garrard (l. to r.) about to leave for Cape Crozier in search of the eggs of the emperor penguin. The Antarctic winter is illuminated by Ponting's flash. (ABOVE)

30. The Cape Crozier party – return. Wilson, Bowers, and Cherry-Garrard (l. to r.). 'The Crozier party returned last night after enduring for five weeks the hardest conditions on record,' wrote Scott on 2 August 1911. 'They looked more weather worn than anyone I have yet seen.' (BELOW)

31. The *Terra Nova* imprisoned in the ice. To reach the Antarctic, the *Terra Nova* had to navigate a course through the pack ice which forms around the continent each year. Herbert Ponting chose this photograph as the frontispiece for his book about the expedition, *The Great White South* (London, 1921). (LEFT)

32. The castle berg. The most striking berg seen by the expedition was frozen into the ice about a mile from the hut at Cape Evans, and resembled a medieval castle. (BELOW)

33. Ice cave. Probably the most famous of Ponting's photographs. By great good fortune, the entrance to the ice cave framed the *Terra Nova* a mile away for a few hours. (LEFT)

34. Mount Erebus. The volcano, named after one of the ships used on Sir James Clark Ross's pioneering southern voyages between 1837 and 1843, dominated the landscape around McMurdo Sound. The *Erebus* was lost with Sir John Franklin during the search for the North-West Passage. (BELOW)

35. 'The Stony Stare' and 'The Glad Eye'. Adelie penguins were the leading actors in H. G. Ponting's successful lectures at the Philharmonic Hall in 1914. Ponting followed the penguins' customs and courtship rituals. Charlie Chaplin's first film, *Making a Living*, was released in the same year.

36. 'Ponko' the penguin. One of the earliest examples of film merchandise, produced to accompany Ponting's Philharmonic Hall lectures. 'Ponko' was Ponting's nickname among the crew of the *Terra Nova*.

37. Dr George Simpson preparing a balloon. George Simpson carried out pioneering meteorological research during Scott's last expedition. Here, Dr Simpson prepares a balloon which measured air-currents in the upper atmosphere. (LEFT)

38. *Iridescent Clouds North from the Ramp on Cape Evans, 9 August 1911.* Edward Wilson's watercolours captured the mystery of Antarctica. He completed this painting only eight days after returning from his epic winter journey to the penguin rookery at Cape Crozier. (BELOW)

VICTORY AND DEATH.

" : . . The white South has thy bones ;
And thou,
Heroic sailor-soul,
Art passing on thy happier voyage now
Toward no earthly pole ! "

This photograph was taken at Guildford on March 28, 1901, just before Captain Scott sailed on the Discovery. He was visiting some friends, and the children, with whom he was always a prime favourite, coaxed him to go into the garden to discover the "South Pole," which they had made with the remains of a fall of snow. He is seen after planting a Union Jack upon it, an action which afforded the youngsters the keenest delight.

39. 'Victory and Death'. Many early reports of the disaster adapted Tennyson's epitaph for Sir John Franklin by changing 'North' to 'South'. (ABOVE)

40. Scott and the Pole. An early twentieth-century photo-opportunity. Scott is shown planting a Union Flag on the remains of a snow fall in a Guildford garden on 28 March 1901, before the departure of the Discovery. (LEFT)

· CHAPTER SIX ·

'FOR THE HONOUR
OF OUR COUNTRY'

T HE Antarctic disaster inspired a deluge of second-rate poetry, but the worst verse was probably composed in Nottingham:

> Strong in their love of noble deeds,
> They strove to conquer where; –
> They could unfurl their country's flag,
> And plant it firmly there.[1]

The story of Scott of the Antarctic was decorated with flags. Before his first voyage south, Scott was coaxed to 'discover' the South Pole in a Guildford garden, planting a flag on the remains of a snow-fall. A union flag served as a tablecloth for Scott's last birthday dinner, sledges in the Antarctic flew personalized banners, and a 'poor slighted Union Jack' fluttered forlornly over the shoulders of the dead in the photographs they took at the Pole.

Captain Scott and his companions died, in Scott's words, 'for the honour of our country'. But what did the many British celebrations of Antarctic heroism reveal about national character on the eve of the First World War?

Over the last twenty years, historians have begun to unravel the cords which bound the United Kingdom together. Protestant-ism and the Constitution (the subordination of the monarch to the will of Parliament) were central to representations of the nation which circulated through the eighteenth century: com-mentators at home and abroad hailed the British commitment to liberty, a land free from the tyranny of popes and kings. The war of American Independence called this commitment into question, but the successful campaign for the abolition of slavery reaffirmed Britain's providential role as champion of liberty. Britons were forged, as English, Scots, and Welsh alike embraced this national mission.

Many have argued that the nation was transformed in the second half of the nineteenth century, by the inexorable rise of an imperialist ideology: Military, Monarchy and Empire superseded Protestantism, Parliament, and Liberty as the dominant features of a new popular culture.[2] The mass media fuelled this transformation, bombarding vast audiences with royal spectacles and imperial adventure stories.

The ways in which a Royal Naval officer, Royal Indian Marine, seaman, cavalry officer, and civilian were hailed as heroes, expose the very heart of the nation on the eve of the First World War, offering insights into the status of the armed forces, the role of monarchy, and the relationship between England, Scotland, and Wales. The celebration of Antarctic heroism reveals a more finely textured national tapestry than the imperial monolith of many recent accounts.

The Spectre of Decline

Outlining his plans to the RGS in 1910, Scott claimed that the conquest of the South Pole would serve as an 'outward visible sign that we are still a nation able and willing to undertake difficult enterprises, still capable of standing in the van of the army of progress'. The explorers' willingness to suffer in a noble cause and the bravery with which they faced death were widely celebrated as affirmations of national virility in an age haunted by the spectre of decline.

The expression of fears about the health of the nation has been a recurring response to the pressures of modernity, a reaction to international competition, and the social tensions generated by rapid industrialization and urbanization. Even Queen Victoria's Diamond Jubilee celebrations in 1897, the most spectacular nineteenth-century expression of imperial grandeur, inspired Rudyard Kipling's sombre 'Recessional', with its reminder of the fall of Nineveh and Tyre. Classical allusions were common, with many writers predicting a British re-enactment of the Roman drama of collapse and imperial *coup d'état*.[3]

Mapping the fluctuation of concerns about the health of the nation is difficult, not least because each period defines its own malaise against an idealized past. Evidence from a compelling range of sources, though, suggests that fears of decline, of the deterioration of the masses and the decadence of the elite intensified in the 1900s. Perhaps most significantly, the humiliations of the South African War, when two tiny republics frustrated the best efforts of the British empire, seemed to bear out Kipling's prophecy. The war inspired a search for national efficiency, prompting the establishment of an Inter-Departmental Committee on Physical Deterioration and the formation of a rash of voluntary societies, such as the National League for Physical Education and Improvement.

The achievements of polar explorers had long offered opportunities to test national character. The *Cornhill Magazine* declared in 1874 that George Nares's Arctic expedition 'would show the world that some great sparks of the spirit of our forefathers still glow in our island', while, in 1899, Clements Markham believed the launch of a National Antarctic Expedition would support his 'conviction that the spirit which influenced the patriotic adventurers of the Elizabethan age was still alive among us'.[4]

But the tenor of praise for polar exploits shifted after the return of Scott's *Discovery* in 1904. The direct challenge posed by German naval ambitions provided a focus for the frustrations of the South African campaign. The amendment of the German Navy Law in 1908, pushing up the rate of capital ship-building from three to four per year, intensified the Edwardian arms race, and provided a back-drop to news of Shackleton's triumphant failure in 1909. Arthur Conan Doyle, creator of Sherlock Holmes and polar enthusiast, predicted that 'when the trouble comes our cry will be for men, not ships. We can pass the eight Dreadnoughts, if we are sure of the eight Shackletons.'[5] Shackleton's Antarctic adventures offered a display of national vigour uncomplicated by the moral dilemmas associated with heroic activity in South Africa.

The desire to repudiate the prophets of decline superseded the emphasis on the provision of peace-time training for the Royal Navy, which had been such a prominent feature of Clements Markham's rhetoric in the 1890s. On the eve of the *Terra Nova*'s departure, Leonard Darwin declared that 'Captain Scott is going to prove once again that the manhood of the nation is not dead, and that the characteristics of our ancestors, who won this great Empire, still flourish amongst us'. The Admiral of the Fleet, Sir Edward Seymour, wrote that he had been persuaded of the value of the expedition, after some initial misgivings, by Scott's declared intention 'to show an example of enterprise, and of facing risks and hardship, much needed in these days when money and pleasure are the things most desired and worshipped. These things will as surely ruin us as they ruined the Roman Empire.'[6]

The health of the nation was at the forefront of public debate in 1913. The imperialist author Sidney Low, friend of Curzon and Cecil Rhodes, considered whether the 'arrest of the reproductive instinct among the higher stocks', combined with 'the increase of

State-Socialism', would lead to 'race suicide'.[7] When news of the Antarctic disaster reached London in February, R. H. Benson had just published a withering assault on standards at Eton, a bill to permit the permanent detention of 'feeble-minded' unmarried mothers dependent on poor-relief was passing through Westminster, and Lord Roberts was about to embark on an extensive lecture tour in support of compulsory national service.

Scott's 'Message to the Public' focused reports of the disaster directly on the fear of decline. Scott had written how the explorers had 'shown that Englishmen can endure hardship, help one another and meet death with as great a fortitude as ever in the past'. This passage more than any other helped transform defeat in the race for the Pole into a moral victory, not only as an example of idealism, but also as a demonstration that the indomitable spirit of the nation lived on.[8]

'There has been too much talk of late of the decadence of our country,' argued the *Daily Graphic*. 'As long as England can produce men like Captain Scott and his comrades we may laugh at this silly talk.' John Scott Keltie summed up such sentiments in a letter to his French colleague Charles Rabot: 'We are often taunted in England with being a degenerate race, but when such deeds as these are possible still among us, I think we may cherish the belief that after all our degeneration has not proceeded very far.'[9]

Supporters of Eton College seized on Captain Oates's example to counter Benson's criticisms. The *Eton Chronicle* declared that Oates's magnificent death demonstrated that Etonians 'have no reason to fear that our standard is deteriorating either in quantity or quality'. Teddy Evans drew a huge audience when he lectured at Eton in October 1913. Six months later, Prince Alexander of Teck returned to the theme while unveiling a memorial tablet designed by Kathleen Scott in the College's library cloister. 'It is often said that we live in an age which refuses pain and shrinks from hardship and that the spirit of luxury is unduly fostered in our School. Well, we at least can point to Oates as an abiding witness that Eton is no trainer of feather-bed soldiers.'[10]

These diagnoses equated the health of the nation with a particular vision of vigorous masculinity. From the pulpit of St Paul's Canon Alexander described his 'revived and renewed belief in the virility of our race', while the rector who unveiled Lois Evans's memorial to her late husband in Glamorgan noted that the explorers had 'taught afresh to a world growing more luxurious and effeminate, the glory of a soldier's endurance and capacity for stern duty and the possession of scientific courage to the last'.[11] A common vocabulary recurs in these discussions, in which virility, courage, endurance, hardihood, and duty are celebrated in opposition to the effete, the flaccid, the luxurious, the materialistic, the nerve-ridden, the degenerate, and the decadent.

'Let us tell the children how Englishmen can die'

Many considered Scott's story an ideal tonic for the nation's ailing youth. 'What a privilege, too, it is for our children to have known him,' wrote one friend to Scott's sister, Lady Ellison-Macartney, 'there is nothing now that one can wish better for Cuthbert than that he should in his life follow even in some small degree your brother's noble example.'[12] Commentators constantly emphasized the inspirational legacy the explorers had bequeathed to British boys and girls.

Barely forty-eight hours after the announcement of the disaster, the London *Evening News* appealed for Scott's story to be read to schoolchildren to coincide with the St Paul's memorial service.

'Let us tell the children how Englishmen can die . . ., let us not lose a great opportunity; let us not forget to implant this glorious memory in the hearts of the children that will succeed our own.'[13] The editor, Walter Evans, rushed the proposal onto the agenda of the London County Council's education committee, which agreed to distribute copies of an article commissioned by the newspaper to LCC head teachers. The sole proviso was that no advertisement for the *Evening News* be included. The initiative was taken up throughout the country, with education officers in Bristol, Leeds, Liverpool, and Nottingham directing headmasters to arrange for Scott's story to be read in their schools.[14]

As the bells of St Paul's struck twelve and the cathedral memorial service began, 1,500,000 children in elementary schools in London, and at least fifty other towns and cities, gathered to hear 'The Immortal Story of Capt. Scott's Expedition – How Five Brave Englishmen Died', by the writer and folklorist Arthur Machen. The story began:

> Children: You are going to hear the true story of five of the bravest and best men who have ever lived on the earth since the world began.
>
> You are English boys and girls, and you must often have heard England spoken of as the greatest country in the world, or perhaps you have been told that the British Empire . . . is the greatest Empire that the world has ever seen . . . when we say that England is great we are not thinking of the size of the country or of the number of people who live in it. We are thinking of much more important things, and if you listen to the story that is to be read to you, you will find out what greatness really does mean.

After a brief narrative of the expedition and the march to the South Pole, Scott's account of Oates's death and the final section of the 'Message to the Public' were quoted in full. The story concluded:

> So these brave men died; and now you know what we mean when
> we say that they were great. They feared no danger, they never
> complained, they did their very best, each one was willing to give
> up his life for the others, and when they knew that there was no
> hope for them they laid down their lives bravely and calmly like
> true Christian gentlemen.[15]

Reports stated that 750,000 pupils in LCC schools, and a further
750,000 children in towns from Invereighty in Forfar to Calstock
in Devon were read the story of Scott of the Antarctic on Friday,
14 February 1913.[16]

Numerous other schemes were proposed to exploit the didactic
potential of the disaster. The theatrical impresario Sir Herbert
Beerbohm Tree suggested a 'commemorative hall or gallery . . . in
which the great and heroic deeds of all Englishmen could be
recorded pictorially. Think of the educational value such a thing
would have!'[17] St Catherine's Press swiftly published a 30-page
booklet, which included a brief history of the expedition, biographies of the dead, and, most importantly, Scott's 'Message to the
Public'. The concluding lines asserted that 'The nation's loss is also
the nation's splendid gain. The bones of heroes are also the glorious
seeds of heroes to come.' Although priced at a shilling, the first
edition of 3,000 copies sold out in three days and, by the end of
February, 2,500 copies of a second edition had been sold.[18]

The volume of print directed at young people increased
massively in the forty years before the First World War, with tales
of polar exploration a staple ingredient of this expanding juvenile
literature: between 1909 and 1916, the *Boy's Own Paper* published
seventeen feature articles about polar exploration, in addition to
miscellaneous cartoons and photographs (**Fig. 6.1**). Following
Scott's death the *Boy's Own Paper* published an account of
Antarctic exploration by a regular contributor, W. J. Gordon, in

The Pole really found at last!

6.1 'The North Pole'. Polar images and stories were a regular feature of the *Boy's Own Paper*, one of the leading illustrated weeklies for boys. Here the *Boy's Own Paper* responds to Frederick Cook and Robert Peary's rival claims to have reached the North Pole.

three parts: ' "Southward Ho!" To the Pole – Antarctica, or the Land of the Snow Queen.' The final instalment recounted Scott's last march, emphasizing how the explorers 'met their fate as men who are really men should do. Never was higher courage shown, never a better guide for those who would be really worthy of their race.'[19]

The *Boy's Own Paper* focused attention on Captain Oates in particular, an indication of the magazine's preoccupation with English public schools. Oates was an ideal *Boy's Own Paper* hero: Old Etonian, cavalry officer, war hero, polar explorer, and now national martyr. Another boys' magazine with a liking for exclamation marks, *Young England*, also singled out the 'story of self-sacrifice, in the case of poor Oates – that will surely inspire men for all time!' 'He never returned! He had walked to his death for the sake of his comrades! "Greater love hath no man than this, that a man lay down his life for his friends!" ' Just after the outbreak of war, the *Boy's Own Paper* published a special colour reproduction of J. C. Dollman's painting of Oates, *A Very Gallant Gentleman*, which they recommended 'should find an honoured place in the den of every B. O. P. reader'.[20]

The Boy Scout movement, recently founded by the hero of the South African War, Robert Baden-Powell, proved particularly active in disseminating Scott's story among children. Baden-Powell had founded the Scouts in 1908 in part out of concern for the deteriorating health of urban youths. The tragic tale of Antarctic exploration perfectly expressed the movement's ethos of duty, comradeship, and strenuous outdoor activity. The Scout Association endorsed the *Evening News'* proposal that Machen's account of the disaster be read to every Scout troop, and large numbers of Scout-masters applied for copies. In Scotland, the Greenock Division organized a special memorial service, while Edinburgh Scouts handed out 4,000 leaflets advertising a performance in aid of the Scott memorial fund.[21] Almost 200 Scouts from eleven troops attended a special service at St Matthew's church, Cheltenham, on the Sunday after the announcement of the disaster. The Rector praised those who searched 'out the secrets of His glorious creation . . . Scouts were they all in farthest point South, in farthest point of endurance. Ye who seek to be pioneers – learn how Englishmen can seek and struggle, can dare and die.' A Union Jack was draped over the pulpit, alongside a laurel wreath tied with royal purple.[22]

Baden-Powell himself frequently referred to the disaster,

emphasizing that the dead men were doing actual Scout work in exploring the icefields of the South. When two Sea Scouts were killed during a voyage on their yacht the *Mirror* just after the publication of *Scott's Last Expedition*, Baden-Powell argued that

> If Captain Scott and his brave companions showed an example of dying for their duty our brother Scouts have shown also that boys can die like men in carrying out their orders calmly in the face of danger, even to sacrificing their own lives, as Sea Scout Witt and Assistant Scoutmaster Carnall did, in helping their comrades to safety. They passed the greatest test to which a man can be put, and they passed it with honour.

He declared that Scott had 'died proving himself one of the most energetic Scouts of our nation'.[23]

Baden-Powell returned to Scott's story again in the new year. After lamenting the decline of Britain's domination of international sport ('last week another English boxer was defeated by a Frenchman'), Baden-Powell found consolation in the Antarctic disaster. 'Are Britons going downhill? No! . . . There is plenty of pluck and spirit left in the British after all. Captain Scott and Captain Oates have shown us that, too.'[24]

Baden-Powell drew inspiration from his attendance at the lectures of both Teddy Evans and Herbert Ponting. While Ponting and Evans would argue about the expedition for another fifteen years, both men agreed on the educative value of Scott's story. Evans suggested that 'A copy of my late leader's message should be in the possession of every British school boy', while Ponting believed 'the example set by Captain Scott and his companions, should be the example which every British boy should endeavour to reach, when he is called upon to face the "Grim Shadow" face to face'. With the cheapest seats at Evans's Nottingham lecture going for a shilling, opportunities for children to attend were limited.

But a 13-year-old Louis Mountbatten heard Evans perform and wrote to his mother that the lecture 'was probably the best I was ever going to hear in my life'. Half a century later he told one of Scott's biographers, Reginald Pound, that 'I am inclined to think that my forecast has been fulfilled'.[25]

Three Englishmen, a Scotsman, and a Welshman

Captain Scott and his companions died in the service of the nation, their courage offering both reassurance to an anxious age and inspiration to the generation which would succeed them. Scott's story furnished an effective instrument to groups eager to inculcate a constellation of values regarding courage, comradeship, and duty. But duty to what?

Scott himself referred only to England in the crucial passages of his journal. A revivified English pride flourished in the second half of the nineteenth century, as institutions such as the *Oxford English Dictionary* (begun in 1879) and *Dictionary of National Biography* (begun in 1882) presented a very English vision of the national past. Acclamations of English character figured prominently in literature, history, and political thought. So did the story of Scott of the Antarctic reinforce the creeping hegemony of Englishness before 1914?

Many reports followed Scott's lead. The *Daily Mail* praised the 'true and faithful servants of England', while the *Daily Chronicle* declared that 'English heroism has given to the world yet another epic'. An 11-year-old girl, Mary Steel, composed a poem which concluded

> Though nought but a simple cross,
> Now marks those heroes' grave,

Their names will live forever!
Oh England! Land of the Brave![26]

But this Anglo-centric vision was not projected throughout Britain. The relative freedom of local government and civil society from central interference fostered municipal, regional, Scottish, and Welsh traditions. The efflorescence of cultural nationalism was a European phenomenon, vibrant in Scotland, Wales, and Ireland, as well as England. Scott's own words proved no obstacle to the description of the explorers as Britons and the disaster as a British tragedy. The *Illustrated London News* declared the explorers had 'proved once more the inherent heroism of British men of action', while the *Observer* argued that 'there has never been a more strictly heroic vindication of British character'.[27]

The presence of both a Welshman (Edgar Evans) and a Scotsman (Henry Bowers) among the dead encouraged the celebration of the disaster throughout the nation. Immediately after news reached London, the *Scotsman* highlighted the donation of a sledge by the boys of Kelvinside Academy in Glasgow, the presence of Kathleen Scott's brother, the Revd R. Douglas Bruce, as Rector of St Anne's Episcopal church in Dunbar, Bowers's home in Rothesay, and his widowed mother's residence in the Ardberg district. 'It is remembered with pride that more than one of these heroes and martyrs of the Antarctic, including Captain Scott himself, claimed connection by birth or descent with Scottish soil.' J. M. Barrie's biographical introduction to a single volume of extracts from Scott's journals, published by Smith, Elder in 1914, described how the explorer's great-great-grandfather was the Scott of Brownhead whose estates were sequestered after 1745. His dwelling was razed to the ground and the family fled, eventually settling in Devon.[28]

Memorial funds received donations from all over Scotland,

from Stranraer to Inverness. The *Aberdeen Express* declared that the passing of Captain Oates would take its 'place along with the story of the Highland regiment that stood unflinchingly on the deck of the sinking *Birkenhead* as the boats bore away the women and children to safety'.[29]

While some thus claimed the disaster as a distinctively Scottish tragedy, others emphasized the Welsh connection. One of the officers hoisted two large leeks alongside the Welsh flag when the *Terra Nova* sailed out of Cardiff harbour in 1910 and Teddy Evans steered a course close to the coastline, to allow the citizens of the Vale of Glamorgan to see the ship.

When Commodore Royds unveiled Albert Hodge's statue in August 1925, a Welsh reporter urged the citizens of Cardiff to remember Scott's last expedition and

> the glow of pride and glory that came at the presentation to Commander Evans of the strident, triumphant Welsh Dragon flag . . . Commander Evans took that flag to the confines of the Pole, and now it sways from the dome of the Council Chamber of the City Hall, whose corridors are also adorned with pictures of the lines of craft that sailed out of Cardiff, wishing the *Terra Nova* godspeed.

The correspondent recommended that all Cardiff schoolchildren be taken to the City Hall to learn the story of the expedition.[30]

Speakers at the civic reception in Cardiff which greeted the return of the *Terra Nova* moved easily between proclamations of allegiance to Wales, England, Britain, and the empire. The Lord Mayor, Alderman Morgan Thomas, 'gloried in the fact that Great Britain could produce such heroes as those who had sacrificed their lives in the Scott expedition', while Daniel Radcliffe declared he 'felt immensely proud of what they had done for the empire. While they had men like the officers and crew of the *Terra*

Nova England would never die, but her flag would continue to wave over every ocean.' The most prominent of the Cardiff memorials, the clocktower in Roath Park, carried the inscription 'Britons All. And Very Gallant Gentlemen', the only monument to inscribe the explorers as 'Britons'.[31]

The adulation of Captain Scott and his companions testifies not to the hegemony of Englishness, but to the vitality of Scottish and Welsh allegiances in 1913. 'The country has been held together,' Brian Harrison argues, 'not by propagating a composite United Kingdom nationality, but by a somewhat informal and untrumpeted acquiescence in national diversity.'[32] The cultural forms through which the identity of the nation was expressed were generated by a wide range of official and quasi-official bodies, voluntary associations, and commercial schemes. The plurality of agency promoted many visions of the nation. The *Terra Nova* sailed into Cardiff harbour with the arms of the City of Cardiff at her foremast, the Welsh Dragon at her mainmast, the Royal Yacht Squadron burgee at her mizzenmast, and the White Ensign at her peak, a fitting symbol of the range of allegiances capable of expression through the expedition.[33]

But if English, Scots, and Welsh alike could embrace Scott's story, not all were welcome in the national visions projected through the disaster. Scott's death struck a chord in Ireland, but Catholics always occupied an uneasy position in a Protestant nation. And the story of Scott of the Antarctic painted the nation white. Part of the appeal of Scott's story was aesthetic: the Antarctic offered a pure stage for the performance of heroic drama. The only non-Caucasian face on the expedition was the ship's cat, 'Nigger'. The inclusion of the cat on one souvenir plate may have been a playful expression of a national preoccupation with animals. But the central location of 'Nigger' throws the achievements of the white men in the white south illustrated on the four panels into bold relief. Although impossible to quantify, the overwhelming whiteness of the story of Scott of the Antarctic must have reinforced colour prejudice in Edwardian Britain.

Outpost of Empire

The racial dynamic which complicated Robert Peary's conquest of the North Pole with an African-American, Matthew Henson, and, later, Sherpa Tenzing Norgay and Edmund Hillary's ascent of Mount Everest, was absent from Scott's last expedition, where class, not race, structured social relations. Journeys through an unpopulated Antarctica did not generate the same questions about colonial exploitation set by Arctic exploration of Inuit lands, or mountaineering in the Himalayas.

But Great Britain was an imperial nation in 1913, ruler of a vast overseas empire bound together by the sea. The Antarctic disaster furnished another dramatic episode in the rough island story, a tale of maritime exploration and expansion. 'This country of ours is so great, its Empire so wide,' wrote J. E. Hodder Williams in *Like English Gentlemen*, 'because throughout the long years, Englishmen, everywhere, have fought and struggled and died to possess that unknown land, and to plant their flag on its topmost height.'[34]

The family histories of the dead show how empire shaped people's lives through the nineteenth century. Three of Scott's uncles served in the Indian army, while his brother Archie became private secretary to the Governor of Lagos, and joined the Hausa Force administering law and order in West Africa. At the age of 19, Bowers's father Alexander captained his tea-clipper *Geelong* to an inland port further up the Yangtse-kiang than any British ship had penetrated. Edgar Evans's father, Charles, sailed barques carrying coal from Swansea across the Atlantic Ocean and round Cape Horn, to obtain copper ore. Lawrence Oates had served in Egypt, India, and South Africa with the Inniskilling Dragoons, before he sailed to the Antarctic. Oates's father William was an enthusiastic big-game hunter in South Africa, while his uncle Frank was said to have been only the fifth white man to see the Victoria Falls. Edward Wilson had misgivings about the morality of British imperial rule, but he had only been accepted for the *Discovery* expedition thanks to the intercession of his uncle Charles, a Major-General in the Royal Engineers, who served in Palestine, Anatolia, Egypt, and, most famously, on the failed expedition to relieve General Gordon at Khartoum.

The departure of the *Discovery* was accompanied by a postcard event, which portrayed the expedition as a distinctively imperial enterprise.[35] The London publishers E. Wrench issued four post-cards about the expedition in their 'Links of Empire' series. For a subscription of 2s., the cards would be posted back to the subscriber, first from London on the ship's departure; then from Simonstown, South Africa, and Lyttelton, New Zealand, as the *Discovery* sailed south; and finally, from Lyttelton again, on the expedition's return from the Antarctic.

Imperial rhetoric also pervaded the organization of Scott's last expedition. The fund-raising brochure opened by proclaiming that 'The main object of this Expedition is to reach the South Pole, and to secure for the British Empire the honour of that achievement'. At the RGS reception before the departure of the *Terra Nova*, Scott explained that he had 'tried to make this an empire expedition' and was confident he had gathered 'a set of men who will represent the hardihood and the energy of our race' from Toronto, Australia, and New Zealand. He lamented that he had missed many, such as the 'hard men who wrestle with the difficulties of frontier life' in Canada and the 'hardy mountaineers' from the northern parts of India.[36]

Scott's invocation of empire was a seasoned fund-raising ploy. Imperial rhetoric could mobilize contributors who were wary of English expansionism: citizens of Cardiff and Christchurch could join an imperial endeavour without compromising their allegiance to Wales and New Zealand. The expedition certainly captured the imagination of New Zealanders. The *Terra Nova* received numerous donations of supplies, and Ponting's film of large crowds lining the pier at Lyttelton suggests that the expedition generated considerable interest. Pledges of money, however, were disappointing and Scott raised much less from the colonies than he had hoped: £2,500 from the Commonwealth of Australia (half the sum given to Shackleton), £1,000 from the New Zealand government, and a mere £500 from the South African government, supplemented by a further £500 from the citizens of Johannesburg and Cape Town. The citizens of Cardiff donated more than the whole of South Africa. Only a personal donation of £2,500 from a Sydney businessman, Samuel Horden, salvaged the expedition's finances. The lukewarm response suggests that fifteen years of Antarctic expeditions had hardened potential donors against grandiose imperial rhetoric.

The possession of a vast empire, encircling the globe from Tasmania to Calcutta, from the Sudan to Honduras, exerted a profound influence over Britons' sense of their place in the world. After the announcement of Amundsen's success in 1912, a Cardiff ship supplier wrote to the RGS on hearing a rumour that Scott had ordered equipment from Norway: 'We, as Britishers, cannot quite swallow this. Is this correct? We shall be glad if you will kindly enlighten us in this matter.'[37] Such instinctive assumptions of

British superiority, founded in part on the sheer size of the empire, figured prominently in reports of the Antarctic disaster.

Some extolled the explorers' demonstration of the imperial spirit. J. C. Ross wrote in *The Times* that Scott and his companions had shown 'the temper of men who build Empires, and while it lives among us we shall be capable of maintaining the Empire that our fathers builded [*sic*]'. The *Evening News* published a poem claiming Antarctica as an 'Outpost of empire', which concluded:

> Their deaths have sanctified that lonely place,
> And in that great white land
> As Empire's furthest post their monument shall stand.

The *Daily Express* condemned a German newspaper which had both emphasized the expedition's substantial debts, and dared to ask why Scott had not tried to stop Oates leaving the tent. 'The comments of the *Lokalanzeiger* will amaze and disgust the world,' wrote the *Express*. 'They will earn the contempt of Germany itself. But we are bound to observe that the ignorance of idealism thus betrayed makes us marvel less at the flaw of character which has prevented German success in colonisation.'[38]

Winston Churchill believed that Scott's story spoke with special force to 'our kith and kin in the Colonies and Dominions of the British Empire'. New Zealanders, in particular, exploited Scott's story to encourage imperial allegiance. A public meeting in Oamaru opened a fund to support a Scott memorial essay prize, to 'stimulate the historical imagination of the young, kindle their patriotic ardour, and exert no little influence in cultivating their pride in Imperial citizenship'. The 42nd company of senior cadets, Queenstown, raised funds to place two marble tablets on a massive boulder transported from the Humboldt mountains by the Wakatipu glacier. Public subscriptions paid for the erection of a tapered column, surmounted by an anchor, on a headland overlooking the harbour at Port Chalmers.[39]

Outside New Zealand, public monuments were erected less frequently, but donations from Australia, Canada, and South Africa flowed freely to the Mansion House fund. I. Plotz & Co., the largest proprietors of amusement concerns and novelty owners in South Africa, also constructed three life-size tableaux showing the explorers at the Pole, the relief party, and the five heroes, which they proposed to take on a national tour. The company offered the RGS 5 per cent of the profits, in return for the Society's patronage. The offer was politely declined.[40]

The story of Scott of the Antarctic thus resonated powerfully in an imperial nation. But as reference to an imperial dynamic offers only a partial explanation for the course of British exploration at the turn of the century, so a focus on empire does not do justice to the range of meanings communicated through Scott's story.

The extent to which the disaster was configured as an explicitly imperial story should not be exaggerated: most commentators did not depict the Antarctic as an outpost of empire. Only six out of forty-one leading articles on the expedition published in thirteen newspapers between 10 and 16 February 1913 made any reference to the British empire. And one of those six articles argued that 'too commonly the valour by which we are directed to take guidance is the valour of destruction rather than the valour of creation, the spectacular courage of the soldier or the Empire-builder rather than the quiet courage of the man of science, the healer of wounds, the martyr for his fellows'.[41] With a circulation of over 500,000, the *Daily News and Leader*'s emphasis on the quiet courage of the man of science directly contradicted J. C. Ross's reference to 'the temper of men who build Empires', which appeared in *The Times* on the very same day.

This trend reflects the broader pattern of reports in more than 100 newspapers and periodicals. Out of more than twenty-five poems I have found published in the press, for example, only three (including 'Outpost of Empire') made any reference to the empire. References to the health of the nation alluded, of course, to the maintenance of British dominion overseas, without explicitly mentioning empire. But it is striking that, while Ross's leader shows how a polar disaster was capable of mobilizing an aggressive imperialist rhetoric, such propaganda was rare.

Official accounts did not configure the disaster as a specifically imperial episode. Scott did not write of empire in his 'Message to the Public', and neither did the three cables from New Zealand, nor Clements Markham's preface to Scott's Last Expedition. Teddy Evans's Royal Albert Hall lecture made no mention of the British empire, even when describing the hoisting of Queen Alexandra's little silk Union Jack at the South Pole. Similarly, neither the programme notes nor any of the descriptions of the 152 photographs on display at the Fine Art Society exhibition of Herbert Ponting's work mention the empire. Nor did the programme published to accompany Ponting's lectures in the Philharmonic Hall in 1914. Ponting's photographs and films, which dominated the iconography of the disaster, consistently presented the expedition as a scientific enterprise and the tragedy as another episode in man's heroic struggle against nature.

References to the imperial value of Scott's story only appeared when Ponting tried to sell his film to the nation during the war. The first page of a promotional booklet Ponting published declared that 'As propaganda for inspiring our own youth to brave and noble deeds and for use in foreign countries to show that the spirit which made our Empire is still warm in the hearts of true Britons, the Record and the accompanying explanatory lecture have never been equalled'.[42] Again, the most extravagant examples of imperial rhetoric occur while fund-raising.

Imperial propagandists sang loudly, but they were only one part of the chorus of voices which commemorated Captain Scott and his companions. The Antarctic disaster caused such a sensation in Britain, not by mobilizing a dominant imperial ideology, but because those who celebrated 'the temper of men who build Empires' and those who hailed the 'quiet courage of the man of science', could *both* find inspiration in the story of Scott of the Antarctic.

Killed in Action

The expansion and maintenance of empire was dependent on military achievement and the commemoration of the Antarctic disaster also illuminates the peculiar cultural status of the British armed forces before 1914. Historians continue to debate the extent to which Britain was a militaristic society on the eve of the First World War. Some, like John MacKenzie and Michael Paris, highlight the prominence of military themes in popular culture and the proliferation of paramilitary organizations. Others join Niall Ferguson in emphasizing the relatively small membership of such movements: the National Service League never exceeded 100,000 members, while no more than 2.7 per cent of the male population aged 15–49 were members of the Volunteer Force.[43]

In contrast to the German empire, British officers neither held nor aspired to the status of an elite governing class. Opposition to national service also remained deeply entrenched. One article celebrating Scott's example lamented the lethargy of nationalist sentiment in Britain: 'It is easy to deride the Territorials, but how can we hope for success when the mass of the nation regard those who join the forces as being much on a par with "the girl who took the wrong turning"?' [44] But the armed forces also commanded great respect among many, with the Royal Navy in particular raised as an emblem of the nation.

The press widely reported that the families of Scott and Evans were to be offered pensions as if the men had been killed in action, and many commentators emphasized that four of the dead explorers were members of the services. The Secretary of State for War, Colonel Seely, declared to a gathering of the National Reserve at Hammersmith that 'We shall never forget those brave sailors who laid down their lives in the cause of this country's honour as truly as a soldier who lays it down in the battlefield'. [45]

The First Lord of the Admiralty, Winston Churchill, proclaimed the value of the explorers' sacrifice, when he took the chair at the Queen's Hall for Teddy Evans's first public lecture on 4 June 1913. The explorers, Churchill declared, had demonstrated that 'if ever other tests should be applied to the naval system upon which the British Empire depends, the officers and men of the sea service, and their comrades of the Army, will not fail this country or the Empire in the hour of need'. [46]

The representation of Captain Scott, Captain Oates, and Petty Officer Evans both drew on and reinforced the stereotypes of inspirational leader, gallant cavalry officer and hardy blue-jacket. One profile of Scott in the *Daily Graphic* suggested that 'Nine people out of ten, seeing him, would have said, "Naval officer" ', noting his 'strength and vigour and quickness', 'his clear-cut features, his healthy face'. The *Daily Telegraph* described Scott as 'a sailor of the new era – scientist as well as seaman'. The mobilization of such stereotypes obscured the impulsive, brooding, and fatalistic character who has subsequently emerged. With his journal littered with references to man's powerlessness in the face of an implacable fate, one author later judged Scott 'more like an ancient Greek than a modern naval captain'.[47]

Kathleen Scott chose to depict her dead husband in sledging gear, but images of Scott as a Royal Naval officer also circulated widely. Scott had commissioned Maull & Fox of Piccadilly to take a formal portrait photograph of him in uniform, and, after the announcement of the disaster, the company issued a souvenir plate priced 5s., with a proportion of the profits going to the Mansion House fund.[48]

While Scott thus exemplified the Royal Naval Captain, Oates was hailed as the 'the *beau ideal* of the English soldier'.[49] A number of newspapers reported on Oates's exploits during the South African War, when he refused to surrender after leading his patrol into an ambush. The enemy eventually pulled back, but not before Oates had been shot in the thigh. Frank Taylor's poem, ' "No Surrender Oates" ', described how the valiant men who had served with the Inniskilling Dragoons at Waterloo and Balaclava looked on with approval at the manner of Oates's death.[50] Scott had picked Oates for the polar party to represent the army, and his journal again directed reports to the appropriate interpretation, noting that Oates 'took pride in thinking that his regiment would be pleased with the bold way in which he met his death'.

Commentators debated whether Oates's actions should be condemned as an act of suicide. While some cultures venerated suicide as the highest form of sacrifice, the Protestant inheritance stigmatized the active pursuit of death. Discussions, however, pointed out that Oates's primary intention was not to kill himself, but to save his comrades. If by some miracle Cherry-Garrard and Dimitri Gerof had reached the polar party with their dog-team, Oates would have welcomed his rescuers with open arms.[51]

Indeed, many singled out Oates's self-sacrifice as the defining moment of the disaster. The *Daily Mail* asserted that if 'there was a contest in heroism between Captain Oates and his comrades . . . the final honour lies with Captain Oates'. 'Is there anything finer in all the romantic literature of the world than Captain Oates's last words?', asked the *Daily Graphic*.[52]

Yet Scott remained the pre-eminent hero of the disaster. The repetition of his name to characterize the expedition – *Scott's Last Expedition, With Capt. Scott, RN, to the South Pole*, the Scott memorial fund, the Scott monument, the Scott book, and so on – repeatedly emphasized Scott's role as the leading actor in the Antarctic drama. Scott himself was also the expedition's principal narrator, with his journals describing a personal quest. Attention focused directly on Captain Scott father, husband, and son, during the debates about provision for the bereaved.

By contrast, far fewer personal details were available about the unmarried Captain Oates. His mother Caroline was crushed by her loss. Driven by grief, she ordered his diary destroyed and shunned publicity. Every night she slept in her son's bedroom and kept one of his regimental epaulettes in her handbag. Some have suggested that, after interviewing members of the expedition, she blamed Scott for the disaster, but kept silent out of a sense of duty.[53] Oates enjoyed a fraught relationship with his commander, under pressure as guardian of the ponies on whom so much depended, but frustrated by their poor condition and Scott's erratic behaviour. 'He is not straight,' Oates wrote to his mother in one outburst, 'it is himself first the rest nowhere.' Through interviews and her son's correspondence, Caroline Oates gained insights into Scott's volatility and the tensions of polar life initially denied to the public. But although the destruction of her son's diary leaves a dramatic suggestion, hard evidence for Caroline Oates's motivation remains elusive.[54]

Scott generated a rich iconography, but few photographs of Oates – essential currency in the age of a mass circulation pictorial press – appeared in 1913, with the *Daily Graphic* forced to resort to an awful artist's impression for one front cover. Ponting rarely caught Oates on camera: just two portrait photographs (one head-shot and one full-length in the pony stalls), and only fleeting appearances in the film of the expedition. Of twenty-eight memorial postcards identified by Margery Wharton, ten pictured Scott alone, while only one focused solely on Oates. No painting of Oates was placed in the National Portrait Gallery and no waxwork in Madame Tussaud's, while the first biography was not published until 1933.

Oates did, however, inspire a number of public monuments, as the armed forces proved particularly active in commemorating their dead comrades. Officers of the Fleet, the Royal Indian Marine, the Inniskilling Dragoons, and servicemen in Devonport, Chatham, and on board HMS *Britannia*, organized and paid for the establishment of a range of tablets, statues and schemes. The Inniskilling Dragoons held a memorial service each year on the Sunday closest to Oates's death. The regiment was serving in India on the first anniversary, when the commanding officer, Neil Wolseley Haig, sent a package to Oates's mother, containing a canvas embroidery of 'the last scene' by Private Ricketts. An embarrassed Haig had given Ricketts his word he would send the embroidery, but considered the work very morbid and urged Mrs Oates 'not to bother to open it, but just burn it straight away'.[55]

The representation of Scott's last expedition as another triumphant episode in the history of the armed forces was reinforced by reference to an extensive roll-call of dead heroes. 'As long as nations wish to be found worthy, more inspiring for all life to come than all else in the lives behind us, shall be the great deaths', reported the *Observer*. 'Of the root of Christianity we need not speak. With the names which have Nelson for chief, with the memories of Grenville and Franklin and Gordon, are those of Scott and Oates.'[56] Such cross-referencing was a common feature of the heroic mode.

Sir John Franklin provided the principal model for Captain Scott, with comparisons heightened by the parallel between the dutiful grieving widows, Jane and Kathleen. Franklin's polar sacrifice offered a template for the story of Scott of the Antarctic in the brief period between the first announcement on the afternoon of Monday, 10 February, and the receipt of Scott's 'Message to the Public' in the early hours of Tuesday morning.

The other heroes invoked were nearly all soldiers or seamen who had died in battle, principally Admiral Horatio Nelson (who died at the battle of Trafalgar in 1805) and General George Gordon (who died after the fall of Khartoum in 1885), but also Sir Philip Sidney (who died after the battle of Zutphen in 1586), Sir Richard Grenville (who died after his ship *Revenge* had fought alone against a Spanish squadron in 1591), Sir Francis Drake (who died on an expedition near Porto Bello in 1596), Admiral Robert Blake (who died after a series of naval engagements in 1657), General James Wolfe (who died at the battle of Quebec in 1759), Sir John Moore (who died at the battle of Corunna in 1809), and Brigadier-General Sir Henry Lawrence (who died during the siege of Lucknow in 1857). The principal exceptions were Captain James Cook (who died on an expedition in Hawaii in 1779) and Dr David Livingstone.

This roll of martyrs was, unsurprisingly, exclusively male. All had died at their post, either in battle or on an expedition: to be resolute when confronting danger in the service of the nation was the highest form of heroism. The comparisons underline the uniqueness of Scott's 'Message to the Public'. Last letters and dying words were not uncommon by-products of heroic endeavour. But as an exposition composed in the face of death, Scott's 'Message to the Public' was unprecedented, both in length and power of expression, the ultimate articulation of heroic sacrifice.

The commemoration of the Antarctic disaster exposes the Janus-face of the armed forces in British society before 1914. Service on sea and land called forth the most admired qualities of manhood: duty, comradeship, and courage in the face of death. Heroic tales of military endeavour, from Kipling's poetry through the *Boy's Own Paper* to W. H. Fitchett's *Deeds that Won the Empire* (a favourite on the *Terra Nova*), permeated popular culture. Yet reverence for the armed forces also generated an array of troubling associations, recalling the continental despotism of Bonaparte, Kaiser, and Tsar, against which the British commitment to freedom and liberty had been defined.

In this context, the Royal Navy proved a particularly effective national symbol. The popular image of the army improved in the second half of the nineteenth century, but the regimental structure militated against the development of a resonant corporate army identity. Each regiment had its own distinctive traditions and history, consecrated in the regimental chapel. (The Dean of Gloucester cathedral hung Edward Wilson's sledge flag alongside the flags of the Gloucester Regiment in the Lady Chapel, which was somewhat ironic given Wilson's abhorrence of violence.[57]) While the officers of the fleet paid for Scott's statue in Waterloo Place, the monuments organized by representatives of the army were all regimental initiatives.

The navy offered a less fragmented repository for national virtue. Moreover, the nation's maritime heritage was rooted as much in skilful seamanship, exploration, and trade as in seaborne combat. As Scott and his companions arrived at the South Pole, the *Captain's* correspondent F. H. Stafford described the merchant service as 'a noble profession [which] has made England what she is'. 'Training in a sailing ship is still looked upon as the best possible . . . There is nothing to equal it. It develops all that is finest in the British character – courage, self-reliance, resourcefulness, agility, keenness of observation, and a hundred and one qualities that go to form a sturdy, manly character.'[58]

Explorers such as Cook, Franklin, and Scott could exhibit courage, hardihood, and endurance in the service of the nation, without inspiring hostility from the opponents of that continental vice, militarism.

Monarchy and Nation

The memorial service at St Paul's cathedral marked the formal induction of Scott and his companions into the pantheon of national heroes. The intonation of the names of Robert Falcon Scott, Lawrence Edward Grace Oates, Edward Adrian Wilson, Henry Robertson Bowers, and Edgar Evans (the order determined neither by age nor alphabet, but social rank) inscribed the dead explorers on the nation's roll of martyrs.

The national memorial service, the Prime Minister's pledge to provide for the bereaved, the King's award of a title to Kathleen Scott and the Polar medal to the crew of the *Terra Nova*, the exhibition of Scott's journal in the British Museum and portrait in the National Portrait Gallery, secured the Antarctic disaster as a sacrifice for the nation. Ceremonies were staged and relics displayed in the nation's sacred spaces, adorned with flags, uniforms, and anthems.

Yet while Franklin, Nelson, and Gordon were invoked most frequently, the institutions in which the dead were honoured offered a diverse picture of the nation, a diversity too often obscured in accounts which pick out only the most extravagant examples of imperial or military propaganda. The armed forces featured prominently in St Paul's, with twenty-three naval and fifty military memorials listed in 1909. Yet the cathedral housed more than seventy other memorials to statesmen, ecclesiastics, writers, architects, engineers, and painters, including Christopher Wren, Samuel Johnson, and J. M. W. Turner.

Scott's journals were placed on display in the manuscripts saloon of the British Museum alongside Nelson's plan for engaging the French fleet at Trafalgar and Gordon's last letter from Khartoum. The saloon, however, primarily honoured not military but literary achievement, with copies of *Beowulf*, the *Anglo-Saxon Chronicle*, and Chaucer's *Canterbury Tales* on display, in addition to documents bearing the signatures of Shakespeare, Spenser, Milton, Pope, Gibbon, Gray, Byron, Walter Scott, Newman, Tennyson, and George Eliot.[59] Scott's journals were a fitting addition to this literary expression of national character. The National Portrait Gallery exhibited a similarly diverse selection of the faces of Britain, with literary achievement again accorded particular significance. The Gallery's prize possession was its very first acquisition: the Chandos portrait of William Shakespeare.

Arguably the most significant commercial exhibition of national history was Madame Tussaud's gallery of waxworks, one of the most popular tourist attractions in the capital since the mid-nineteenth century. Two polar incidents had been displayed in 1897 (Fridtjof Nansen's encounter with Frederick Jackson, and Salomon Andrée's ill-fated attempt to balloon over the North Pole), and a waxwork of Captain Scott was exhibited after the announcement of the disaster.[60]

Madame Tussaud's, like the National Portrait Gallery, placed the monarchy at the heart of national life. This exhibition of seamless continuity, with Charles I placed next to Oliver Cromwell, exemplified what Stefan Collini has described as the 'muffling inclusiveness' of the English past.[61] Political, commercial, and military success insulated England from the liberationist nationalism which emerged out of defeat in continental Europe through the eighteenth and nineteenth centuries. With relatively stable constitutional development since 1688, England did not experience the fundamental ideological cleavage which turned all aspects of society's history into material for partisan dispute. After 1789, by contrast, the French past became an ideological battleground upon which royalists and republicans competed for authority, with fierce debate, for example, over the content of flag and anthem.

In the absence, therefore, of the fundamental religious and political divisions which structured French life, the story of Scott of the Antarctic was not harnessed to any specific or sectional definition of the nation. The decision to hold the national memorial service in St Paul's, for example, was not contested: Westminster Abbey did not project an alternative vision.

The monarchy proved central to this muffling inclusiveness. The royal family took an active interest in polar exploration and Scott's expeditions in particular. Queen Victoria herself wished the National Antarctic Expedition success in 1899. King Edward VII and Queen Alexandra came on board the *Discovery* at Cowes in 1901, and Scott was invited to lecture at Balmoral. Royal permission was granted for Scott and Kathleen Bruce to be married in the Chapel Royal at Hampton Court Palace in 1908, thanks to the intervention of Kathleen's aunt, Zoe Thompson, widow of the Archbishop of York. The new King George V received Scott before he sailed for the Antarctic a second time, and photographs of George and Mary adorned the wardroom of the *Terra Nova* and the expedition's base camp at Cape Evans.

The commemoration of the disaster was also punctuated by royal interventions, beginning with George's message of condolence to Lord Curzon and attendance at the national memorial service. Oriana Wilson presented the King with two sketches her husband had drawn at the Pole, while Queen Alexandra purchased the first print of the Maull & Fox souvenir plate. Teddy Evans, Herbert Ponting, Kathleen and Peter Scott, and the entire crew of the *Terra Nova* were entertained at Buckingham Palace. The royal seal of approval was firmly stamped on the story of Scott of the Antarctic.

Yet, apart from brief messages of condolence, the King himself was silent. The disaster was not harnessed to an explicit ideology. Schoolchildren in Bermondsey and Galashiels, ratepayers in Cardiff and Cheltenham, newspaper readers in Leeds, and cinemagoers in Edinburgh were free to imagine their own nation under the crown. The monarchy acted as a powerful 'symbol of unity in diversity' precisely because royal ceremonial transcended party strife, inspiring allegiance from political enemies. The figure of the King, both sovereign and constrained, was ambiguous: 'Emperor of India' and constitutional monarch of a 'crown'd republic'. Not that the King was an empty vessel, capable of investment with an infinite range of meanings. The monarchy both drew strength from and reinforced conventional attitudes towards gender relations, social hierarchy, and morality. But the King's detachment, both from formal politics and from any explicit nationalist agenda, was essential to the unifying power of royal ceremonial.

The commemoration of the Antarctic disaster offers some penetrating insights into the distinctive contours of national identity in Britain before the First World War. The sacrifice of Captain Scott affirmed the virility of the nation, in an age haunted by the spectre of decline. A diverse range of individuals and associations harnessed the disaster to transmit ideological messages, but no central authority co-ordinated these representations to craft a single myth of Scott of the Antarctic.

The vitality of localism, not the coercive power of invented traditions, secured the allegiance of the inhabitants of Devon, Cardiff, Edinburgh, and Belfast to King and Country. Individuals could assemble their own nation from a cornucopia of national images animated in a range of sacred sites: the literary genius of William Shakespeare, the scientific insight of Isaac Newton, the artistic imagination of Joseph Turner, the determination of Oliver Cromwell, the imperial vision of Benjamin Disraeli, the military prowess of the Duke of Wellington, the missionary fervour of David Livingstone, the technical achievement of Isambard Kingdom Brunel – myriad faces of the nation were in cultural circulation, invested with a miscellany of meanings, and inspiring allegiance across social, political, and geographical boundaries.

Captain Scott shone brightly within this kaleidoscope of national character, the light catching different contours as viewers changed perspective. Winston Churchill believed the tragedy demonstrated that officers of the armed forces would not fail the empire in the hour of need. But at the annual meeting of the Peace Society in May 1913, the Chief Rabbi hailed Scott as a hero for pacifists, prepared to sacrifice his life in a peaceful cause. Dr Hertz declared his hope that 'military virtues would no longer be glorified, that the non-military virtues – those displayed by Captain Scott for example – the non-military virtues will be glorified and force will no longer be resorted to'.[62]

Scott's waxwork was not placed beside General Gordon in Madame Tussaud's, but between General Booth, founder of the Salvation Army, and Captain Smith of the *Titanic*.

· CHAPTER SEVEN ·

'THESE WERE MEN'

C APTAIN SCOTT had been dead for only two weeks when, at around 11.40 p.m. on Sunday, 14 April 1912, the passengers on the deck of the *Titanic* felt a slight shudder, as an iceberg tore a broken gash approximately 200 feet long on the starboard side of the ship. Over 1,500 of the 2,200 passengers and crew on board the *Titanic* died in the Atlantic over the next few hours. 'When the supreme sacrifice was asked of them they made it with invincible heroism,' exclaimed the *Daily Mirror*. 'They died superbly. They have added glory and lustre to the record of their sea-fighting race.'[1] The *Mirror* referred not to Captain Scott and his companions, but to the victims of the *Titanic* disaster.

The veneration of suffering reached its apogee before the First World War. A resonant language of heroic sacrifice emerged, which drew on classical, chivalric, and religious models, Roman warriors, Arthurian knights, and Christ himself. This language of sacrifice, in which failure was redeemed by the exhibition of heroism in the face of death, rang out after the sinking of the *Titanic*, but found its most sonorous expression in the response to the death of Captain Scott. Socialists, suffragettes, and Irish nationalists joined in the celebration of Scott's sacrifice, united by the belief that character was forged through struggle.

Heroes of the *Titanic*

The responses to the sinking of the *Titanic* and the death of Captain
Scott displayed many similarities. Both disasters inspired a range of
special ceremonies, newspaper editions, poems, books, and monuments. The *Titanic* memorial service in St Paul's offered a model
for the Scott service ten months later. Not only was Scott's waxwork placed alongside the *Titanic*'s Captain Smith in Madame
Tussaud's, but Scott's widow was chosen to sculpt a statue of
Smith, which was unveiled near Lichfield cathedral in July 1914.
A Mansion House fund raised a massive £440,000 to provide for
the bereaved. But, as with the Antarctic disaster, churches and
local councils proved the most effective agents of collective
remembrance: no permanent London memorial to all the dead
of the *Titanic* existed until 1995, when the National Maritime
Museum dedicated a garden to the victims.[2]

Commentators in Britain and America celebrated the heroism
of the *Titanic*'s passengers: the language of sacrifice resonated on
both sides of the Atlantic. 'All the great virtues of the soul were displayed . . .', wrote Philip Gibbs in *Lloyds Weekly*, 'courage, self-
forgetfulness, self-sacrifice, love, devotion to the highest ideals.'
Edward Reaves, a Baptist preacher in South Carolina, hailed the 'nobility of the brave men who faced death calmly while helping others'.[3]

Particular attention was paid to the gallantry of men who gave
up their lifeboat places for women and children. Benjamin Guggenheim was reported to have instructed a steward to tell his wife:
'I am willing to remain and play the man's game if there are not
enough boats for more than the women and children.' The *Daily
Mirror* published a double-page spread of photographs under the
headline 'Greater Love Hath No Man Than This, That A Man Lay
Down His Life For His Friends'.[4]

Harvard University celebrated its own *Titanic* heroes, the painter Francis Millet and millionaires John Jacob Astor and Harry Widener, whose widow endowed Harvard's Widener Library in her dead husband's memory. Tributes moved from expressions of sorrow to 'glory that Harvard still has sons who can die as well as live like noblemen'.[5] The London press hailed Captain Smith who was reported to have stayed at his post as the ship went down, exhorting the passengers to 'Be British!' Captain Smith 'was a typical British seaman,' declared the *Daily Graphic*, who showed 'valour and coolness in the last hour of trial.' Such Anglo-Saxon self-control was often set against the hysterical reaction of the 'Latin races': one Italian was alleged to have survived by dressing up as a woman.[6]

Reports about the *Titanic* explored three themes which were to figure prominently in the response to Scott's death. First, many raised the heroism shown on board the ship as a triumphant retort to the prophets of national decline. 'Amidst all our sorrow,' declared the *Daily Telegraph*, 'it comes as a great relief to learn definitely that England still breeds men who will in the hour of danger surrender their lives to save the women and children.' Pelham and Wright's popular music-hall song, 'Be British', also celebrated the persistence of national vigour, concluding with a quotation from Corinthians, 'O Grave where is thy victory – O death where is thy sting?' Zonophone re-released 'Be British' in 1913, with a tribute to Scott, ' 'Tis a Story That Shall Live Forever', on the other side of the record. The *Leicester Mail* compared the two disasters, noting that the loss of the *Titanic* had first shown 'how Englishmen can behave in the face of sudden and terrible calamity, and now comes this story of the Antarctic heroes which utterly confounds the pessimists'.[7]

Second, the *Titanic* disaster offered a stage for acts of chivalry which reinforced established gender roles. The *Daily Mirror* devoted a front cover to Captain Smith's wife Eleanor and daughter

Melville: 'Though no woman could have lost her husband in more tragic circumstances, she has borne her overwhelming grief with a bravery which compels admiration'.[8] For Eleanor Smith read Lady Jane Franklin and Kathleen Scott, icons of wifely devotion, whose tragic stoicism underscored their husbands' heroism.

Third, the sinking of the *Titanic*, like the death of Captain Scott, was portrayed as an episode in humanity's historic struggle with nature. One leader in the *Daily Mirror* reminded people that 'Nature . . . is our real enemy . . . In face of such disasters as that the world mourns over now, we feel the derisive absurdity of man warring against man, while his real enemy is always ready with her superhuman engines against him.'[9] The article struck a pacifist and humanitarian note, alongside the patriotic celebration of Captain Smith's Anglo-Saxon virtues.

Ten months later, Scott's death prompted the *Observer* to consider the powerlessness of humanity in the face of Nature:

> It is what modern men are not willing to reflect on, but they have had their lesson twice in the last few months. Though the first example was upon an appalling scale, the second is greater. . . . In each case the mighty elements that have for ice their symbol annihilated man and his handiwork and brought the world back to some things learned at our mothers knees.

'Nature, "red in tooth and claw",' concluded the *Cambridge Independent*, 'has once more, as in the case of the *Titanic*, asserted its supremacy over man.'[10]

There was no single myth of the *Titanic*, as there was no single myth of Scott of the Antarctic, but, rather, an array of overlapping and, at times, contradictory narratives. But, while the disasters provoked similar responses, a number of contrasts help us identify the distinctiveness of Scott's story. The *Titanic* disaster was a messier affair than the death of Captain Scott. The sheer scale sparked more diverse reactions, such as the *Titanic* toasts composed by African Americans, which Henry Louis Gates Jnr. has described as 'the most popular poem[s] in the black vernacular'.[11] Five different versions of the death of Captain Smith appeared in 1912, ranging from the critical (shooting himself on the bridge) to the absurd (rescuing a baby, before going down with the ship).[12] Scott's journal, by contrast, served as an anchor around which narratives of the Antarctic disaster drifted.

Many commentators interrogated Scott's methods, but the conviction that his death was worthwhile was very widely held: courage exhibited in the face of death turned tragedy into triumph. An assault on the South Pole, though, was a markedly different endeavour from a trans-Atlantic cruise. Explorers expected to suffer, innocent passengers did not. The presentation of the *Titanic* disaster as a triumph, as something worthwhile, proved more problematic, dissent more widespread.

From 15 April 1912, the *Titanic* served as an emblem for incompetence, hubris, and cowardice, as well as heroism. Only a couple of days after the announcement, the *Daily Mirror* led its front page with the headline 'Why Were There Only Twenty Lifeboats For 2,207 People On Board The Ill-Fated Titanic?,' and called for the Board of Trade to insist upon a larger number of lifeboats on great liners.[13] The popular press vilified Bruce Ismay, chairman and managing director of the White Star Line, for escaping in a lifeboat rather than going down with his ship.

George Bernard Shaw, G. K. Chesterton, and Joseph Conrad all challenged heroic readings of the *Titanic* disaster. Chesterton hoped England would follow America on this occasion, and aggressively enquire into the causes behind the loss of the ship. While Joseph Conrad's criticisms appeared in the *English Review*, a literary periodical of limited circulation, George Bernard Shaw voiced his opinions in the popular *Daily News and Leader*. Shaw derided the sentimental press coverage:

> an explosion of outrageous romantic lying . . . Writers who had never heard of Captain Smith to that hour wrote of him as they would hardly write of Nelson . . . But is it necessary to assure the world that only Englishmen could have behaved so heroically, and to compare their conduct with the hypothetic dastardliness which lascars or Italians or foreigners generally – say Nansen or Amundsen or the Duke of Abruzzi – would have shown in the same circumstances?[14]

Shaw's comments indicate the high esteem in which foreign explorers were held in Britain.

Arthur Conan Doyle protested at this unjustified criticism of heroes, but Shaw responded by asking

> what real value heroism had in a country which responds to these inept romances invented by people who can produce nothing after all but stories of sensational cowardice? . . . Heroism is extraordinarily fine conduct resulting from extraordinarily high character. Extraordinary circumstances may call it forth and may heighten its dramatic effect . . . but none of these accessories are the thing itself.

Shaw concluded by stating he would have expressed himself even more strongly, but refrained because 'the facts are beating the hysterics without my help'.[15]

Dissenting Voices?

George Bernard Shaw, paragon of Edwardian iconoclasts, does not appear to have publicly criticized either Scott or the press coverage of the Antarctic disaster in 1913. His later friendship with Kathleen Scott would not have developed, as her biographer points out, had he coruscated her late husband. His views, though, did emerge in the 1920s through his friendship with Apsley Cherry-Garrard, as we shall see.

Did others dissent from the celebration of Antarctic heroism in 1913? If we seek for voices that questioned the heroism of Captain Scott and his companions, we would expect to find them among the infamous triumvirate of Edwardian troublemakers: Irish nationalists, radical socialists, and militant suffragettes. Yet even those most committed to challenging the Edwardian status quo acknowledged the heroism of Scott, Bowers, Evans, Oates, and Wilson.

Scott's death occurred at the height of the campaign for women's suffrage in Britain. Interviewed in April 1913, Roald Amundsen expressed his support for the suffragettes, explaining that 'Englishmen treat women no better than Esquimaux'.[16] The campaign had made gradual progress since the 1860s, when John Stuart Mill first presented a petition supporting the enfranchisement of women to the House of Commons. The landslide Liberal election victory in 1905 raised hopes, but the government prevaricated and campaigners grew increasingly frustrated. The militant Women's Social and Political Union (WSPU) organized a series of attacks on cricket pavilions, golf clubhouses, and racecourse stands, and burnt down a house being built for the Chancellor, David Lloyd George. Dean Inge considered the campaign 'the most appalling example of epidemic moral insanity that our age has witnessed'.[17]

The Women's Freedom League had planned a series of protests for Friday, 14 February 1913, but postponed the disturbances, which would have clashed with the Scott memorial service in

St Paul's. 'Without joining in the gush of maudlin sentimentality which has almost succeeded in bringing ridicule on the dead, women suffragists did not fail to pay their tribute to the brave adventurers.'[18]

Not all protests were cancelled: *Votes for Women* recorded assaults on no fewer than seventeen golf courses early on Friday morning. Militants also disrupted Teddy Evans's first public lecture on the expedition, motivated by the presence of the First Lord of the Admiralty, Winston Churchill, in the chair.[19] These protests, though, expressed no criticism of the Antarctic explorers. Indeed, in a remarkable article in the *Suffragette*, Christabel Pankhurst claimed Scott and Oates as kindred spirits:

> There is, indeed, nothing to match the spirit of the militants, unless it be the spirit shown by Captain Scott and his brave companions. There is universal mourning for these dead heroes, but it is only the militant women who really understand and share the spirit that moved them in their work and in their death. Captain Scott and his band in the Antarctic, the militant women at home, standing at danger-point, have shown the same indomitable courage; and when we say this, we pay the highest tribute that has yet been paid by any to the memory of these men.

Pankhurst placed the Antarctic explorers alongside militant suffragettes like Constance Lytton, heroes who were willing to die in a noble cause.[20]

Militant suffragettes staked a claim for the place of women in the pantheon of heroism. A further article asked if women would have the courage to do what Captain Scott did. The article highlighted the election of thirty-six women as RGS fellows, women who showed a courage and daring equal to that of male travellers. The author, though, reserved special commendation for Kathleen Scott, who helped organize the expedition, shared her husband's anxieties, and had her hopes dashed by his death. 'As every woman knows, it needs even more courage to stay behind than to go forward.'[21]

Sacrifice was a central theme of suffragette discourse, to which Christabel Pankhurst continually returned during the most intense phase of the WSPU campaign. On 4 June Pankhurst's prophecy of fatalities in the struggle was fulfilled, when Emily Wilding Davison threw herself in front of the King's horse at the Epsom Derby. Davison's action was widely criticized, both in the popular press and by moderates, but militant suffragettes celebrated the first true martyr to the cause, drawing on the images of sacrifice inspired by the Antarctic disaster four months earlier. *Votes for Women* hoped that Davison's death would 'bring home to all the men and women united in service to this movement the realisation that in sacrifice it was created, in sacrifice it has thriven, and by sacrifice alone it will triumph'.[22]

While suffragettes were frustrated at Prime Minister Asquith's procrastination, the elections of 1910 had made his Liberal government reliant on the support of Irish nationalist MPs and forced the Irish Question back to the top of the political agenda. Home Rule for Ireland appeared a realistic prospect for the first time in nearly twenty years. The Unionist press unsurprisingly celebrated the Antarctic disaster in familiar terms. 'Not in British history, and perhaps not in the history of mankind, is there to be found a document that breathes such a spirit of selfless heroism,' wrote the *Ulster Guardian* of Scott's last message. 'Once more a great example of human courage and endurance – noble, unselfish, and patriotic – has been given to mankind,' declared the *Irish Times*. 'The sympathy of every Irish heart will go out to Mrs. Scott'.[23]

But Irish nationalists, too, joined in the tributes to Antarctic heroism. The principal nationalist paper, the Dublin-based *Freeman's Journal and National Press*, hailed the 'martyrs of progress' who 'met death unfearing . . . They have enriched the world and have left a monument to the nobility of man at his best'. Two leading nationalist MPs, John Redmond and T. P. O'Connor, attended the St Paul's service, while the *Freeman's Journal* judged that 'the heroic tragedy has touched the hearts and imagination of the public in a degree without parallel in recent times'.[24]

If Christabel Pankhurst and John Redmond paid homage to the Antarctic heroes, what of the representatives of the labour movement? In 1912 trade union membership stood at nearly 3,500,000, and 40,890,000 working days were lost due to industrial disputes, a number exceeded only twice over the rest of the century.[25] So, did the labour juggernaut question the heroism of Captain Scott and his companions? No, dissent from the chorus of praise was rare. The newspapers and periodicals which expressed the views of organized labour joined in the celebration of Scott's sacrifice. The *Daily Herald* concluded that the explorers had left 'a heritage and names of imperishable glory,' while the *Labour Leader* suggested their 'bravery has ennobled the whole human race.' In Robert Blatchford's idiosyncratic weekly, the *Clarion*, Alex Thompson wrote how 'The men who do start Labour and socialist papers undertake the work in the spirit which led Livingstone to Central Africa and Scott to the South Pole. They knowingly accept the risks and discouragements of a thankless service because of their sense of duty.'[26] As Christabel Pankhurst claimed Scott as a hero for militant suffragettes, so Alex Thompson claimed Scott as a hero for socialists.

Edwardian radicals did, though, express disquiet at the sentimentality of the popular press. The socialist A. R. Orage's weekly review *New Age* vividly condemned 'the gush which the press has vomited over' the dead men, the hounding of their families, and the 'ghoulish conjectures' as to whether Kathleen Scott had received news of her husband's death.[27] And many commentators drew attention to the unacknowledged heroism of ordinary working men, who risked their lives every day in factories and mines. Although he paid tribute to Captain Scott, Alex Thompson also complained that the *Worksop Guardian* had recently closed its fund for relatives of the fourteen victims of the Rufford pit disaster after raising only £2,000. 'But if her husband had been a Polar explorer,' asked Thompson, 'would the subscription list have been thus restricted?'[28]

A leader in the *Daily Herald* captured this tension in radical reports of the Antarctic disaster, praising the explorers, but calling for people to get on with their lives after a week of frenzied press coverage. Scott and his companions had 'done service and brought honour not simply to Britain – we are tired of these pretentious and unreal race distinctions – but to humanity and its seeking and soaring spirit. All the world, feeling more or less proud of them, may also feel somewhat braver, somewhat more trustful of its better self.' Yet the article concluded by suggesting that the disaster had inspired 'too much sympathy and pathos . . . there are thousands of heroes and pioneers nearer home than the Antarctic. And there are other Poles to be reached.'[29]

I have examined more than a hundred newspapers and periodicals and uncovered only one article which found no redemptive qualities in the sacrifice of Captain Scott. In response to praise of the British explorers in *Le Temps*, Maurice de Waleffe savaged the expedition in the Parisian *Midi*:

> Say that you are going to the Pole to indulge in winter sports, but do not pretend that you go there because you are thirsting to serve science or your country . . .

> No, young Frenchmen, Captain Scott is *not* a model to imitate.
> He would have been better employed in modestly serving his
> country in his own rank and station . . .
>
> Any Englishman who honestly earns his living and supports
> his family appears to me to deserve more admiration . . . than he
> who runs after an empty glory.

F. Moulder sent the article to the *New Age* commenting that while
'we may well be proud of the spirit in which Scott and his companions faced death under terrible conditions, but is it not time we
asked ourselves of what practical utility are such expeditions?'[30]

The utilitarian critics of polar exploration, heard so frequently
during Scott's fund-raising campaign, were largely silent in the
aftermath of the disaster. But de Waleffe gave blunt expression to
their views. Even Moulder, however, leavened his criticism with
praise for the explorers' courage in the face of death. And A. Morley
Davies wrote to *New Age* to expose the hypocrisy of socialists who
criticized polar exploration on the grounds of 'practical utility':
'why do those who are so ready to charge scientific workers with
being the tools of capitalists complain of them just as much when
they obviously are not?'[31]

Roman Warriors, Chivalrous Knights, and Christian Martyrs

Socialists, suffragettes, and Irish nationalists expressed the deep
imprint of the language of sacrifice upon Edwardian culture, a
belief in heroic martyrdom which drew on a host of classical,
religious, and chivalric models.

One public monument pictured Edward Wilson as a polar
knight. Wilson's brother-in-law, Bernard Rendall, ran Copthorne

School in Sussex, which had donated a dog sledge for use on the expedition. After the announcement of the disaster, the school invited subscriptions and commissioned a memorial window for the school chapel. Dedicated on 21 September 1913, the window showed Wilson on his knees with his hands clasped and a ski stick resting against his shoulder, recalling a medieval knight at prayer before battle.[32] But most memorials were not so explicit. Rather, tales of chivalry offered both a vocabulary and plotlines for the story of Scott of the Antarctic. The polar party was frequently described as a 'little band,' alluding to the speech of Shakespeare's Henry V at the battle of Agincourt: 'We few, we happy few, we band of brothers'. Sir Clements Markham, who had designed heraldic sledging flags for use on the National Antarctic Expedition, hailed Captain Scott as a 'true and spotless knight'.[33]

The Elizabethan soldier, statesman, and poet Sir Philip Sidney offered a chivalric model for the Antarctic heroes. Sidney removed his leg-armour before the battle of Zutphen in 1586 in case it detracted from his courage, and refused a cup of water on his death-bed because another dying soldier's need was greater. The Oxford Professor of English Literature Sir Arthur Quiller-Couch declared that the Antarctic heroes had displayed the same spirit as Sidney, while the *Daily Mirror* predicted that Scott's last words would be as 'Immortal as the words of Sir Philip Sydney and of Nelson,' describing the South Pole as the 'southernmost goal of modern chivalry'.[34]

The principal chivalric influence over representations of the disaster was exerted through the model of the knightly quest. The *Evening News* described the explorers as 'knights errant' engaged 'on the great quest of that which is beyond, and ever beyond', while the *Daily Telegraph* proclaimed the search for the South Pole as the 'great quest of ages'.[35]

The male quest romance had emerged as a distinctive literary genre in the later nineteenth century in the writings of authors such as G. A. Henty, Rudyard Kipling, and H. Rider Haggard. Novels like Rider Haggard's hugely successful *She* explored themes of imperial domination, male bonding, and female sexuality in exotic settings. The story of Scott of the Antarctic offered a distilled version of the genre (heroic band struggles against forces of nature in quest for South Pole), staged in a rarefied Antarctic atmosphere, associated with purity and cleanliness.

Commemorative poems in particular explored the dramatic possibilities of the Antarctic as mythical foe, the dragon to Scott's St George. H. W. Aubrey offered a gothic vision of an Antarctic littered with bones in 'The Snow Queen's Toll'. Drawing on a range of feminine stereotypes, Aubrey describes how the snow queen casts her spell 'o'er brave men's hearts' to lure them away from home and hearth.' After the explorers reach the Pole, the 'outraged' queen 'laid her curse on the hero band', dispatching blizzards and pestilence to slay them.[36]

Aubrey's snow-queen recalls the harpies of Greek mythology, and classical models offered a further source of inspiration for accounts of the disaster. Heroic sacrifice was a regular feature of Greek and Roman literature, and Sir W. B. Richmond of the Royal Academy praised the explorers 'whose heroism reads like a page of Homer'. But narratives of the Antarctic disaster that drew explicit classical comparisons were primarily confined to the public school educated elite. Two of the three poems published by the *Eton Chronicle* to honour Captain Oates, for example, found inspiration in Greek history.[37]

A single book offered the principal resource for representing the disaster as a heroic sacrifice: the New Testament. Christians were not alone in venerating sacrifice: Judaism, Islam, Hinduism, and

Buddhism share a common investment in the idea of sacrifice, of life through death, as John Bowker has observed. Speaking in the East London synagogue after the disaster, Rabbi Michelson highlighted the 'sacrifice they made for the sake of one another. Heroism could not go further than theirs. It was all in the true spirit of the Rabbinic apophthegm "What shall a man do that he may live – kill himself!" '[38]

But a common Christian inheritance offered the deepest well of inspiration for the language of sacrifice in Britain and America. Both private letters and published tributes directly compared Scott to Christ. Jane Stirling-Hamilton consoled her friend Lady Ellison-Macartney by emphasizing how 'Their deaths were *necessary* to God's great purpose – nothing has made me understand so clearly the meaning of Perfect [*sic*] through suffering and the glory of the sacrifice'. 'God must have been very near them in that lonely, icy land when the end came and they seemed forsaken,' wrote Jane Pearson. 'There seems so much to me like our dear Lord's death in a way.'[39]

Canon Rawnsley encapsulated the spirit of sacrifice which pervaded accounts of the disaster. Rawnsley described how, as Scott awaited death,

> . . . Christ stood by and pitifully smiled,
> Showing the crown of thorns and wounded feet.
> But ere the brave heart stiffened into ice
> The tent became a palace filled with light
> Wherein we met the warriors of the Pole,
> Who welcoming cried, 'Lo! life is sacrifice,
> Failure so born is victory in the fight,
> And true submission manhood's kingliest goal.'[40]

Christ himself stands beside Scott, displaying the signs of his suffering. The 'warriors of the Pole' exult in their demise, proclaiming the courageous acceptance of failure as the highest expression of manhood.

Clergymen exploited the disaster to emphasize the muscularity of the Christian faith. The Baptist preacher C. H. Spurgeon had complained in 1898 that 'There has got abroad a notion, somehow, that if you become a Christian you must sink your manliness and turn milksop'. The crew of the *Terra Nova* proved otherwise. Many clerics seized on Scott's reference to the will of providence in his last message, while the secretary of the evangelical White Cross League drew attention to Bowers's membership of the League and his strenuous efforts in the cause of purity.[41]

Wilson and Bowers were devout Christians, whose faith infused their endeavours in the Antarctic. But the faith of the rest of the crew, and of Scott in particular, is open to question. The shore party faced their first Antarctic winter with only seven hymn books, after forgetting to unload more from the *Terra Nova*. Cherry-Garrard recorded how a rendition of 'Onward Christian Soldiers' degenerated into giggles, after the crew began singing in the wrong key.[42] And Scott himself was probably an agnostic, if not an outright atheist.

Indeed, it is tempting to contrast Scott with his Victorian fore-bears, Henry Havelock, Dr Livingstone, and General Gordon, whose religious conviction was the cornerstone of their heroic reputations. Many commentators represented Havelock's story as a religious quest for faith, while Horace Waller's biography pictured Livingstone dying with his hands clasped in prayer, and William Hamo Thornycroft's statue in Trafalgar Square showed Gordon with a bible tucked beneath his arm.

Yet to erect Scott as a secular hero for a secular age would be misleading. The commemoration of the Antarctic disaster exposes the pivotal role of the Church in national life on the eve of the First

World War. Churches remained the central sites for commemorative activity as we have seen, repositories of national virtue, staging services, collecting donations, and erecting memorials. Moreover, celebrations of the explorers' heroism reveal how a language of sacrifice with deep religious roots pervaded Edwardian culture.

Two biblical passages, frequently cited after the loss of the *Titanic*, proliferated in reports of the Antarctic disaster. First, 1 Corinthians 15: 54–5, 'Death is swallowed up in victory. O death, where is thy sting? O grave, where is thy victory?', furnished a number of headlines.[43] Second, John 15: 13, 'Greater love hath no man than this, that a man lay down his life for his friends', was cited even more frequently, with particular reference to Captain Oates. The tablet commemorating Oates in St Anne's church, Eastbourne, for example, included this passage, which the Archdeacon took as his text at the unveiling.[44]

Frances Stafford, a friend of Scott's sister, wrote of the inspiration she had drawn from Scott's example.

> To how many today they 'being dead, yet speak' – speak of the high victory over self born of strong self discipline, – speak of the thought of *others* up to the very last – 'Greater love hath no man than this that he lay down his life' – speak of the absolute submission to God's way born of a long obedience, a long faithfulness to duty. . . . Yrs in deep sympathy & gt. envy.[45]

The correspondence transcends the formal platitudes of many condolence letters. Stafford makes no mention of scientific progress or national decline, but is inspired simply by the selflessness of the dead.

Church ceremonial invested the disaster with a sacred aura, while the Christian message of sacrifice, that death was not only inevitable but essential and invigorating, rendered Scott's story a source of inspiration and even envy. 'Of such tragedy we needed more,' declared Archdeacon H. S. Wood on the second anniversary of Scott's death. 'It was the salt of life.'[46]

'To Play the Man'

Heroic martyrs might display many qualities: bravery, comradeship, courage, gallantry, nobility, fortitude, daring, honour, valour, and so on. But one characteristic was paramount. In 1914 Smith, Elder published a single volume of extracts from Scott's accounts of the *Discovery* and *Terra Nova* expeditions, arranged by Charles Turley. Scott's old friend, J. M. Barrie, supplied a biographical introduction which exposed the core of the Edwardian heroic ideal: self-control.

None of his teenage contemporaries predicted fame for Robert Scott: the young seaman was idle, distracted, untidy, and a bad loser. But the Scott whom Barrie befriended after the return of the *Discovery* was a man transformed.

> The faults of his youth must have lived on in him as in all of us, but he got to know they were there and he took an iron grip of them and never let go his hold. It was this self-control more than anything else that made the man of him of whom we have all become so proud. . . . He had become master of his fate and captain of his soul.[47]

Barrie took his cue from Scott himself. In one of his last letters, published in *Scott's Last Expedition*, Scott had urged his wife to guard their son 'against indolence. Make him a strenuous man.

I had to force myself into being strenuous, as you know – had always an inclination to be idle.'[48]

One of the principal attractions of polar exploration was as a test of self-control. Before sailing on the *Terra Nova*, Edward Wilson complained that he was 'getting more and more soft and dependent upon comforts, and this I hate. I want to endure hardness and instead of this I enjoy hotel dinners and prefer hot water to cold.'[49] Scott himself considered that there was no way of life 'quite so demonstrative of character as an Antarctic expedition. One sees a remarkable reassessment of values. Here the outward show is nothing, it is the inward purpose that counts.'[50]

Self-control was the core of heroic character. Scott's other admirable qualities emanated from this self-mastery, which allowed him to respond in appropriate fashion to every circumstance confronted. But self-control alone was not enough, for the captain of his soul might exercise his powers for personal gain. With his final plea to 'look after our people', Scott exhibited the essential complement to self-control: selflessness. 'The end of Con's diary', wrote Kathleen Scott, 'is the most wonderful thing I ever read – so invigorating and self-forgetting.' Two aspects of the story underlined this selflessness. First, the expedition's scientific aims: 'they died on no mere quest of gold.' And, second, the explorers' comradeship. 'Has anything ever been more fine', asked the *Daily Express*, 'than the refusal to seek safety at the expense of comrades?'[51]

Class, race and gender inflected this heroic ideal. A number of accounts questioned the working-class Petty Officer Edgar Evans's character as we have seen. Most importantly, the story of Scott of the Antarctic ultimately reinforced established gender stereotypes.

Women's involvement in public life had increased steadily up to 1913, but progress generated reaction. In the aftermath of the South African War, many campaigners for national efficiency propagated a domestic vision of women's roles as constrained as the mid-Victorians. One prominent educationalist wrote in 1911 that boys needed instruction in 'courage, self-control, hard work, endurance, and the protection of the weak', while girls needed to be taught 'gentleness, care for the young and helpless, interest in domestic affairs, and admiration for the strong and manly character in men'.[52]

Scott's story appealed strongly to anti-feminists, who, unlike Christabel Pankhurst, desired not to emulate his sacrifice but to pay homage to his manly character. The society magazine *Queen* believed the disaster had an 'especial poignancy for women'. Citing Kipling, the author noted that men dying in battle always referred, as Captain Scott had done, to their mothers, the inspiring source of their bravery. 'The age of chivalry is in this respect necessarily with us always. It is indeed Nature's recompense to women that they can never be disassociated from – but must on the contrary be regarded as inseparably related to – the most splendid achievements of men.'[53]

Taking their lead from Scott's last message, the numerous memorial appeals placed the bereaved at the centre of representations of the disaster. Photographs of Kathleen and Peter Scott appeared on the front pages of many newspapers and periodicals. The accomplished sculptress Kathleen Scott was reduced to the role of grieving widow, her character defined by the achievements of her husband.

While Kathleen Scott was represented as a devoted wife in the tradition of Lady Franklin, the explorers were hailed as exemplars of manliness. In his review of *Scott's Last Expedition*, Henry Leach explained that the 'reason why Scott must be a vast influence . . . is because of the supreme manliness of character that he exhibited throughout his life and in the moments of his lonely death'. *Punch* hailed *Scott's Last Expedition* as 'a wonderful tale of manliness', and

Scott as 'a man among men', while a leader in the *Manchester Guardian* was titled simply 'These Were Men'.[54]

Condolence letters echoed this incessant journalistic refrain. Teddy Evans told Caroline Oates that her son had 'died as he had lived – a magnificent MAN.' Carsten Borchgrevink, the first person to set foot on Antarctica, described Scott to John Scott Keltie in similar terms: *'he was a man'*.[55] And, in his 'first and only signed statement' on the disaster, Roald Amundsen declared 'Captain Scott left a record, for honesty, for sincerity, for bravery, for everything that makes a MAN. And this to me is greater even than having discovered the Pole!'[56]

Many exhorted their audience to follow Captain Scott and 'play the man'. *The Times*, for example, urged 'Every man who aspires to play a man's part, and every boy who would be a man' to take Scott's words to heart.[57] The choice of phrasing is instructive. Heroism was a performance. The hero responded to adversity by sticking resolutely to the script. And Scott's last message served both as a supreme exhibition of manly self-control in the face of death, and as a script for others to emulate. One sermon delivered at the Royal Naval College in Dartmouth raised Scott's journal as a sacred text: 'it is a sermon in itself, it should teach us all how to live and die.' The minister drew three lessons from the disaster: 'The sacredness of duty, The glory of self-sacrifice, The blessing of failure.' He also quoted several lines from Rudyard Kipling's 'If –', which he hoped the boys would learn by heart before leaving Dartmouth.[58]

The only penetrating critique of this heroic ideal which I have found appeared in a moderate Catholic periodical. The *Tablet*, published in London from 1840, mocked the popular canonization of the Antarctic heroes: 'A nation that must have a substitute for religious relics must also have proxies for its saints.' The *Tablet*

praised the explorers' fortitude in typical fashion. But the article
then moved on to question the 'unmeasured newspaper praise of
men of adventure, men to whom the face of danger *was* alluringly
bright, as if indeed courage were wholly physical, or at least as if
physical courage were the sole stuff out of which are made heroes'.
The *Tablet* pointed out that 'a million wives and mothers, devotees
of duty, and even the city clerk (we forebear to clinch the argument
by citing the cleric) doing his dull routine, are exemplars of a heroism not inferior to that of the man of adventure. Daily drudges,
mated to monotony, and with no aid or inspiration such as comes
from the knowledge that their deeds are to make history, these are
they who have the martyr's pang without the palm. And if in the
face of death they are not calm, they even falter, may not fear be,
after all, the beginning of wisdom?'[59]

Edwardian radicals joined in the celebration of the story of Scott
of the Antarctic. They were not united by patriotism; indeed, many
expressed their hostility to the vacuous bombast of the popular press.
But they shared a common investment in the idea that adversity
offered the truest test of character. And to confront death was the
ultimate inquisition.

Admiration for Scott's achievement was not universal. Certain
journals greeted the disaster with silence. The weekly 'organ of
social democracy', *Justice*, for example, failed to mention either
the conquest of the South Pole in March 1912 or Scott's death
in February 1913, considering both as irrelevant distractions from
more pressing concerns. My research has focused on published
narratives, but the media always offer an imperfect reflection of
public attitudes. The utilitarian critique of polar exploration as a
waste of time and money must still have been widely held in 1913.
And, the following year, the popular *Pimple* series of comic films

turned to polar exploration with the release of *Lt. Pimple's Dash to the Pole*. Although satirizing an expedition to the North Pole, the film indicates a popular irreverence obscured in the aftermath of the disaster.[60]

But the absence of open dissent, in marked contrast to the loss of the *Titanic*, is striking. Radicals called for recognition of the hardihood, endurance, and courage of militant suffragettes, or working men in mine, factory, and mill, but still paid tribute to Scott and his companions. The *Tablet* stood almost alone in painting a less romantic picture of heroic endeavour, praising instead the 'daily drudges, mated to monotony'.

Scott's story supports the contention that the idea of character shifted in the second half of the nineteenth century, from a mid-Victorian concern with inward spirituality, to a coarser Edwardian preoccupation with physical hardship. Earlier evangelical conceptions of character forged on the battlefield of the soul receded, displaced by a more muscular ideal forged during imperial service in desert, jungle, or polar wasteland. The tremendous popularity of Scott and Shackleton, whose expeditions had no missionary aims, testifies to this shift, which was driven in part by the appetite for sensation of the new mass media.

In an age of anxiety, of geopolitical tension and social conflict, the idea of sacrifice, always a facet of the language of character, assumed particular prominence, energizing examples of martyrdom drawn from antiquity, chivalry, and the Christian tradition. Scott's sacrifice offered a beacon of idealism to dispel the darkness of modernity, to renew faith in a soulless Darwinian universe. 'There is no room in evolutionary theory for the growth of this spirit of self-sacrifice,' declared the Catholic *Month*. 'Evolution . . . could never have developed such altruism as was shown in the tragedy of the Antarctic.'[61]

In May 1914, Prince Alexander of Teck arrived at Eton College to unveil Kathleen Scott's memorial to Captain Oates. Soon to take up his new post as Governor General of Canada, the Prince spoke of the lesson Oates had bequeathed to his old school: 'It may not be for many of us – perhaps not for any of us here – to respond to so stern a call as summoned him to those icebound fields; but occasions will surely arise – special in their opportunity for each one to stand forward and play the man.'[62] Barely three months later, opportunities to play the man abounded throughout Europe.

· CHAPTER EIGHT ·

'SO MANY HEROES'

'How many of the three millions who volunteered, within a year of war breaking out, owed the deciding impulse to that glorious example of Robert Scott and his companions?'

Arthur Pollen, 'The Spirit of the Nation',
Dublin Review, 159 (1916), 47

'So Many Heroes'

O N 21 September 1914 the greatest British orator of the age delivered his first major speech after the outbreak of war. David Lloyd George confessed that he envied the nation's youth. 'For most generations', he lamented, 'sacrifice comes in drab and weariness of spirit. It comes to you today, and it comes today to us all, in the form of the glory and thrill of a great movement for liberty, that impels millions throughout Europe to the same noble end.' The Germans had mocked the decadent and degenerate British, and Lloyd George agreed that many had indeed been too comfortable, too indulgent, and too selfish. But he believed war would inspire the 'great everlasting things that matter for a nation – the great peaks we had forgotten, of Honour, Duty, Patriotism, and, clad in a glittering white, the great pinnacle of Sacrifice pointing like a rugged finger to Heaven'.[1] Lloyd George spoke in London's Queen's Hall, the very auditorium in which Teddy Evans had given the first public lecture on the sacrifice of Captain Scott fifteen months earlier.

The story of Scott of the Antarctic reverberated through the First World War, when sacrifice became commonplace. The willingness of the explorers to risk their lives on a scientific quest offered a powerful model for the British war effort in defence of an idea, liberty, rather than territory, helping define a peace-loving Britain against a brutal, militarist Germany. Scott and Oates exemplified the idealism, comradeship, and courage required in war. Kathleen Scott received scores of letters from soldiers describing how the story of her dead husband had sustained them during the conflict.[2]

Fourteen months after the outbreak of war, the First Lord of the Admiralty, Arthur Balfour, unveiled Kathleen Scott's Fleet memorial statue in London. 'What the Fleet has done for the safety of these shores, for the greatness of this Empire, and for freedom throughout the world, is a commonplace among the English-speaking peoples,' explained Balfour. 'We sometimes are apt to forget how much it has done in the unwarlike and yet most dangerous work of exploration, travel, and of wresting from nature secrets most jealously held.'[3] Balfour noted with approval the placement of the monument near statues of two other naval martyrs, Captain James Cook and Sir John Franklin.

The New Zealand government commissioned a marble replica of the Fleet memorial for the centre of Christchurch. It had a vast Union Flag draped over the statue like an imperial toga, and a number of speakers extolled the value of Scott's example for an empire at war. The Mayor believed it was no surprise that 'a service of which Captain Scott was a member was enabled to keep the Germans bottled up in Kiel canal'. The semi-private London ceremony, with no notice given to the public, was in marked contrast to the strident celebration of Scott's inspirational legacy in Christchurch.[4]

The British government made more public use of Scott's story in May 1916, when Prime Minister Asquith unveiled a tablet in St Paul's, designed by S. Nicholson Babb. The tablet contained a portrait of Scott, a relief panel of the polar party, and three figures representing 'Discipline', 'Courage', and 'Glory'. Lord Curzon composed the inscription: 'Inflexible of purpose – steadfast in courage – resolute in endurance in the face of unparalleled misfortune – their bodies are lost in the Antarctic ice – but the memory of their deeds is an everlasting monument.' Curzon originally suggested that the inscription conclude 'their example is unforgettable and unforgotten'. But Lionel Earle, Secretary of the Board of Works, objected that 'such phrasing smacks a little too much of the Kaiser, who is always referring in his speeches to the never-to-be-forgotten deeds of his ancestors and the Teutonic heroes of the past'.[5]

Asquith echoed Balfour, by calling for the nation to honour the memory of these peace-time heroes. In the midst of the bloodiest war in the nation's history, the Prime Minister declared that 'there is no figure of our time who holds and will retain the same enduring place in the admiration and gratitude of his countrymen' as Captain Robert Falcon Scott.[6]

Many other commemorative projects were realized during the war. In September 1915 the Duke of Newcastle dedicated a memorial window in St Peter's church, Binton, near Stratford-upon-Avon, where Scott's brother-in-law Rosslyn Bruce was the vicar. A few days after the ceremony, Bruce entertained wounded soldiers from three local hospitals in the rectory. He showed the soldiers the window, drawing special attention to the pane depicting Captain Oates. After singing the national anthem, the soldiers left Binton cheered on by local schoolchildren.[7]

Almost the entire crew of the *Terra Nova* saw action in the war.[8] Among the civilians and scientific staff, Raymond Priestley served

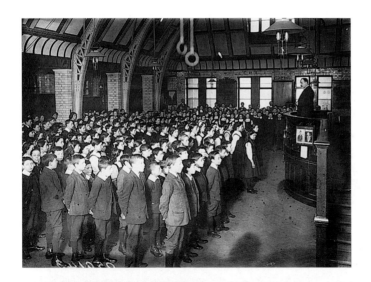

41. Scott's story in school. The headmaster reads Arthur Machen's account of the expedition to the pupils at Hugh Myddleton London County Council Elementary School. The London *Evening News* commissioned Machen and distributed his account to schools throughout the country, to coincide with the national memorial service at St Paul's. (TOP)

42. *A Very Gallant Gentleman* (1914). Readers of the *Cavalry Journal* were invited to purchase copies of J. C. Dollman's famous portrait of Captain Oates, while the *Boy's Own Paper* issued a special plate of the painting just after the outbreak of the First World War.

43. A flagship for Wales. The Captain Scott Society campaigned unsuccessfully for the construction of a full-scale sea-going replica of the *Terra Nova*, which had foundered off the coast of Greenland in 1943, to serve as a centrepiece for the regeneration of Cardiff Bay in the 1990s. The *Discovery*, by contrast, returned to Dundee to the sound of bagpipes in 1986, and is now one of the city's leading tourist attractions. (TOP)

44. Souvenir plaque. One of the many souvenirs produced to commemorate the disaster. Captain Scott can be seen in the top left-hand corner, his wife Kathleen in the top right-hand corner, his son Peter in the bottom left-hand corner, and the ships' cat 'Nigger' in the centre of the silvered memorial plaque. Cheaper copper versions were also sold.

Captain Robert Falcon Scott RN CVO FRGS
Leader of the National Antarctic Expeditions 1901–1904 & 1910–1912
Born June 6th 1868 Died March 1912

45. *The Departure of the Terra Nova from Cardiff* (1911). This painting by Richard Short, a retired naval captain who had witnessed the scene, was specially commissioned to commemorate Cardiff's involvement with the expedition, and was hung with black crepe following the announcement of the disaster. (ABOVE)

46. *Captain Robert Falcon Scott, RN.* Maull & Fox of Piccadilly secured Kathleen Scott's approval for the issue of an autograph plate priced 5s., with a proportion of the profits going to the Mansion House Scott memorial fund. Queen Alexandra was reported to have purchased the first plate. (LEFT)

47. Captain Oates with the ponies. Ponting rarely caught Captain Oates on film. This photograph shows Oates in the stalls constructed on the *Terra Nova* to shelter the nineteen Siberian ponies taken to the Antarctic. (ABOVE)

48. Captain Scott at Madame Tussaud's. First published in the *Daily Graphic* on 22 February 1913. Captain Smith of the *Titanic* stands on the floor between Scott and General Booth, founder of the Salvation Army. Scott remained on display in Madame Tussaud's until the 1960s. (LEFT)

"THOSE WHO DEPEND UPON US": CAPTAIN SCOTT'S LAST WISH.

49. 'Those Who Depend Upon Us'. Scott's mother, Hannah, vied with Kathleen and Peter as the relative featured most prominently in reports of the disaster. (LEFT)

50. Captain Scott, the Edwardian Marlboro Man. Alcohol and tobacco companies frequently exploited iconic images of manliness: John Robertson & Son's Dundee whisky traded on the 'race for the North Pole' in the 1890s. This advertisement's emphasis on purity plays on Antarctic associations with cleanliness. (BOTTOM LEFT)

51. 'The Goal'. This *New York World* cartoon, reprinted in the *Daily Mirror*, formed the basis of a private memorial in the notebook of P. D. Hobson, a Royal Naval midshipman serving on HMS *Colossus*, now in the Royal Naval Museum. (BOTTOM RIGHT)

AMERICA AND CAPTAIN SCOTT.

All the world has joined in paying tribute to the heroism of Captain Scott and his four brave comrades. This drawing, which is reproduced from the *New York World*, is entitled "The Goal," the skulls illustrating the terrible price which was paid.

52. Kathleen Scott's statue for the Scott Polar Research Institute. Frank Debenham apologized to Kathleen Scott for the poor condition of the statue when she visited the Scott Polar Research Institute in 1938. The arms invited frequent visits from robins. (LEFT)

53. Memorial window in St Peter's church, Binton. The Duke of Newcastle unveiled this elaborate stained glass window in Binton, Warwickshire, to commemorate the Antarctic disaster. Kathleen Scott's brother, Rosslyn Bruce, was the vicar at St Peter's church. (BELOW)

54. Cigarette cards on polar exploration. John Player & Sons issued two series of twenty-five cigarette cards devoted to polar exploration in 1915–16. The second series focused on Scott's and Amundsen's expeditions, and depicted a wide range of polar activities.

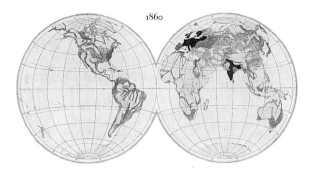

1860

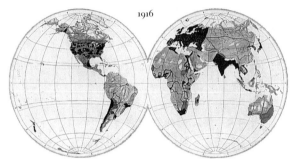

1916

55. The Royal Geographical Society's Map Curator E. A. Reeves, produced two maps to illustrate the rapid progress of exploration between 1860 and 1916.

■ 1. Mapped from accurate Topographical Surveys

■ 2. Mapped from Less-Reliable Surveys (chiefly Non-topographical)

□ 3. Mapped from Route Traverses and Sketches

□ 4. Entirely Unmapped

56. Scott and Shackleton. This front cover from *The Times*'s tabloid section, shows how Shackleton's reputation has eclipsed Scott's in recent years.

in signals with the Royal Engineers; and Charles Wright served as a wireless officer, winning the British Military Cross and the French Légion d'honneur. Of the Royal Naval officers, Victor Campbell won the DSO in the Dardanelles, while the conflict turned Teddy Evans into an authentic war hero: Evans of the *Broke*. Commanding the destroyer HMS *Broke* alongside only one other British ship in 1917, Evans confronted six German destroyers intent on bombarding Dover. After some bloody hand-to-hand fighting, three of the German destroyers were sunk, three retreated, and more than a hundred prisoners were taken. 'Remember the *Lusitania!*', Evans was reported to have shouted to the Germans clamouring to be rescued from the sea.

Herbert Ponting applied to the War Office through Lord Curzon for a job on the photographic staff, but was not offered a post. He then applied to the Foreign Office, but was informed that he would be doing far better work if he were to continue his Scott lectures in England. Ponting gave occasional performances, before embarking on a new series at the Philharmonic Hall in October 1916. Box-office takings were poor, however, and Ponting was forced to end the run after four months, estimating he had lost £1,200 on the venture.[9]

The poor attendance was not surprising. He had given hundreds of performances at the Philharmonic Hall in 1914 alone, so Ponting's lectures were old news by now. Ponting simply could not compete with sensational films from the front. He did, though, claim to have lectured free to many thousands of wounded soldiers. 'Lady Waterlow has just this minute rung me up to state she is bringing some more *blind* men next Saturday,' Ponting told Kathleen Scott. 'She has brought dozens. They simple love the strong.'[10]

Ponting's films were also shown to over 100,000 officers and men of the British army in France. His promotional material during and after the war quoted a letter from the Revd F. I. Anderson, Senior Chaplain to the Forces:

> I cannot tell you what a tremendous delight your films are to thousands of our troops. The splendid story of Captain Scott is just the thing to cheer and encourage out here . . . The thrilling story of Oates' self-sacrifice, to try and give his friends a chance of 'getting through,' is one that appeals so at the present time. The intensity of its appeal is realised by the subdued hush and quiet that pervades the massed audience of troops while it is being told. We all feel we have inherited from Oates a legacy and heritage of inestimable value in seeing through our present work.[11]

The provision of entertainment behind the lines, including sports, films, and theatrical performances, played a vital role in maintaining troop morale.

While most members of Scott's last expedition survived, at least three of the *Terra Nova*'s crew were casualties of war. Henry Rennick was lost with HMS *Hogue* in the North Sea, while Harry Pennell went down with HMS *Queen Mary* at the battle of Jutland. And Alf Cheetham, a boatswain who had survived all four of Scott and Shackleton's great expeditions, sailing to the Antarctic and back on board the *Discovery*, *Nimrod*, *Terra Nova*, and *Endurance*, drowned in the North Sea in 1918, when his trawler was torpedoed.

Nor did Clements Markham live to see the end of the war. The man most responsible for sending Robert Scott to the South Pole died at the age of 81. 'It is characteristic of Markham', wrote H. R. Mill on the hundredth anniversary of the foundation of the RGS, 'that his manner of leaving this world was the direct result of his unfaltering adhesion to old habits.'[12] As a young seaman, he learned to read in his hammock with a book in one hand and a candle in the other, a practice he continued into old age. But one night in 1916 the candle dropped, the bed caught fire, and Markham died from his injuries. An unlit electric bulb hung above his head.

In the last entry of his diary, Markham recorded meeting young Peter Scott. 'I often think of his dear father', the old man wrote, 'and the men he has trained to fight his country's battles.'[13] Many believed the Antarctic disaster had braced the nation for war. In one remarkable article, Agnes Egerton Castle presented Scott and his companions as biblical prophets:

> before God permitted this passion of the human race in which, reverently be it said, the Lord Christ is once more crucified in all Christianity and the forces of evil are let loose in hideous conflict against the powers of good, He sent His precursor . . .
>
> Like John in the desert, austere prophets, were they not sent to make straight the paths, to bid our manhood face undeviatingly the road to Calvary that lay so close before them . . . to teach our youth how to count life cheap and duty dear; that he who saves his life shall lose it, and that no greater love has any man than to lay down his life for his friends.
>
> We have so many heroes among us now, so many Scotts and Wilsons and Oates, holding sacrifice above gain, and long endurance, patience, grit, courage in the very teeth of failure, beyond everything else human nature reckons dear . . .
>
> Englishmen are dying like gentlemen every day; sticking to their dying companions, showing that the spirit of pluck and the power to endure have not passed out of the race.[14]

The sacrifice of Captain Scott had prepared the ground for the sacrifices required in Flanders and the Dardanelles.

Writing a few months later in the *Dublin Review*, Arthur Pollen also mused on the inspiration the explorers had bequeathed the nation. Scott had 'told the rising generation in a most singular and arresting manner', Pollen wrote, 'how a sailor could face death with perfect willingness and assurance, not for his country's safety, but only for her honour. How many of the three millions who volunteered, within a year of war breaking out, owed the deciding impulse to that glorious example of Robert Scott and his companions?'[15]

Dr John Fraser was one of Edward Wilson's closest friends during his student years. After the announcement of his death, Fraser wrote to Wilson's father that Edward's 'intense purity and entire unselfishness with his genius made him, I believe, one of the finest and best men that has ever lived'. During the war, Fraser won the DSO, the Military Cross, and the Croix de Guerre for his conspicuous acts of bravery.[16] We can only speculate about the influence of Wilson's example.

The naval surgeon Edward Atkinson, who had taken command of the expedition after the polar party failed to return in 1912, believed the disaster came at an 'appropriate time . . . Many a man has been wounded and lain out in No Man's Land since then to close his life in pain and discomfort. Perhaps the example set by the fate of the Polar party and the way in which they met it may have served its purpose as an example to the rest.' One of the officers commanding the remnant of the Newfoundland Regiment annihilated on the Somme told Atkinson it had.[17]

Atkinson himself served in the Royal Naval division at Gallipoli, and fought on the Somme, where he was awarded the DSO and mentioned three times in dispatches. In 1918 he was knocked briefly unconscious when his ship HMS *Glatton* was torpedoed in Dover harbour. Blinded and with his leg scarred by shrapnel, the naval surgeon crawled around the ship treating others before escaping himself, an act of bravery for which he earned the Albert Medal.

Egerton Castle and Pollen interpreted the disaster as a grand patriotic gesture. But the power of Scott's story, as with all great heroic reputations, lay in its flexibility: even those disillusioned with nationalist hyperbole, could draw inspiration from Scott's sacrifice. The Labour politician and Christian socialist George Lansbury, for example, who supported conscientious objection, declared in 1916 that Scott and Oates had shown how 'human nature, inspired by the example of our Lord, is, even in this sordid, miserable time of competition and greed, capable of rising to the most sublime heights of sacrifice and love in the service of others'.[18]

The cigarette company John Player issued a series of twenty-five cigarette cards on Antarctic exploration in 1916. Four of the cards focused on Amundsen's Norwegian expedition, with one card declaring 'no decent minded Englishman grudged the modest men of the Viking breed their well earned prize'. Amundsen was described as 'the beau ideal of a Polar explorer. Strong, skilful and daring; possessed of a keen sense of humour, and with kindly steel blue eyes'. The series included cards devoted to Bowers, Oates, Wilson, Teddy Evans, the dog-driver Dimitri, and even the assistant paymaster, Francis Drake. But not one of the twenty-five cards mentioned Petty Officer Edgar Evans, the working-class seaman who was frequently forgotten or blamed for the disaster. Around this time F. Whelan Boyle's retelling of Scott's story in the *Boy's Own Paper* claimed again that 'but for the collapse of Seaman Evans the rest of the party might have got back to the base in safety'.[19]

The most intriguing cigarette card was Number 1: 'Captain Scott'. The card praised 'the most complete scientific expedition that ever left for the Polar regions', and concluded that Scott's message had 'stirred the heart of the whole civilised world'. But, unlike the card of Amundsen, the description included no heroic adjectives, no mention of bravery or sacrifice. Card Number 1 captures something of Scott's influence during the First World War. We can imagine soldiers poring over cigarette cards to pass the hours of boredom between attacks and behind the lines. This unadorned card simply shows a man in uniform whose eyes suggest suffering, a screen onto which both officers and men could project their own conceptions of courage and comradeship, sticking it out to the bitter end.

Polar Tales

Nearly all the 6 million men from England, Scotland, Wales, and Ireland who served in the armed forces stuck out the war to the bitter end. For one in eight, the end meant death. Many authors have argued that nineteenth-century ideals of duty, honour, and sacrifice were buried with the corpses of the Western Front. The naive idealists who greeted war enthusiastically in 1914, so the story goes, had their beliefs stripped away at the Somme and Passchendaele. A new modern mode of consciousness emerged from the war, rejecting idealism and embracing irony, the only appropriate voice for representing the terrible absurdity of modern warfare.

So did the story of Scott of the Antarctic ebb away after the war, a fading echo from a vanished era? Herbert Ponting certainly enjoyed mixed fortunes. He mounted yet another lecture series in 1919, but box-office takings were again poor. Ponting retired from lecturing and devoted his remaining years to producing three feature-length versions of his Scott films. He lobbied incessantly for the films to be purchased by the nation, citing glowing press reports, the endorsements of both the King and the former US President Theodore Roosevelt, and a letter from a representative of the Board of Education in Washington, who hoped 'every boy and young man in this city and throughout this country could see these pictures'.[20]

Ponting edited the various series of *With Captain Scott to the South Pole* into a single feature, *The Great White Silence*, which attracted some complimentary reviews but little public interest in 1924. He repackaged the silent feature as *The Epic of the South Pole* in 1929 when, largely thanks to the efforts of his old adversary Teddy Evans, the Scott films were at long last purchased by the nation.

After a special screening in the Royal Albert Hall, the Duke of York accepted the films to inaugurate an Empire Library for the recently formed British Empire Film Institute. But the project petered out with Ponting again out of pocket, receiving only half the £10,000 promised. Ponting persevered and re-edited the footage yet again into *Ninety Degrees South*, the first sound version, released in 1933. Considerable technical difficulties had to be surmounted to transfer silent footage to sound, and Ponting claimed to have spent £10,000 and lost 30 pounds in weight during the preparation of the film. But, in spite of such efforts, *Ninety Degrees South* failed at the box office and frustration at wasted opportunities and stolen rewards haunted Ponting until his death in 1935.[21]

Commercial failure, however, indicated not a lack of interest in Scott's last expedition, but the limitations of Ponting's films. He had produced a wonderful record of the Antarctic landscape and wildlife, a seminal work in the development of the nature documentary, but he simply did not have enough footage of Scott, Bowers, Evans, Oates, and Wilson to offer a gripping narrative of the assault on the Pole. The construction of a mammoth 25-feet long picture of the Beardmore Glacier for *Ninety Degrees South* could not compensate for the absence of film of the principal characters. Out of around ninety minutes of footage, only one short scene focused on Captain Oates, cutting the hair of Cecil Meares on board the *Terra Nova*.

But accounts of the Antarctic disaster proliferated after 1918, as words not pictures breathed new life into the story of Captain Scott.[22] Ponting's book, *The Great White South*, proved far more successful than his films, going through eleven reprints between 1921 and 1935. Teddy Evans's *South with Scott*, published in the same year, also sold well, while John Murray, which had absorbed Smith, Elder after Reginald Smith's suicide in 1916, published a succession of versions of *Scott's Last Expedition*, including the first cheap edition in 1923. These accounts recycled the now familiar narrative of heroic endeavour, relying heavily on Scott's journal. *South with Scott* was particularly uninspired, with the war hero Evans no doubt constrained by a desire to conceal his rift with Scott. His biographer Reginald Pound believed Evans destroyed his expedition journal after writing the book.[23]

Apsley Cherry-Garrard, however, yearned for a more honest reckoning. Cherry-Garrard had originally agreed to write an official history of the expedition, but grew increasingly frustrated that the achievements of Bowers and Wilson, his companions on the winter journey to Cape Crozier in search of the eggs of the emperor penguin, had been forgotten. Seeking freedom from committee interference and encouraged by his friend and neighbour George Bernard Shaw, he opted to publish his own independent account of his Antarctic experience.

The crew of the *Terra Nova* produced three works of art which will endure: Scott's journal, Ponting's photographs, and Cherry-Garrard's *The Worst Journey in the World*. Published by Constable in December 1922, *The Worst Journey*, a description not of the assault on the Pole but of the trek to Cape Crozier, remains one of the classic narratives of exploration. Cherry-Garrard skilfully interweaves his personal account with psychological insights, scientific discussions, and meditations on the meaning of exploration in the modern world. *The Worst Journey* is an extended lament for dead comrades, for lost youth, and for the passing of a more noble age, its tone of 'elegiac melancholy', as Sara Wheeler has observed, imbuing the book with a timeless appeal.[24]

Although his contribution was concealed in case it distorted the book's reception, George Bernard Shaw helped Cherry-Garrard revise the manuscript, characteristically pressing for a frank appraisal of the expedition's leader. *The Worst Journey* offered the most rounded consideration of Scott's command published after the war:

> notwithstanding the immense fits of depression which attacked him, Scott was the strongest combination of a strong mind in a strong body that I have ever known. And this because he was so weak! Naturally so peevish, highly strung, irritable, depressed and moody. Practically such a conquest of himself, such vitality, such push and determination, and withal in himself such personal and magnetic charm ... He will go down to history as the Englishman who conquered the South Pole and who died as fine a death as any man has had the honour to die. His triumphs are many – but the Pole was not by any means the greatest of them. Surely the greatest was that by which he conquered his weaker self, and became the strong leader whom we went to follow and came to love.[25]

Many critics immediately recognized a classic: George Mair in the *Evening Standard* doubted whether any other travel book was 'so impelling and authentic in its appeal'. A limited American run attracted little attention in 1923, but wider distribution in 1930 drew considerable critical acclaim. The *New York Times Book Review* hailed Cherry-Garrard's 'remarkable descriptive powers', while the *Bookman* described *The Worst Journey* as 'one of the most thrilling and absorbing narratives in modern literature'.[26]

But his criticisms of Scott also angered many, notably Kathleen, jealous guardian of her dead husband's reputation. When Constable reissued *The Worst Journey* in 1927, Kathleen, now married to the politician Edward Hilton Young, tried unsuccessfully to persuade Cherry-Garrard to remove descriptions of Scott as 'weak' and 'peevish'.[27]

The cleric James Gordon Hayes's *Antarctica* caused further

embarrassment the following year. A chapter on 'Recent Antarctic fatalities' questioned Scott's explanation for the disaster. Gordon Hayes highlighted two principal causes: dietary deficiencies, particularly a lack of vitamins, and the decision to rely on men instead of dogs. Gordon Hayes absolved Scott of blame over diet, given the state of scientific understanding in 1910. Transport, however, was another matter and he concluded that 'Scott's disaster was preventible, by knowledge available at the time'.[28]

Yet Scott's reputation weathered these revelations about his personality and methods. The *Times Literary Supplement* reported how Gordon Hayes 'reluctantly' concluded that the Antarctic disaster 'might have been avoided if there had been an exercise of intelligence in any way comparable with the heroism displayed'.[29] While serious questions were raised about Scott's leadership, his heroism in the face of death remained unchallenged. *The Worst Journey* had exposed a moody and depressive leader, but Cherry-Garrard ultimately followed J. M. Barrie in emphasizing Scott's self-control, his conquest of himself, as the foundation of a truly heroic character.

In part to counter criticism, Kathleen at last sanctioned the first full-length biography by her friend and former admirer, the Irish writer Stephen Gwynn. Bodley Head published Gwynn's *Captain Scott* to rapturous reviews in 1929, placing Scott alongside Drake, Raleigh, and Frobisher in their Golden Hind series. 'Few will think Mr. Gwynn overstates his case,' judged *The Times*, 'when he says that Scott's supreme achievement is that he touched the imagination of his country as no other man has done during the course of this century.'[30]

The book opened by declaring that any technical discussion of polar exploration was 'entirely beyond the competence or intention of the writer of these pages'. Rather than debate the relative merits of the Norwegian and British expeditions, Gwynn declared his intention to explore Scott's inspirational legacy. The final sentence concluded that the explorers' great achievement had been to show that 'outside the common routine of duty lie fields of uncharted endeavour, in which high service may be valiantly rendered, high honour nobly pursued, and high sacrifice heroically accepted'.[31]

At the beginning of 1930, Reinhard Goering's drama based on the expedition opened in Berlin, a further indication of the global appeal of Scott's story. Kathleen travelled to Germany to see the production, which she thought awful. But the *Observer* believed 'No finer tribute has been paid to England by Germany for a long time'. Six months later, a polar exhibition organized by the RGS drew almost 6,500 visitors to Westminster's Central Hall over two weeks in July. Oriana Wilson recalled how she was obliged to shake James Gordon Hayes's hand and was about to be seated beside him at an exhibition function, before Charles Wright spotted her embarrassment and insisted she join his party.[32]

The publication of books on the expedition gathered pace in the 1930s, with popular accounts such as Martin Lindsay's *The Epic of Captain Scott*, and biographies of the other leading players in the Antarctic drama. Predictably titled *A Very Gallant Gentleman*, the first study of Oates by Louis Bernacchi, physicist on Scott's *Discovery*, appeared in 1933. But Caroline Oates, still fiercely protective of her son, refused Bernacchi access to the family papers and, with little new material, the book sold relatively poorly.

George Seaver's *Edward Wilson: Naturalist and Friend*, published with Oriana Wilson's full co-operation in the same year, was far more successful, reprinted over ten times before the end of the decade. Sailing to southern Africa in 1934, Oriana met a missionary teacher who told her that the chairman at an international convention in London had encouraged missionaries to use biographies and devoted his speech to Seaver's work.[33] Encouraged by the book's success, John Murray commissioned Seaver to produce a further study, *Edward Wilson: Nature Lover*, in 1937, and the first biography of Bowers in 1938. Seaver proved an ideal biographer for the two muscular Christians. An unconventional churchman who had served during the war, his books captured the spiritual impulse which drove these two selfless idealists to worship God by communing with nature. Petty Officer Edgar Evans, however, was increasingly marginalized, forgotten, or blamed, the strongest man of the party who failed first. It would be another fifty years before the first biography of Evans was published, by the librarian at Swansea Museum.

By 1935 the story of Scott of the Antarctic was firmly secured in the national canon of heroic tales. Scott and Oates featured in a spectacular film made to commemorate George V's Silver Jubilee, *Royal Cavalcade*, which told the story of his reign by following the path of a penny minted in 1911, to its inclusion in the donations for the King's Jubilee Trust. The producers reconstructed the explorers' arrival at the Pole, and Scott and Oates joined Henry V, Queen Elizabeth, and David Lloyd George among a handful of historical figures represented on screen.

The twenty-fifth anniversary of Scott's death in 1937 provoked a new wave of interest. Robert Baden-Powell secured Scott's *Discovery* for use as a training ship for Sea Scouts. Baden-Powell declared that 'over-civilisation is fast killing the spirit of adventure with its slogan of "Safety First", but here amid the traditions and historic examples enshrined in this ship we hope to breed again in our boys, for generations to come, the high spirit of adventure, of courage, and of loyal self-sacrificing Service'. The Royal Society of St George organized an essay competition about Scott, and were delighted to receive 800 entries. Colonel Jarrott was particularly pleased that so many children understood 'the moral value [of the expedition] to the empire'.[34]

'A hero to all of us'

Far from subsiding, then, the story of Captain Scott pulsed strong after 1918. How can we explain its enduring appeal? In part, the disaster offered an epic of heroism for a generation tired of war. The leading writer Henry Newbolt had composed 'Vitai Lampada' in 1898, anthem of the Edwardian games-ethic, with its command to 'Play up! play up! and play the game!' whether on the cricket pitch or battlefield. Newbolt published five books between 1914 and 1918, celebrating heroic deeds in battle. But in his introduction to *The Book of the Long Trail*, published in 1923, Newbolt expressed his disillusionment with modern warfare. War still shows the finest qualities of men, he wrote, but 'it also shows men at their worst. . . . millions of men killed or mutilated, millions of homes made desolate . . . the life of the world made hideous for years, with the survivors glaring at each other across the ruins . . . War then must stop, and you will, I hope, have no more war stories.'

The Book of the Long Trail focused instead on explorers, including Franklin, Livingstone, and Captain Scott. 'Where will you look for finer men than these, or for more honourable enterprises than those they undertook, or greater dangers and sufferings than theirs, or moments more full of daring and excitement . . . If any men were ever worth your knowing these are they'. Newbolt's introduction concluded: 'I have said little or nothing of Scott: I have been allowed to tell his story mainly in his own words, and I would not add to them if I could. If you do not love him and Wilson and

Bowers and Oates, then this book can be of no use to you. But I think I know you better.'[35]

The Book of the Long Trail captured the ambiguous impact of the First World War on British culture. The sheer scale of suffering made it difficult to generate heroic icons out of the war, but the language of sacrifice was deflected, not destroyed. On the one hand, we see the disillusionment of the ultimate propagandist for a chivalric conception of warfare. But Newbolt's investment in heroic ideals remained intact, transferred from the battlefield to the romantic vistas of the explorer. The death of Scott, Bowers, Oates, and Wilson (Evans is again marginalized) in the pure, icy wastes of Antarctica offered a narrative vehicle for the transmission of ideas of sacrifice uncontaminated by the futile slaughter of the Western Front.

War heroes did not of course disappear in 1919: cultural change takes time. Rupert Brooke's romantic poetry, for example, sold far better than the work of Wilfrid Owen throughout the 1920s. But the experience of modern warfare, the scale and anonymity of mechanized slaughter, the legacy of mutilation and disfigurement, the immobility of trench fighting, the absurdity of a subterranean existence where men starved and rats feasted, rendered such traditional heroic narratives more problematic than they had been before 1914.

It was not surprising, then, that the most acclaimed British hero of the First World War did not fight in the trenches. T. E. Lawrence, who led an Arab uprising against the Turkish rulers of the Ottoman Empire, captivated the public, first through Lowell Thomas's film and lecture heard by over 4 million people, and then through his own classic memoir, *The Seven Pillars of Wisdom*. Where the shattered landscapes of Flanders were stripped of allure, Lawrence traversed an exotic and glamorous desert stage; where regular soldiers followed orders, Lawrence possessed the secret agent's freedom of manœuvre; and where modern technology obliterated armies, Lawrence epitomized a sprit of freedom and individuality. The legend of Lawrence of Arabia reassured an imperial nation, demonstrating the supremacy of the white man among the natives.

Kathleen Scott herself was touched by Lawrence's fame. After sculpting the *Blonde Bedouin*, she suffered an 'acute attack of Lawrencitis', before friendly warnings and an ill-judged letter cured her affliction. George Bernard Shaw helped edit *Seven Pillars*, and introduced Lawrence to Apsley Cherry-Garrard. Following Shaw's public commendation of both men's astonishing synthesis of literature and action, Lawrence wrote (rather disturbingly) to Cherry-Garrard that 'If our sexes had been different (one of us, I mean) we could have pulled off a eugenicist's dream'.[36]

In June 1924 the nation hailed a new set of peace-time heroes. On the third expedition to Mount Everest, organized by the RGS and the Alpine Club in the early 1920s, the experienced climber George Leigh Mallory and young Oxford student Andrew Irvine disappeared during an attempt on the summit. Reaching 29,000 feet into the sky, Everest appeared impregnable. Indeed, height is the mountain's greatest defence. The terrain is less demanding than the most difficult Alpine routes, but at five and a half miles above sea level the physiological challenge is immense: extreme weather conditions, freezing temperatures, and a third less oxygen than at sea level. By a peculiar quirk of fate, the summit lies at the atmospheric limit of what humans can endure. Seven Sherpas died on the British 1922 expedition, after Mallory's first attempt on the summit triggered an avalanche. Everest would claim twenty-two more lives over the next fifty years, and, even armed with the latest equipment, eight climbers died on the mountain in a single night in 1996.

Like so many of his generation, Mallory had been moved by the Antarctic disaster, devouring *Scott's Last Expedition* soon after publication. He recommended the book to his friend Geoffrey Young as 'a solid rock of human experience [which] contains some observations which just sink right into one. Compared with Scott's the other journals accounts seem very futile, except those of the winter expedition. How would −70° suit your finger tips for tying up tent etc.?' A few weeks before returning to the Himalayas for the last time, Mallory met Kathleen Scott, recently married to Geoffrey's brother Edward. The encounter disturbed Mallory, who was beset by premonitions that he would die on Everest.[37]

The Everest disaster mobilized the same language of sacrifice, of death in a noble cause, which had greeted news of Scott's demise a decade before. At a joint meeting of the Alpine Club and RGS at the Royal Albert Hall, the expedition leader, Colonel Norton, grieved for the loss of 'a loyal friend, a great mountaineer and a gallant gentleman'.[38] The press heaped praise on Mallory and Irvine, and the close-knit community of public school masters and Oxbridge fellows mourned the passing of two of their chosen sons.

But the glory of heroic sacrifice did not shine quite as brightly as in 1913. The ghosts of the dead had haunted the nation for a decade, and the Everest disaster failed to ignite the burst of commemorative activity inspired by Scott, Bowers, Evans, Oates, and Wilson. An impressive memorial service was held at St Paul's in October, but no tablet was placed in the cathedral crypt, no Mansion House fund opened, no statue erected on a London street.

The conquest of Everest, although an increasing obsession among some enthusiasts, had failed to capture either the public or the literary imagination before the war. The index for the *Geographical Journal*, for example, listed only nine references to Mount Everest between 1903 and 1912, while the *Boy's Own Paper* published no articles about the mountain before 1914. When the *Boy's Own Paper* finally turned to Everest in the 1920s, one writer complained that 'Quite a lot of people do not seem to realise that the attempt to climb Mount Everest in India is really the greatest adventure in the world. The task is far more difficult and dangerous than was the journey to either of the Poles.'[39] The deaths of Mallory and Irvine would raise the profile of mountaineering in Britain for ever.

Mallory and Irvine left a mystery which continues to fascinate: were they the first men to reach the summit of Everest? J. B. Noel captured the expedition on film, an essential ingredient of modern celebrity. But, like Ponting before him, the climax of the drama eluded Noel's lens: he made no sighting of Mallory and Irvine on the day that they died. And the mountaineers left no document to compare with Scott's journal, the sacred text which could anchor such a range of heroic narratives, emphasizing patriotic service or scientific research, sacrifice or comradeship.

The adaptability of Scott's story was most strikingly demonstrated via the wireless on 11 November 1935.[40] The BBC had broadcast a memorial concert on Armistice Day since 1927, helping to synchronize ceremonies throughout Britain. The appropriate form of the broadcast was much debated, and internal correspondence reveals how the boundary between celebration and commemoration proved difficult to negotiate. After a heated argument, one BBC memo suggested that 'in view of the present militaristic tone of the public ceremonies broadcast on Armistice Day . . . something might be done in the Corporation's own programmes to restore the balance' and emphasize 'the idea of peace and comradeship'.

With this aim in mind, the BBC turned to the story of Captain Scott. The Corporation's Armistice Day programming in 1935 concluded with a play: 'Scott in the Antarctic. An epic retold.

Complied from the Records by Val Gielgud and Peter Cresswell.' Brother of actor John, Val Gielgud had also co-written the screen-play for *Royal Cavalcade*. The *Radio Times* concluded 'Nowadays we are rather shy of the word "hero". For better or worse, Carlyle's Teutonic adoration of the individual is out of favour in this country. But Scott is still a hero to all of us. His glorious life and death are so unrelated to any particular period that it is likely that his reputation will live on far into the future.'[41]

BBC producers had initially been fearful about broadcasting plays on Armistice Day, wary of resuscitating painful memories. But the tremendous success of an adaptation of R. C. Sherriff's stage-play *Journey's End* in 1929 changed their minds. *Journey's End* told the story of a group of officers commanded by Captain Dennis Stanhope on the eve of the German spring offensive in 1918, the darkest hour of the British war effort. A young lieutenant, Raleigh, asks to be posted to the unit led by his sixth-form hero, Stanhope. Stanhope's nerves, however, have been destroyed by nearly four years of fighting, and he survives only by drinking. In contrast to Scott, therefore, the pressures of war have exposed a taint in Stanhope's character. Raleigh's arrival intensifies Stanhope's feel-ings of inadequacy, as he is forced to confront his decline in the eyes of his young admirer. Through the course of the play, Stanhope watches the death of his closest friend, Osborne, and, in the final scene, Raleigh.

With Laurence Olivier making his name as Stanhope, *Journey's End* ran for an unprecedented 593 performances at London's Apollo Theatre. The bleak conclusion caused controversy, with Sherriff accused of pacifism. But *Journey's End* ultimately salvaged heroic qualities from the wreckage of a trench experience, with telling parallels to the trials endured in the Antarctic. Many accounts of Scott's last expedition had suggested a simple link between class and character, as we have seen. The working-class Evans lacked the mental capacity to cope with the stresses of polar exploration, and the 'strongest man' of the party collapsed first, initiating the disaster. Such ideas certainly survived the war. Discussing the expedition with George Seaver in 1929, Cherry-Garrard argued that 'It is a matter of mind rather than body . . . It was the sensitive men, the men with nerves, with a background of education – "good blood" – who went farthest, pulled hardest, stayed longest.'[42]

But the breakdown of thousands of officers during the war had complicated traditional conceptions of heroism, undermining the simple link between class and character. A War Office Committee of Inquiry into shell shock revealed how even the bravest of men, including officers who had consistently demonstrated the highest courage, might suddenly collapse. Mental breakdown and loss of self-control were a natural consequence of prolonged exposure to traumatic experience. The Committee's report in 1922 failed to offer any clear definition of cowardice to a military establishment struggling to discriminate between shell shock and shirking.[43]

The uneducated Petty Officer Evans was said to have been unable to occupy his simple mind during the long Antarctic marches, lapsing into insanity. But the legions of shell-shocked officers undermined pre-war assumptions about the relationship between social status, education, and mental strength. Stanhope envies the lower-middle-class Trotter, suggesting to Osborne that 'all his life Trotter feels like you and I do when we're drowsily drunk'.[44] Trotter lacks the imagination to suffer as intensely as his social superiors, and is insulated from the stresses which drive Stanhope to the bottle.

The upper-class Hibbert, on the other hand, is paralysed by fear after only a few weeks in the lines, and is confronted by Stanhope for faking illness. Stanhope encourages Hibbert by confessing that he feels exactly the same. He asks Hibbert if he could 'ever look a man straight in the face again – in all your life' if he deserted. All men are afraid, but 'just go on sticking it because they know it's – it's the only decent thing a man can do'.[45]

Raleigh's death at the end of the play signals the demise of fantasies of chivalrous combat. But, in spite of his inner torment, Stanhope continues to do his duty and the play concludes with him climbing up to the front line. Stanhope's final words, 'All right, Broughton, I'm coming', are a triumph of self-control in the face of adversity, stripped of romance. Stanhope is a flawed hero, but a hero none the less. The play ultimately reasserts the supremacy of character, a seam of mental endurance which allows Stanhope to see the conflict through to the end.

The story of Scott of the Antarctic could be interpreted in similar terms, for what was Scott's journal but a window on the psyche of a man confronting fear? Colonel Jarrott of the Royal Society of St George emphasized the imperial value of Scott's story, but others found meaning in a less grandiose tale of comradeship and endurance in the face of adversity, of men doing the decent thing. Sherriff hoped to follow *Journey's End* with a play about Captain Scott, but was prevented by Kathleen, who blocked all attempts to dramatize her dead husband's story in Britain.[46]

Exploration and Sacrifice

The *Terra Nova* sailed to the Antarctic at a turning-point in the development of the modern world. King George V postponed his visit to an aeroplane exhibition at Olympia to attend the Scott memorial service in St Paul's. The following day, Percy Lambert was reported to have set a new land speed record in his Talbot car, covering over 103 miles in one hour at the Brooklands track.[47]

Cables had rendered trans-continental communication almost instantaneous, moving images of the Antarctic were projected into picture theatres throughout Europe and America, cars travelled at over 100 miles per hour, and aeroplanes symbolized the techno-logical mastery of nature. And yet, in spite of these myriad advances, when Scott's last expedition departed New Zealand, there was only silence. And an assault on the Pole still relied on animals and men.

The conquest of the South Pole completed the last great quest, extending human knowledge to the ends of the earth. Nowhere else could inspire a comparable enterprise, combining the fulfilment of an ancient quest, with pioneering scientific research. Other realms would fire the imagination, first on Everest and then in space, but the rapid development of motor vehicles and aviation shifted the balance between scientific research and heroic adventure struck by Scott's Antarctic expeditions before the war. When asked on the eve of Scott's departure about the value of polar exploration, the RGS President Leonard Darwin replied 'simply that the good we aim at is knowledge'.[48] This book has, I hope, retrieved the scientific aims of Scott's last expedition from condescension and obscurity.

It was fitting that the most lasting monument to the expedition was not a play, film, book, or statue, but a building: the Scott Polar Research Institute (SPRI). After 1918 the expedition's Australian geologist Frank Debenham campaigned for the establishment of an institute using the balance of the Mansion House memorial fund. Cambridge University approved his proposal in November 1920, and the new centre for British polar research began life in a large attic room in the Sedgwick Museum of Geology.[49]

A few months later, the RGS President, Francis Younghusband, cited neither science nor knowledge when justifying the Society's support for an expedition to Mount Everest. He spoke instead of the spiritual good that would accrue from the ascent, which would 'hearten men in every land and in every occupation, and stir them also to rise triumphant over all impediments which confront them'. Indeed, Younghusband acknowledged that an investigation into 'the exact temperature at which currants will grow is of more importance to geography' than the conquest of Everest. But, by ascending Everest, he argued, mankind would 'test ourselves against the highest mountain in the world'.[50]

Some scientific investigation would be pursued in the Himalayas, and some commentators would highlight its importance. But by 1924, twenty-five volumes of Antarctic research in botany, geology, glaciology, meteorology, physiography, terrestrial magnetism, and zoology generated by Scott's last expedition had been published. Although others contributed, the *Terra Nova's* staff played the principal role in preparing these volumes, which one scholar described as forming 'a new landmark in Antarctic science'.[51] Frank Debenham, Thomas Griffith Taylor, Raymond Priestley, George Simpson, and Charles Wright all built distinguished academic careers upon their Antarctic work. But no scientist would make his name on the slopes of Everest and the shelves of university libraries around the world would not be strained by volumes of Himalayan research.[52]

With the scientific results published and Hodge's national memorial statue unveiled, the Mansion House Scott memorial fund was officially closed in July 1925 and the balance of £13,000 passed to Cambridge University, on condition that a suitable memorial building be erected within ten years.[53] In May 1926 the Institute celebrated its new-found security with a dinner of eight courses attended by twenty-six old polar explorers, including nine veterans of Scott's expeditions and five of Shackleton's. Nansen was to have given the inaugural address, but was prevented from attending by the general strike. Jean Charcot, Erich von Drygalski, Adrien de Gerlache, Otto Nordenskjöld, Charles Rabot, and Knud Rasmussen sent messages of support. Roald Amundsen, though, does not appear to have been invited.[54] The British polar establishment never forgave the most accomplished traveller of his age, not for his use of dogs, but for his deceit.

The institute moved from the Sedgwick Museum to an old house on Lensfield Road the following year. Finally, on 16 November 1934, after a lengthy fund-raising campaign, a new memorial building designed by the renowned architect Herbert Baker was opened on the same Cambridge street, twenty-one years after news of the death of Captain Scott reached London. Two of Kathleen Scott's sculptures have stood outside SPRI ever since: a bust of Captain Scott in a niche above the main entrance, and a full-size statue. Modelled on T. E. Lawrence's younger brother Arnold, Kathleen had originally exhibited the statue as a war memorial at the Wembley Empire exhibitions of 1924–5, with the inscription '1914–18. These had the most to give.' Arnold Lawrence later became Professor of Archaeology at Cambridge, and must be one of the few British academics to have cycled past a life-size statue of his naked body on a regular basis.[55]

A number of senior administrators, however, strongly objected to the association of the Institute with the statue. The Master of Downing College, Albert Seward, was anxious 'to avoid undue stressing of the idea of sacrifice', while Frank Debenham feared that passers-by would associate the building too strongly with the tragic aspects of polar exploration.[56] After debating whether to refuse Kathleen Scott's gift, or hide it in a secluded memorial garden, they finally agreed to erect the statue in front of the new building, provided it was emphasized that the statue was a memorial to the five dead explorers, and not a representation of the spirit of polar exploration. H. R. Mill later described the statue as representing 'Aspiration' rather than 'Sacrifice', and a hedge was grown to replace the railings which initially guarded the Institute.

The dispute exposed a profound change in the relationship between geography, travel, and exploration. The RGS ceased funding geography at Oxford and Cambridge in the early 1920s, after thirty-five years of support. The rapid development of higher education offered a new institutional framework to supervise the production and distribution of geographical knowledge, culminating in the establishment of the Institute of British Geographers in 1933, a deliberate strategy to bypass the influence of the RGS.[57] Here, the study, not the field, was supreme. Geographers would be measured by their professional qualifications, not their manly character. The measurement of the world was divided from the measurement of manliness.

On 5 January 1922 Scott's old rival Ernest Shackleton suffered a fatal heart attack. He died, not huddled in a tent on the Great Ice Barrier, nor in the depths of a crevasse on the glacier he had named after his first patron, William Beardmore, but in a ship's cabin in the South Atlantic. Shackleton's plans for an Arctic voyage in search of land near the North Pole had been thwarted by the Canadian Vilhjalmur Stefansson, and he turned south motivated primarily, it seems, by the simple desire to get out of England. There was talk of looking for Captain Kidd's treasure in South Trinidad, of circumnavigating Antarctica, perhaps of finding some mineral deposit which would help pay off his mounting debts. The name of the ship on which the most charismatic of all the polar heroes passed away, served only to underline the faded ambition of his final endeavour: *Quest*.

Aviators superseded explorers as the most celebrated heroes after

1918. The knights of the air were not engaged in scientific research, but in demonstrating the soaring potential of the human spirit, man mastering machine again after machines had obliterated so many men. The remarkable Roald Amundsen would join their ranks. Always ahead of his time, he obtained the first Norwegian civilian pilot's licence and, aged 53, set yet another record flying to a new 'farthest north' of 87° 44' in 1925. The American Commander Richard Byrd beat him to the North Pole the following year, but Amundsen had his sights on a different prize. A few days after Byrd's return, Amundsen commanded a small crew, including the pilot Umberto Nobile, on the first flight across the Arctic continent in the airship *Norge*. Given that the claims of Byrd, Peary, and Cook have subsequently been questioned, it is possible that Amundsen was not only the first man to stand on the South Pole, but also the first to gaze on the North.

Amundsen retired at the height of his fame, but was dogged by debts and set out again in 1928 to search for Nobile, who had gone missing on a new Arctic flight. Twenty-five years after he had completed the North-West Passage, Amundsen's poorly equipped plane disappeared into fog over the Polar Sea and the great Norwegian was never seen again.

In 1929 Richard Byrd became the first man to travel over the South Pole since Scott and Amundsen. The American's plane carried three foreign flags, one Norwegian, one British, and one French, for the country's hospitality to aviators. Byrd sent a personal message to Peter Scott through the National Geographical Society in Washington and his achievement was celebrated throughout the world.

But the greatest of the aviator heroes, indeed arguably the most fêted individual of the twentieth century, was Charles Lindbergh. The first solo pilot to cross the Atlantic non-stop from New York to

Paris, Lindbergh's flight on the *Spirit of St Louis* triggered an unprecedented global frenzy in 1927. The hours of uncertainty as the pilot struggled to stay awake over the Atlantic beyond all communication heightened tension to fever pitch. Vast crowds greeted Lindbergh in Paris, Brussels, and London. The *New York Times* received 2,000 unsolicited poems in his honour in a single week.[58] A young man from the Upper Mississippi Valley was invested with the dreams of his age, the triumph of the individual, renewed faith in technological progress, and friendship between Europe and America. Lindbergh played the hero's part to perfection, patting the cheek and shaking the hand of a young Princess Elizabeth, brought down by her nurse to meet the American aviator in Buckingham Palace. His decorum and manners appealed to the old world, while his deed and celebrity appealed to the new. 'He represents all that a man should say,' said Winston Churchill, 'all that a man should do, and all that a man should be.'[59]

And Lindbergh lived. Charles Nungesser and François Coli had disappeared after taking off from Paris two weeks before the *Spirit of St Louis* left New York. The heroism of the two French war aces was acknowledged, but Lindbergh's victory eclipsed their martyrdom. There had been so many martyrs, so much talk of sacrifice, and the world thrilled to a living hero.

The Antarctic disaster had also resonated around the world in 1913, but the global echoes of Scott's story diminished after the war. In 1918, Marguerite Cope had informed the RGS that her freshman class at Judson College in Alabama were studying *Scott's Last Expedition*. 'I do not know of any story of adventure in real life,' Cope wrote, 'that sets forth the splendid endurance of the Englishman more forcibly than this.'[60] It seems doubtful that freshman classes in the American south would have spent much time on Scott a decade letter.

Yet the story of Scott of the Antarctic retained a special appeal in Britain between the wars. Other heroes would inspire. T. E. Lawrence, like Lindbergh, was chased by the press along the path from heroic icon to modern celebrity, while the language of sacrifice rang out again after the death of Mallory and Irvine. But patriots and pacifists, imperialists and missionaries, scoutmasters, scientists, and priests alike still gathered to tell the story of Scott of the Antarctic, a story both transcendent and of its time, a story which had a braced a nation for war in 1914, and a parable of courage and comradeship. And, beneath all these stories, Scott's pencil marks in the cold.

EPILOGUE

W HEN war engulfed Europe in 1939, ministers would not express their envy at the opportunities for sacrifice offered to young men, but Captain Scott's story would again prove useful. The Ministry of Information identified Scott as an ideal subject for films showcasing British life and character, emphasizing independence, toughness of fibre, and sympathy with the underdog.[1] The National Book Council recommended Cherry-Garrard's *The Worst Journey in the World* as suitable reading for troops, while Penguin published a cheap edition of Gwynn's *Captain Scott* and George Seaver added *Scott of the Antarctic* to his collection of polar biographies.

In the immediate aftermath of the war, Ealing Studios finally persuaded the surviving crew and relatives of the dead to sanction a feature film based on Scott's last expedition. Both the Colonial Office and the newly formed Falkland Islands Dependencies Survey supported the production, hoping that the film would promote Britain's polar interests. Antarctica had emerged as an important arena of imperial competition, as Argentina, Chile, and the United States pushed their territorial claims in the South Atlantic.

After an arduous production schedule in Switzerland, Norway, and the Antarctic itself, *Scott of the Antarctic*, with John Mills in the title role, graced the annual Royal Command Performance at the Empire Cinema, Leicester Square, in November 1948. Kathleen Scott had died the previous year, leaving instructions for her grave-stone to be inscribed: 'No happier woman ever lived'. But Lois

Evans and her family, who had received so much less support from the Mansion House fund a generation earlier, were among the guests of honour at the premiere. The *Sunday Dispatch* believed the film would reassure those who feared the collapse of the British empire 'that ours is the finest breed of men on this earth'. But, with mixed reviews and moderate audiences, such grandiose rhetoric failed to inspire as it had done in 1913. The grim story of polar endurance, already familiar to so many, offered no escape from the austerity of a post-war Britain preoccupied with its own fuel shortages and inadequate rations.[2]

Scott's reputation survived the war, as new surveys and old classics told the story of the heroic age of polar exploration. The fiftieth anniversary of the disaster prompted a predictable burst of attention, including the 'Ladybird' children's book through which I first learned about the expedition. Reginald Pound's biography broke new ground in 1966. Pound was the first author to be allowed access to Scott's original sledging journal, and his book exposes the volatile, fatalistic, and ungenerous temperament of its subject, publishing Scott's harsh assessments of both colleagues and competitors. The book also raised the question of how far Scott had pressured Oates to take the final step for which he is remembered. Pound, though, ultimately followed Apsley Cherry-Garrard, exposing Scott's personal failings while acknowledging his heroism.

But, as society experienced profound changes, so the resonance of Scott's story was transformed after the war. Clement Attlee's pioneering administration entrenched social democracy in Britain, and the experiences of the ordinary seaman, Petty Officer Edgar Evans, began to receive belated recognition. The Royal Naval Gunnery School in Portsmouth named an accommodation block after Evans in 1964 and a string of new memorials honoured one of Swansea's most famous sons. Captain Scott, in contrast, became a target for satirists and social critics. Many schools had put aside their hostility to the distractions of the picture palace to organize special trips to *Scott of the Antarctic*, and the explorer increasingly came to symbolize a fossilised Englishness of stiff upper lips and unthinking deference. Peter Cook lampooned Scott for the Cambridge Footlights Revue in 1959, in a sketch titled 'Polar Bores'. The Monty Python team followed a decade later with 'Scott of the Sahara', a parody of Hollywood sensationalism, in which a half-naked Oates grappled with a giant electric penguin. And the radical playwright Howard Brenton's *Scott of the Antarctic* was performed at Bradford Ice Rink in 1971, with the Norwegians effortlessly navigating the stage on skates, while the British stumbled around on foot.

By the 1970s, therefore, Scott's complex personality had been revealed and his methods questioned. His personal contribution to the disaster, including his failure to use more dogs and his impulsive decision to take an extra man to the Pole, had been widely debated. Roland Huntford supplemented these criticisms with extensive original research and, where others had pulled their punches, he lashed out. The novelty of his 1979 biography, *Scott and Amundsen*, lay in his attitude to Scott's journal. While many had criticized Scott in the past, all had paid tribute to his heroism in the face of death. Huntford, however, saw only deceit in Scott's last message, the shameful self-justification of a man who had led his comrades to disaster.

Huntford's most lasting legacy was to erect Scott as a hero for a nation in decline, an emblem of the amateurism and incompetence which, he argued, had encumbered Britain through the twentieth century. With rising unemployment, social tensions, and a diminished international role, debates about decline took centre stage in the 1970s and 1980s. Trevor Griffith's television adaptation of Huntford's biography, *The Last Place on Earth*, hammered home the message that Scott exemplified the arrogant mindlessness of a generation. The fate of Scott's last expedition was cast as a metaphor for a wider national failure to embrace modernity.

The rediscovery of Ernest Shackleton at the end of the 1990s revived this interpretation, as Scott has been sacrificed on the altar of Shackleton worship. 'It is, after all, Shackleton who deserves our praise,' argued Lucy Moore in the *Observer*, '. . . a hero for our time, a man who, like millennial Britain, has learned to crave the winning (even when it doesn't), rather than just the playing of the game.'[3] Shackleton's bravado and charismatic leadership define a modern Britain, which has shaken off the straitjacket of class prejudice and preoccupation with heroic failure represented by Captain Scott. When the BBC recently asked viewers to nominate the greatest Britons ever, Shackleton came eleventh. Scott came fifty-fourth.

Explanations of decline based on the cultural failings of a ruling elite remain seductive, both in their simplicity and in their critique of a class whose practices often appear ridiculous or contemptible to modern eyes. Yet raising Scott as an emblem of decline reveals more about current concerns than about past history. Although national peculiarities require further attention, heroic martyrs were the currency of many nations, from Joan of Arc to General Custer. The Antarctic disaster struck a chord around the world, as we have seen. The argument that the British, uniquely, developed a cult of the loser cannot be sustained. 'The English people were never prone, as some other peoples have been, to glorify the defeated', wrote Stephen Gwynn in 1929. 'They have, in truth, never needed to do so.'[4] Although Britain's recent sporting history has compelled a closer relationship with gallant losers, Gwynn offered an accurate assessment of British confidence between the wars.

The extraordinary response to the death of Captain Scott in February 1913 was generated by the conjunction of an exceptional set of circumstances: the unique place of the South Pole in the public imagination; the particular stage of development of transport and communications, where cables carried news of the disaster around the world in a matter of hours, but an assault on the Pole relied on animals and men; and Scott's skill at articulating the heroic fantasies of his generation. None of the other martyrs of modern British history, Nelson, for example, or General Gordon, left a testament of comparable drama or pathos. Scott's genius was to present the assault on the Pole as a heroic sacrifice for an age which venerated struggle.

But even as he lay dying in the Antarctic, this unique combination of factors was drifting apart. After listening to one of Herbert Ponting's first lectures on the expedition, the journalist Filson Young considered whether the world was losing its sense of wonder. He had relaxed after dinner in the centre of London watching seals and penguins at play, waves breaking on Antarctic icebergs, and the sun shining on the slopes of Mount Erebus. 'It all seemed unreal, like an entertainment got up to fleet the passing hour. Things that never happened are now made so real to us that we are unable truly to apprehend the reality of things that have happened.'[5] The progress of technology extracted the price of disenchantment.

A decade earlier, in the depths of an Antarctic winter, Edward Wilson had also mused on the development of the modern world. Wilson believed that 'when Polar exploration became possible to any form of motor transport or flying machine its attraction to most people would be finished, and would interest an entirely different mind'.[6] His two companions, Robert Scott and Ernest Shackleton, heartily agreed. They were wrong. The last great wilderness continues to seduce the curious, adventurous, and restless. But the meaning of journeys to unknown lands has altered for ever. Vast areas remain uncharted, principally the dark depths of the oceans. But the conquest of the South Pole marked the symbolic completion of the map of the world. Men and women would still make their name travelling into the unknown, but their exploits lacked the grandeur of the last great quest. Few people today remember Vivian Fuchs, fewer still Wally Herbert.[7] As technological advances have reduced the risks involved in the observation of the natural world, so explorers have mutated from scientific travellers to seekers of sensation, from Captain Scott to the adventurer Ranulph Fiennes and yachtswoman Ellen Macarthur. Their sensational exploits provide rich fodder for an insatiable media, while their bravery inspires admiration. But they do not extend the boundaries of our world. All are doomed, as Joseph Conrad predicted, to follow in the beaten tracks of the pioneers.

The peculiar combination of heroic endeavour, scientific research, and national glory expressed by Scott's Antarctic exhibitions, has been energized only once since the conquest of the South Pole: in the race to the moon. But the exploration of space has proved a very different enterprise from voyages to the Antarctic. Although President J. F. Kennedy said nothing of science when he announced that Americans would walk on the moon before the end of the 1960s, travel beyond our planet has generated impressive scientific results. The administrators of the space programme argued over the scientific content of missions, just as Clements Markham and J. W. Gregory had argued before the voyage of the *Discovery* in 1901. The geologist Jack Schmitt collected rock samples on the last Apollo mission, a Frank Debenham for the lunar age. But while Scott's scientific crew had no option but to sail around the world, unmanned space probes can now transmit data across millions of miles.

The race to the moon was primarily an expression of the

awesome power of the modern nation-state. Charles Lindbergh himself surprised the crew of Apollo 8 on the eve of their mission in 1968. Lindbergh calculated that the massive Saturn V rocket which would propel the men beyond the earth's atmosphere would burn ten times more fuel in a single second than the *Spirit of St Louis* had consumed during its entire flight from New York to Paris. Four hundred thousand people worked to achieve the immense technological leap necessary to send Neil Armstrong and Buzz Aldrin to the moon a year later. Such astronomical investment would have been inconceivable without the impetus of the Cold War and a dead President's promise.

The Apollo astronauts themselves were very different creatures from the polar explorers of the 1900s. Sealed in metal boxes astride giant bombs, their lives rested less on their own ingenuity and powers of endurance than on the successful operation of a chain of thousands upon thousands of mechanical and human components. If the chain operated smoothly, they would not suffer great physical hardship: boredom and stress, certainly, but not the relentless treadmill of a polar journey testing both mind and body. The heroism of the astronaut is the heroism of nerve, the possession of the right stuff, the willingness to gamble that the chain will not break, and to retain composure in those brief moments of decision when the fate of the mission lay in his or her hands. As veteran astronaut Pete Conrad observed to Andrew Chaikin, he 'wasn't an explorer; he was a test pilot'.[8]

We live now amidst the rubble of a Victorian culture fractured by two world wars. Insights drawn from psychology, the science of the mind, have superseded nineteenth-century discussions of character, while medical research into post-traumatic stress disorder has exposed the physiological bases of mental breakdown. Our more cynical age views heroes with suspicion, as instruments of propaganda or tools of deception. The everyday heroism of ordinary men and women, as Alex Thompson and Christabel Pankhurst had hoped, is now more readily acknowledged. But ideas of character and sacrifice still pervade our imagination. Tom Hanks shakes uncontrollably at the horror of the Normandy landings in Stephen Spielberg's *Saving Private Ryan*, but, like Captain Stanhope, he sticks by his men to the bitter end, the only decent thing a man can do.

Captain Scott is out of fashion today. A visit to Eton College last year uncovered Kathleen Scott's memorial to Captain Oates hidden behind a sofa in the library. But the tragic story of the men who lost the race to the South Pole will endure. For this featureless spot on the surface of the earth where scientific curiosity and romantic imagination collide, retains its allure. And in our jaded, disorienting times, some will always seek enchantment in the south with Captain Scott, turning the pages of the last great quest.

APPENDIX
BRITISH MEMORIALS COMMEMORATING
THE ANTARCTIC DISASTER, 1913–1925

THIS appendix lists expedition relics and objects created specifically to commemorate the Antarctic disaster. Many communities also used souvenirs, or pictures from illustrated newspapers and periodicals as memorials.

Each memorial commemorated Scott, Bowers, Evans, Oates, and Wilson, unless otherwise stated.

Form of Memorial:	*Location (Date):*
E. A. Wilson's sledging flag	Gloucester cathedral (1913)
R. F. Scott's sledging flag	Exeter cathedral (1913)
City of Cardiff flag	City Hall, Cardiff (1913)
Welsh flag	National Museum of Wales, Cardiff (1913)
Stained-glass window	Royal Naval Barracks chapel, Devonport (1913)
Stained-glass window [Wilson]	Copthorne School chapel, Crawley (1913)
Memorial tablets [Oates]	St Anne's church, Eastbourne (1913)
Memorial tablet [Oates]	Meanwood church, Leeds (1913)
Memorial tablet [Oates]	St Mary's church, Gestingthorpe (1913)
Flag and flagstaff	St Bartholomew's church, Southsea (1913)
Figurehead of the *Terra Nova*	Roath Park, Cardiff (1913)
Various [Wilson]	Gonville and Caius College, Cambridge (from 1913)
Various [Wilson]	Cheltenham College, Cheltenham (from 1913)
Memorial tablet [Bowers]	HMS *Worcester*, Greenhithe (1913–14)
Memorial tablet [Evans]	St Mary's church, Rhosili (1914)
Memorial tablet [Bowers]	St Ninian's Church, Rothesay (1914)

Memorial tablet	St George's church, Chatham (1914)
Memorial tablet [Oates]	Eton College Library, Windsor (1914)
Memorial tablet [Oates]	Eton College ante-chapel, Windsor (1914)
Statue [Wilson]	Promenade, Cheltenham (1914)
Statuette [Oates]	Cavalry Club, London (1914)
Bust [Scott]	Municipal Buildings, Devonport (1914)
Stained-glass window	St Peter's church, Binton (1915)
Statue	Waterloo Place, London (1915)
Memorial tablet	City Hall, Cardiff (1916)
Bed	Royal Hamadryad Hospital, Cardiff (1916)
Memorial tablet	St Paul's cathedral, London (1916)
Clocktower	Roath Park, Cardiff (1918)
Fountain	Glen Prosen, Angus (1918)
Scott Polar Research Institute	Cambridge (1920; Memorial Building 1934)
Picture [Evans]	St Helen's School, Swansea (1921)
Stained-glass window [Scott]	Emmanuel church, Exeter (1924)
Statue	Mount Wise, Devonport (1925)

MESSAGE TO THE PUBLIC

As he waited to die at the end of March 1912 in a freezing tent on the Great Ice Barrier, Captain Robert Falcon Scott wrote a 'Message to the Public' at the back of his sledging journal. The journal was retrieved by the search party which found the bodies of Scott and his two companions, Henry Bowers and Edward Wilson, seven months later.

Message To Public

The causes of the disaster are not due to faulty organisation, but to misfortune in all risks which had to be undertaken.

1. The loss of pony transport in March 1911 obliged me to start later than I had intended, and obliged the limits of stuff transported to be narrowed.
2. The weather throughout the outward journey, and especially the long gale in 83° S., stopped us.
3. The soft snow in lower reaches of glacier again reduced pace.

We fought these untoward events with a will and conquered, but it cut into our provision reserve.

Every detail of our food supplies, clothing and depôts made on the interior ice-sheet and over that long stretch of 700 miles to the Pole and back, worked out to perfection—the advance party would have returned to the glacier in fine form and with surplus of food, but for the astonishing failure of the man whom we had least expected to fail. Edgar Evans was thought the strongest man of the party.

The Beardmore Glacier is not difficult in fine weather, but on our return we did not get a single completely fine day; this with a sick companion enormously increased our anxieties.

As I have said elsewhere, we got into frightfully rough ice and Edgar Evans received a concussion of the brain—he died a natural death, but left us a shaken party with the season unduly advanced.

But all the facts above enumerated were as nothing to the surprise which awaited us on the Barrier. I maintain that our arrangements for returning were quite adequate, and that no one in the world would have expected the temperatures and surfaces which we encountered at this time of the year. On the summit in lat. 85°/86° we had −20°, −30°. On the Barrier in lat. 82°, 10,000 feet lower, we had −30° in the day, −47° at night – pretty regularly, with continuous head wind during our day marches. It is clear that these circumstances come on very suddenly, and our wreck is certainly due to this sudden advent of severe weather, which does not seem to have any satisfactory cause. I do not think human beings ever came through such a month as we have come through, and we should have got through in spite of the weather but for the sickening of a second companion, Captain Oates, and a shortage of fuel in our depôts for which I cannot account, and finally, but for the storm which has fallen on us within 11 miles of the depôt at which we hoped to secure our final supplies. Surely misfortune could scarcely have exceeded this last blow. We arrived within 11 miles of our old One Tom Camp with fuel for one hot meal and food for two days. For <u>four</u> days we have been unable to leave the tent: the gale howling about us. We are weak, writing is difficult, but for my own sake I do not regret this journey, which has shown that Englishmen can endure hardships, help one another, and meet death with as great a fortitude as ever in the past. We took risks, we knew we took them; things have come out against us, and therefore we have no cause for complaint, but bow to the will of Providence, determined still to do our best to the last. But if we have been willing to give our lives to this enterprise, which is for the honour of our country, I appeal to our countrymen to see that those who depend on us are properly cared for.

Had we lived, I should have had a tale to tell of the hardihood, endurance, and courage of my companions which would have stirred the heart of every Englishman. These rough notes and our dead bodies must tell the tale, but surely, surely, a great rich country like ours will see that those who are dependent on us are properly provided for.

NOTES

· INTRODUCTION ·

1 The search party consisted of Atkinson, Cherry-Garrard, E. W. Nelson (biologist), Tryggve Gran (Norwegian ski-expert), Dimitri Gerof (dog-driver), and the naval seamen Thomas Crean, F. J. Hooper, Patrick Keohane, William Lashly, and Thomas Williamson.

2 A. Cherry-Garrard, diary, 2 January 1913, MS 559/10, SPRI, records that Victor Campbell, one of the naval officers in the shore party, had pushed for the inclusion of a text because 'he says that women think a lot of it'.

3 H. R. Mill, *The Record of the Royal Geographical Society, 1830–1930* (London, 1930), 210, listed 'seven problems of discovery, the solution of which was held to be nearly impossible', adding the summit of Mount Everest and the South Pole.

4 *Illustrated London News*, 18 May 1912, 757.

5 *Manchester Guardian*, 15 February 1913, 10.

6 *The Times*, 17 August 2000, 9.

7 R. Campbell-Johnson, 'Where are the Heroes Today?', *The Times*, 7 December 1998, 22.

8 See Paul Theroux's introduction to the latest edition of Huntford's *Scott and Amundsen*, retitled *The Last Place on Earth: Scott and Amundsen's Race to the South Pole* (London, 2000), pp. vii–xii.

9 Scott's last expedition does receives passing mentions in E. J. Hobsbawm, *The Age of Empire, 1875–1914* (London, 1987), 13, and P. F. Clarke, *Hope and Glory: Britain, 1900–1990* (London, 1996), 89.

10 For recent examples of these claims see, among many, M. de-la-Noy, *Scott of the Antarctic* (Thrupp, 1997), 59–60 on manhauling; and C. Alexander, *The Endurance: Shackleton's Legendary Antarctic Expedition* (London, 1998), 9, on Barrie's involvement in the publication of Scott's journals.

11 *The Times*, 16 June 1914, 7.

12 Many historians have utilized the concept of 'myth' in recent years, frequently drawing on Roland Barthes, *Mythologies* (London, 1972). See, for example, A. Calder, *The Myth of the Blitz* (London, 1991) and R. Slotkin, '*The Fatal Environment: The Myth of the Frontier in the Age of Industrialisation, 1800–1890* (Middletown, Conn., 1986). But the word 'myth' is so strongly associated with deceit in popular usage, that I have preferred to write about the 'story' of Scott of the Antarctic, in order to emphasize the narrative construction of Scott's heroic reputation, without suggesting conscious manipulation as strongly as myth.

· CHAPTER ONE ·
MEASURING THE WORLD

1   L. Beaumont to K. Scott, 15 March 1913, MS 2, SPRI.

2   'Britain's Duty', *Daily Chronicle*, 13 February 1913, 6.

3   *The Times*, 11 February 1913, 10.

4   The following account draws principally on P. van der Merwe *et al.* (eds.), *South: The Race to the Pole* (London, 2000), 8–20.

5   Report, 24 May 1830, 'The Raleigh Club, 1827–54', Add. papers 115, RGS.

6   T. Jeal, 'David Livingstone: A Brief Biographical Account', in J. M. MacKenzie (ed.), *David Livingstone and the Victorian Encounter with Africa* (London, 1996), 36–7.

7   *Manchester Guardian*, 18 April 1874, 7.

8   Quoted in F. Driver, 'Henry Morton Stanley and his Critics: Geography, Exploration and Empire', *Past and Present*, 133 (1991), 144, and I. Cameron, *The History of the Royal Geographical Society 1830–1980: To the Farthest Ends of the Earth* (London, 1980), 87.

9   R. A. Stafford, *Scientist of Empire: Sir Roderick Murchison, Scientific Exploration and Victorian Imperialism* (Cambridge, 1989), 28–9.

10 B. Riffenburgh, *The Myth of the Explorer: The Press, Sensationalism and Geographical Discovery* (Oxford, 1994). See also R. G. David, *The Arctic in the British Imagination, 1818–1914* (Manchester, 2000), ch. 4.

11 F. Driver, *Geography Militant: Cultures of Exploration and Empire* (Oxford, 2001).

12 S. Smiles, *Self-Help: With Illustrations of Conduct and Perseverance* (London, 1908), pp. x–xi.

13 Ibid. 316.

14 J. M. MacKenzie, 'Empire and National Identities: The Case of Scotland', *Transactions of the Royal Historical Society*, 6th ser., 8 (1998), 225.

15 Smiles, *Self-help*, 285 on Livingstone, and 473–4 quoting Parry on Franklin.

16 S. Collini, *Public Moralists: Political Thought and Intellectual Life in Britain, 1850–1930* (Oxford, 1991), 100.

17 Quoted in Riffenburgh, *Myth of the Explorer*, 31, and F. Spufford, *I May Be Some Time: Ice and the English Imagination* (London, 1996), 174.

18 Quoted in F. Fleming, *Barrow's Boys* (London, 1998), 424.

19 J. Conrad, 'Geography and Some Explorers', in *Last Essays*, ed. R. Curle (London, 1926), 19–20. The essay was originally published in 1923 under the title 'The Romance of Travel' and published in *National Geographic* the following year.

20 Ibid. 1–2.

21 Ibid. Conrad, 'Travel', 128 and 134.

22 Quoted in Cameron, *Farthest Ends*, 200.

23 A. Geikie, 'Geographical Evolution', Proc. RGS, NS 1 (1879), 423–4.

24 RGS council minutes, 9 June 1879, RGS. Also see scientific purposes committee minutes, 16 June 1879, RGS. C. R. Markham, *The Fifty Years' Work of the Royal Geographical Society* (London, 1881), 108, notes that Coles's course involved 'the use of the transit-theodolite, ordinary 5-inch theodolite, sextant and artificial horizon, hyposometrical apparatus, manner of plotting a traverse-survey by means of the prismatic compass, and map construction'.

25 'Proceedings of the Geographical Section of the British Association, Sheffield Meeting, 1879', *Proc. RGS*, NS 1 (1879), 602–3. See also C. R. Markham, 'The Field of Geography', *GJ*, 11 (1898), 2.

26 Scientific purposes committee minutes, 17 March 1884, RGS.

27 C. R. Markham, 'The Present Standpoint of Geography', *GJ*, 2 (1893), 504.

28 Calculated from annual figures given in 'RGS council reports, 1830–96' (bound pamphlet), Publications Collection, RGS; C. R. Markham, 'Address to the Royal Geographical Society', *GJ*, 4 (1894), 23–4.

29 D. W. Freshfield, H. H. Godwin-Austen, and J. K. Laughton (eds.), *Hints to Travellers*, (5th edn., London, 1883), p. iv.

30 RGS council minutes, 11 June, 1883 RGS.

31 'Instruments Lent to Travellers', vol. 1, RGS. This volume lists the name of the explorer, date of withdrawal, and destination of the expedition, but not the instruments borrowed.

32 'Instructions to Mr. Thomson', inserted in expedition committee minutes, 8 December 1882, RGS. See also expedition committee minutes, 27 October and 16 November 1882, RGS. In spite of Livingstone's legacy, missionary enterprise was strikingly absent from the RGS agenda, in part because missionary endeavour was so amply supported by other institutions.

33 Quoted in R. I. Rotberg, *Joseph Thomson and the Exploration of Africa* (London, 1971), 244.

34 Expedition committee minutes, 1 March 1888, RGS. When Thomson applied for the additional £100, he was offered only £50 and asked to supply the Society with certain observations. Thomson withdrew his application and received no additional contributions.

35 Calculated from RGS council reports, 1874–96.

36 H. R. Mill, *The Record of the Royal Geographical Society, 1830–1930* (London, 1930), 251, records that the RGS contributed £7,500 to support geography at Cambridge between 1883 and 1923, and £11,000 at Oxford between 1887 and 1924.

37 C. R. Markham, 'Royal Geographical Society' (unpublished MS *c.*1903), 449, Special Collection, CRM 47, RGS.

38 R. Strachey, 'The Annual Address on the Progress of Geography: 1887–8', *Proc. RGS*, NS 10 (1888), 408–9.

39 'Presentation of the Royal and Other Medals', *Proc. RGS*, 22 (1877–8), 298, and 'Presentation of the Royal Medals', *Proc. RGS*, NS 7 (1885), 477.

40 'Presentation of the Royal and Other Awards', *Proc. RGS*, 20 (1875–6), 368–9.

41 'Presentation of the Royal Medals', *Proc. RGS*, NS 9 (1887), 453–4.

42 Presentation of the Royal Medals', *Proc. RGS*, NS 8 (1886), 466.

43 Markham, 'Field of Geography', 4–5.

44 'Proceedings of the Geographical Section of the British Association, Sheffield Meeting, 1879', *Proc. RGS*, NS 1 (1879), 604, and Markham, 'Field of Geography', 4–5.

45 'Presentation of the Gold Medals to Lady Franklin and to Captain Sir F. L. M'Clintock', *Proc. RGS*, 4 (1859–60), 111.

46 'Presentation of the Royal awards', *Proc. RGS*, 13 (1868–9), 257–8.

47 'Presentation of the Royal and Other Medals', *Proc. RGS*, 21 (1876–7), 399.

48 J. T. Walker, 'Four Years' Journeyings through Great Tibet, by one of the Trans-Himalayan Explorers of the Survey of India', *Proc. RGS*, NS 7 (1885), 92. A-K's real name was Kishen Singh.

49 'The Geographical Dinner to Mr. H. M. Stanley', *Proc. RGS*, NS 12 (1890), 495.

50 E. Said, *Orientalism* (New York, 1979), 3.

51 Driver, *Geography Militant*, 39.

52 A. H. Markham, *The Life of Sir Clements R. Markham* (London, 1917), 253–4.

53 RGS council minutes, 24 November 1884, RGS.

54 M. E. Grant Duff, 'The Annual Address on the Progress of Geography: 1891–92', *Proc. RGS*, NS 14 (1892), 359; RGS council minutes, 23 February 1885, RGS. E. A. Reeves, The *Recollections of a Geographer* (London, 1933), 87–90, estimated that 1,700 people took the 6–12-week course between 1902 and 1933, including 890 candidates from the Colonial Office.

55 Grant Duff, 'Annual Address on the progress of geography', 358.

56 D. R. Stoddart, *On Geography and its History* (Oxford, 1986), 61.

57 J. R. Seeley, *The Expansion of England: Two Courses of Lectures* (London, 1883), 123.

· CHAPTER TWO ·
THE RACE TO THE SOUTH POLE

1 Quoted in D. Middleton, *Victorian Lady Travellers* (London, 1965), 39.

2 D. W. Freshfield to M. E. Grant Duff, 10 August 1892, Add. papers 93, Box 1, RGS. The RGS archives hold an extensive collection of papers on the dispute.

3 Transcript of 24 April 1893 meeting, Add. papers 93, Box 1, RGS.

4   'The Geographical Dinner to Mr. H. M. Stanley', *Proc. RGS*, NS 12 (1890), 495.

5   *The Times* archives do not record the identity of the correspondent, but there are three strong indications the '*bona fide* traveller' was Freshfield: (1) the detailed account of the dispute could only have come from someone with access to the RGS council. In an unpublished letter to *The Times*, 2 June 1893, Cave described the '*bona fide* traveller' as the 'mouthpiece of the Council', 12 June 1893, Cave corr. block 1881–1910, RGS. (2) The arguments put forward by the '*bona fide* traveller', repeat arguments Freshfield uses elsewhere. (3) Freshfield's letter to *The Times* of 3 July 1893 was a direct reply to Curzon's response to the '*bona fide* traveller', but makes no mention of the '*bona fide* traveller'.

6   'A *bona fide* traveller' to the Editor, *The Times*, 29 May 1893, 7; G. N. Curzon to the Editor, *The Times*, 31 May 1893, 11; D. W. Freshfield to the Editor, *The Times*, 3 June 1893, 6; G. N. Curzon to the Editor, *The Times*, 5 June 1893, 10.

7   *Punch*, 10 June 1893, 269; *Daily Telegraph*, 4 July 1893, G. N. Curzon scrapbook, MSS Eur F 111/131, Curzon Papers, Oriental and India Office Collections, British Library, London (hereafter India Office).

8   1,165 fellows supported the proposal that 'Ladies be eligible for election as ordinary Fellows', 100 supported the election of women 'under diverse restrictions', and only 465 supported the proposal that 'Ladies be absolutely excluded from participation in the Society', Add. papers 93, Box 1, RGS.

9   G. N. Curzon to J. S. Keltie, 18 May 1895, Curzon corr. block 1881–1910, RGS.

10 H. R. Mill, *The Record of the Royal Geographical Society, 1830–1930* (London, 1930), 135, states that the Earl of Northbrook was the council's first choice and that two other 'eminent personalities' were approached before Markham's appointment.

11 C. R. Markham, 'Royal Geographical Society' (unpublished MS *c.*1903), 471–2, Special Collection, CRM 47, RGS.

12 J. Murray, 'The Renewal of Antarctic Exploration', *GJ*, 3 (1894), 26.

13 C. R. Markham, 'The Present Standpoint of Geography', *GJ*, 2 (1893), 483.

14 C. R. Markham to G. N. Curzon, 9 November 1911, MSS Eur F 112/51, Curzon Papers, India Office.

15 A. H. Markham, *The Life of Sir Clements R. Markham* (London, 1917), 331.

16 'The International Geographical Congress', *GJ* 8 (1896), 292.

17 J. W. Gregory, quoted in *Nature*, 64 (1901), 84.

18 T. H. Baughman, *Before the Heroes Came: Antarctica in the 1890s* (Lincoln, Nebr., and London, 1994), p. x. See also, T. H. Baughman, *Pilgrims on the Ice: Robert Falcon Scott's First Antarctic Expedition* (Lincoln, Nebr., and London, 1999), 47, and R. Huntford, *Scott and Amundsen* (London, 1979), 143. Huntford claims 'the Gregory affair was hushed up'. The dispute in fact gained extensive press coverage.

19 See, among many, C. R. Markham, 'The President's Opening Address', *GJ* 13 (1899), 11.

20 C. R. Markham, 'Address to the RGS', *GJ* 4 (1894), 7; C. R. Markham, 'Address to the RGS, 1903', *GJ* 22 (1903), 10.

21 'The National Antarctic Expedition. Instructions to the Commander', *GJ* 18 (1901), 154.

22 C. R. Markham, *Antarctic Obsession: A Personal Narrative of the Origins of the British National Antarctic Expedition, 1901–1904*, ed. C. Holland (Alburgh, 1986), 42.

23 Baughman, *Pilgrims*, 228; D. Yelverton, *Antarctica Unveiled: Scott's First Expedition and the Quest for the Unknown Continent* (Boulder, Colo., 2000), 262. Scott lost his copy.

24 *Parliamentary Debates* (HC), 4th series, vol. cxxii (1903), col. 1808.

25 D. Arlidge, *The Rescue of Captain Scott* (East Linton, 1999) has recently retrieved McKay's role from obscurity. Anxious to claim that the dispatch of the *Terra Nova* had been unnecessary, Scott did not acknowledge McKay's contribution. But the crew's journals also suggest a widespread belief that the release of the ship was primarily an act of providence, rather than, as Arlidge argues, a result of McKay's skilful work.

26 'In the Cause of Science', *Pall Mall Gazette*, 17 September 1904, 1; leader, *The Times*, 10 September 1904, 9.

27 Quoted in H. Ludlam, *Captain Scott: The Full Story* (London, 1965), 102.

28 L. Huxley, *The House of Smith Elder* (London, 1923), 243; 'Farthest South', *Spectator*, 14 October 1905, 566–7.

29 Leader, *The Times*, 10 September 1904, 9; 'Return of the National Antarctic Expedition', *GJ* 24 (1904), 383.

30 J. W. Gregory, 'The Work of the National Antarctic Expedition', *Nature*, 25 January 1906, 297–300; Yelverton, *Antarctica Unveiled*, app. 9, 'The Meteorological Office Blunder'.

31 L. C. Bernacchi, *Saga of the Discovery* (London, 1938), 113.

32 G. E. Fogg, *A History of Antarctic Science* (Cambridge, 1992), 118–20.

33 C. R. Markham to R. F. Scott, 9 October 1903, *GJ* 22 (1903), 688; R. F. Scott, *The Voyage of the Discovery* (2 vols., London, 1905), i. 467–8.

34 R. Gregory to J. L. Bernacchi, 15 January 1940, quoted in R. Pound, *Scott of the Antarctic* (London, 1966), 122.

35 Quoted in D. Preston, *A First Rate Tragedy: Captain Scott's Antarctic Expeditions* (London, 1997), 81.

36 Quoted in R. Huntford, *Shackleton* (London, 1985), 298.

37 J. S. Keltie to G. N. Curzon, 5 January 1914, Curzon corr. block 1911–20, RGS.

38 R. F. Scott to L. Darwin, no date (September 1909), quoted in Pound, *Scott*, 174.

39 R. F. Scott, 'Plans of the British Antarctic Expedition, 1910', *GJ* 36 (1910), 12.

40 Quoted in G. Seaver, *Edward Wilson of the Antarctic: Naturalist and Firend* (London, 1933), 182.

41 Before taking up their posts with the expedition, Simpson worked at the Indian Meteorological Office in Simla; Wright worked at the Cavendish Laboratory in Cambridge; Nelson worked at the Plymouth Laboratory as an invertebrate zoologist; Debenham was a recent graduate from Sydney University; Priestley worked at both the University of Sydney and the University of Cambridge with Prof. Edgeworth David on the geological specimens he had collected on Shackleton's *Nimrod* expedition; Griffith Taylor worked as a physiographer for the Australian weather service; and Wilson worked for the government commission investigating grouse disease.

42 C. R. Markham, Notebook on BAE, 1910–13, MS 715/9, SPRI. Finance committee minutes, 15 July 1910, RGS, also record that the RGS presented Scott with £670 remaining from the *Discovery* fund.

43 *Vanity Fair*, 13 January 1910, and E. R. G. R. Evans quoted in R. Pound,

Evans of the Broke: A Biography of Admiral Lord Mountevans (London, 1963), 57 and 55.

44 Teddy Evans claimed 8,000 applicants in *Scott's Last Expedition* (2 vols., London, 1913), ii 498, but James Lees-Milne, *Ancestral Voices* (London, 1975), 32, records 6,000 as the number related to him by Kathleen Scott.

45 'Luncheon to British Antarctic Expedition, 1910', *GJ* 36 (1910), 21–2.

46 Huntford, *Scott and Amundsen*, 265 and 278–9.

47 Unless otherwise stated, quotations in the following account of the expedition are from the participants' original journals.

48 S. Limb and P. Cordingley, *Captain Oates: Soldier and Explorer* (revised edn., London, 1995), 168–9.

49 J. Fuller, *Troop Morale and Popular Culture in the British and Dominion Armies, 1914–18* (Oxford, 1990).

50 R. Huntford, *Nansen: The Explorer as Hero* (London, 1997), 463–5. Compare with Huntford, *Scott and Amundsen*, 545–6.

51 *With Captain Scott to the South Pole* (first series), programme for London Coliseum, 16 November 1911, uncatalogued folder of ephemera on *Discovery & Terra Nova*, SPRI; 'RN' was not always included in the title of Ponting's films. *Bioscope*, 23 November 1911, 583 and 14 December 1911, 745.

52 Limb and Cordingley, *Oates*, 196.

53 *Punch*, 20 March 1912, 203.

54 *The Times*, 1 April 1912, 8.

55 *With Captain Scott, RN, to the South Pole* (second series), programme for Palace Theatre, 16 August 1912, section (f), MS 280/28/7, SPRI; *Encore* quoted in *Bioscope*, 29 August 1912, p. xxxii.

56 Huntford, *Scott and Amundsen*, 549.

57 *Illustrated London News*, 18 May 1912, 757–71; 'The South Pole', *Manchester Guardian*, 10 March 1912, 6.

58 G. H., 'How the South Pole Was Won. The Last Big Prize Left to the World's Explorers', *Young England*, January 1913, 151; I. S. Robson, 'The Conquest of the South Pole. Dr. Roald Amundsen's Dash into the Antarctic', *Boy's Own Annual*, 35 (1912–13), 281.

59 R. Amundsen, *My Life as an Explorer* (London, 1927), 72.

60 C. R. Markham to K. Scott, 24 July 1912, MS 9, SPRI; R. F. Scott, 'Antarctic Expedition for 1910', 15 September 1909, MS 280/28/3, SPRI.

61   'Mother Earth', *Pall Mall Gazette*, 9 March 1912, 6; C. R. Markham to the
      Editor, *The Times*, 1 April 1912, 11; 'Captain Scott's Expedition', *The Times*,
      2 April 1912, 9.

62   H.G. Ponting to the Editor, *The Times*, 19 November 1912, 7; *The Times*, 16
      November 1912, 6; R. Amundsen, *The South Pole: An Account of the
      Norweigion Antarctic Expedition in the Fram, 1910–1912* (2 vols., London,
      1912), i. 44.

63   C. R. Markham to K. Scott, 12 March 1912, MS 9, SPRI.

64   Copy of L. Darwin to L. Beaumont, 29 October 1912, enclosed with
      L. Darwin to K. Scott, 31 October 1912, MS 1453/71, SPRI; L. Darwin to
      K. Scott, no date [March–April 1912], MS 1453/71, SPRI.

65   A. Cherry-Garrard, *The Worst Journey in the World* (2 vols., London, 1922),
      ii. 443.

66   Quoted in K. Rose, *Superior Person: A Portrait of Curzon and his Circle
      in Late Victorian England* (London, 1969), 73–4. See also M. Bell
      and C. McEwan, 'The Admission of Women Fellows to the Royal
      Geographical Society 1892–1914: The Controversy and the Outcome', *GJ*
      162 (1996), 298–301. By 1912 teaching had been established as a respectable
      middle-class profession, with women accounting for around 75 per cent
      of schoolteachers in England and Wales. The Geological, Linnean, and
      Royal Microscopical Societies had admitted women to full fellowship
      rights in 1904, 1905, and 1909 respectively.

67   Note, J. S. Keltie to G. N. Curzon, 24 October 1913, Curzon corr. block
      1911–20, RGS: 'Between the elections on November 10 and those on
      November 24 we should thus have something like 150 new members
      altogether which means £1200. This, so far as I recollect, is the record.'

· CHAPTER THREE ·
DISASTER IN THE ANTARCTIC

1   This report, attributed to Teddy Evans, was published in many newspapers,
      including the *Daily Express*, 11 February 1913, 1.

2   'Victory and Death', *Daily Express*, 11 February 1913, 4.

3   A. Cherry-Garrard diary, 10 February 1913, MS 559/11, SPRI.

4   I have assembled the account which follows from newspaper reports in

Britain and New Zealand, J. J. Kinsey's correspondence in SPRI, and
Norman Meikle to RGS, 23 February 1970, R. F. Scott, Lbr. MSS 6, RGS.
Meikle recounted a meeting with the telegraphist, who claimed to have
sent the cable from Oamaru.

5   *Pall Mall Gazette*, 10 February 1913, MS 1453/40, SPRI.

6   See correspondence regarding the contract in MS 1453/61, SPRI. The
    agency had originally offered £3,000, but reduced their bid after Scott
    insisted the agency not enter into exclusive contracts with individual
    publications, but instead offer his dispatches to all newspapers at a
    reasonable price; H. Simonis, *The Street of Ink: An Intimate History of
    Journalism* (London, 1917), 169.

7   *Daily Telegraph*, 11 February 1913, 7.

8   The committee comprised Surgeon Atkinson, RN, Lt. Pennell, RN, Lt.
    Victor Campbell, RN, Lt. Wilfrid M. Bruce, RNR, and Francis Drake,
    Assistant Paymaster, RN (retired). A. Cherry-Gerrard diary, 28 January
    1913, MS 559/11, SPRI. The *Daily Express* noted that the report was pub-
    lished in successive special editions up to 6.30 a.m., as it arrived through
    the night on Tuesday, 11 February; *Daily Express*, 12 February 1913, 1.

9   *Daily Express*, 12 February 1913, 2. The entire report, sent from
    Christchurch and signed by Teddy Evans, was published in almost every
    national daily newspaper on Tuesday 11 or Wednesday 12 February. Quota-
    tions from Scott's journals differed slightly from the original verson in
    places.

10 A. Cherry-Garrard diary, 12 February 1913, MS 559/11, SPRI.

11 Kinsey wrote that a cable of 1,381 words was dispatched on 13 February,
    and a cable of 2,280 words on 14 February, J. J. Kinsey to H. Brett, 24 June
    1913, MS 559/164, SPRI.

12 'A Brave Man and an English Gentleman', *Daily Graphic*, 12 February
    1913, 4. For Curzon's letter see, among many, *Daily Chronicle*, 15
    February 1913, 7.

13 'Honour to the Brave', *Aberdeen Express*, (15 February 1913), and *Newport
    Advertiser*, no date, MS 1453/40, SPRI (the scrapbook MS 1453/40 contains
    an extensive collection of press reports on the disaster); *Wide-World
    Magazine*, August 1913, 8.

14 'Circulation of the *Daily Chronicle*', *Advertising World*, February 1914,
    239–40; 'Circulation of the *Daily Mirror*', *Circulation Manager*, February
    1914, 17.

15 *Parliamentary Debates* (HC), 5th series, vol. xlviii, 12 February 1913, col. 993, 14 February 1913, cols. 1430–1; quotations from *Daily Telegraph*, 12 February 1913, 11–12; *GJ* 41 (1913), 221–2; *Evening News*, 12 February 1913, MS 1453/40, SPRI

16 W. R. Inge diary, 14 February 1913, Inge Papers, Magdalene College, Cambridge; *British Weekly*, 20 February 1913, 609 and 603; *Weekly Press* (New Zealand), 19 February 1913, MS 1453/40, SPRI.

17 *British Weekly*, 20 February 1913, 610.

18 K. Scott diary, 25 February 1913, part II D/5, Kennet Papers, Cambridge University Library.

19 *Parliamentary Debates* (HC), 5th series, vol. xlviii, 11 February 1913, col. 718; *The Times*, 12 February 1913, 6. HM Secretary to the Admiralty to HM Secretary to the Treasury, 20 February 1913, T164/404, PRO, stated that the declaration did not affect the level of pension to which Mrs Evans was entitled.

20 L. Beaumont to K. Scott, 15 March 1913, MS 2, SPRI, offers a detailed narrative of the organization of the memorial funds.

21 *Daily Chronicle*, 12 February 1913, 1; *Daily Telegraph*, 12 February 1913, 11.

22 'The People's Tribute to the Heroes of the Antarctic', Pam. 77220, Guildhall library, London; 'For Every One', *Daily Express*, 17 February 1913, 6.

23 *Daily Telegraph*, 12 February 1913, 11. When the *Scotsman* asked subscribers to earmark a specific purpose for their donation, the vast majority indicated provision for the bereaved.

24 'The Debt of Honour', *Daily Express*, 14 February 1913, 4; *Daily News and Leader*, 19 February 1913, 1.

25 *The Times*, 22 February 1913, 5; *The Times*, 25 February 1913, 6.

26 'The Captain Scott Fund – Report of the Committee', MS 1464/5, SPRI. A number of authors have quoted more specific figures, without giving sources. 'Captain Scott Memorial Mansion House Fund – Receipts and Payments Account from 13th February 1913, to 28th April 1926', uncatalogued folder titled 'History of SPRI. Capt. Scott's Antarctic Fund', SPRI, quotes 'Per Mansion House – 76,059.19.4'. In addition to the relatives of the dead, the Mansion House committee also established trust funds for the wife and child of Mr Brissenden, a sailor who drowned while conducting survey work in New Zealand during the expedition, and

the wife of Mr Abbott, a Chief Petty Officer who 'became insane in consequence of the privations endured'.

27 G. Egerton to W. Churchill, 10 April 1913, uncatalogued biographical folder, 'R. F. Scott UDC 92', SPRI.

28 See table titled 'British Antarctic Expedition', T164/404, PRO. Also see 'Private and Confidential, Exhibit C – Circumstances of Dependants', 9 May 1913, uncatalogued folder titled 'History of SPRI. Capt. Scott's Antarctic Fund', SPRI.

29 *The Times*, 19 March 1913, 12 and 21 April 1913, 5. I have used *The Times* as a primary source for information on the fund, because the 'marked copies' in *The Times* archives, which mark the names of authors over anonymous articles, indicate that the secretary of the fund, Sir William Soulsby, wrote the reports about the Mansion House Scott memorial fund for *The Times*.

30 *Truth*, 26 March 1913, 762; *The Times*, 7 August 1913, 8.

31 The Principal of La Martiniere School, Calcutta, to J. S. Keltie, 8 and 9 April 1913, R. F. Scott corr. block 1911–20, file (j) 'Memorial Fund corr.', RGS; Letter to H. Scott, 26 February 1913, MS 1464/23, SPRI; correspondence with K. Scott in MS 1453/162, SPRI; pesos in MS 1453/31, SPRI.

32 *The Times*, 11 February 1913, 10; C. R. Markham, '*Adeste Fideles*: I. Robert Falcon Scott', *Cornhill Magazine*, 34 (1913), 464.

33 D. Freshfield to G. N. Curzon, 10 February 1913, MSS Eur F 112/51, Curzon Papers, India Office; J. Gennings to J. J. Kinsey, 14 February 1913, MS 559/164, SPRI; A. Cherry-Garrard diary, 14 February 1913, MS 559/11, SPRI.

34 Scott actually described Evans as the 'strongest' man of the party, an error corrected in the version of the 'Message to the Public' published in 1913. See Appendix 2.

35 'A Fight against Fatality', *Daily Mail*, 12 February 1913, 4; H. D. Rawnsley, 'In Memory of Petty Officer Edgar Evans', *British Review*, April 1913, 83; G. N. Curzon, 'Address by the Right Hon. Earl Curzon of Kedleston', *GJ* 41 (1913), 212.

36 *Daily Express*, 12 February 1913, 1; *Observer*, 16 February 1913, 8.

37 Anon. [J.E. Hodder Williams], *Like English Gentlemen* (London, 1913), 37, 40–1, and 52. An abridged edition was published in 1916 under Hodder Williams's name.

38 'Captain Scott's End', *Daily News and Leader*, 12 February 1913, 6.

39 *John Bull*, 8 March 1913, 345.

40 *The Times*, 17 February 1913, 6; A. Cherry-Garrard diary, 21 February 1913, MS 559/11, SPRI.

41 'An Awfully Big Adventure', *Daily Express*, 12 February 1913, 4; *Daily Chronicle*, 13 February 1913, 1.

42 R. Huntford, *Nansen: The Explorer as Hero* (London, 1997), 459–60.

43 Note, among many, *Daily Mail*, 11 February 1913, 5 and *Daily Telegraph*, 13 February 1913, 12.

44 H. D. Rawnsley, 'To the Heroes of the *Terra Nova*', *Daily News and Leader*, 12 February 1913, 6 and *British Review*, April 1913, 80.

45 Quoted in R. Huntford, *Shackleton* (1985), 666.

46 S. Solomon, *The Coldest March: Scott's Fatal Antarctic Expedition* (New Haven and London, 2001), esp. 279–81.

47 Handwritten note, 16 April [1913], MSS Eur F 112/51, Curzon Papers, India Office; L. Beaumont to K. Scott, 18 April 1913, MS 2, SPRI.

48 R. Huntford, *Scott and Amundsen* (London, 1979), 560.

49 M. de-la-Noy, *Scott of the Antarctic* (Thrupp, 1997), 60. See also L. Bloom, *Gender on Ice: American Ideologies of Polar Expeditions* (Minneapolis and London, 1993), 122.

50 H. Leach, 'The Heart of Things', *Chambers's Journal*, 7th ser., 4 (1913–14), 50; Markham, '*Adeste Fideles* I. Robert Falcon Scott', 464.

51 I examined the leading articles on the Antarctic disaster published in the *Daily Chronicle* (3 leaders), *Daily Express* (4), *Daily Graphic* (4), *Daily Mail* (4), *Daily Mirror* (3), *Daily News and Leader* (2), *Daily Sketch* (5), *Daily Telegraph* (2), *Evening News* (3), *Manchester Guardian* (3), *Pall Mall Gazette* (2), *Scotsman* (3), and *The Times* (3), between 10 and 15 February 1913.

52 *Manchester Guardian*, 12 February 1913, 7; *Westminster Gazette*, 13 February 1913, 2.

53 *Scotsman*, 18 February 1913, 11; 24 February 1913, 9; 25 February 1913, 9; 28 February 1913, 9.

54 *The Times*, 14 January 1914, 4.

55 A. H. Harrison, 'The Control of British Polar Exploration', *Nineteenth Century*, 71 (1912), 766.

56 A. H. Harrison, 'Antarctic Exploration: A Question of Methods', *Nineteenth Century*, 73 (1913), 528 and 533.

57 Quoted in, G. Seaver, '*Birdie*' *Bowers of the Antarctic* (London, 1938), 250.

58 G. N. Curzon to J. S. Keltie, 21 August 1913, Curzon corr. block 1911–20, RGS.

59 Huntford, *Scott and Amundsen*, 563.

60 Huntford, *Shackleton*, 360. See also Bloom, *Gender on Ice*, 113, and C. Alexander, *The Endurance: Shackleton's Legendary Antarctic Expedition* (London, 1998), 9.

61 K. Scott diary, 27/28 February 1913, part II D/5, Kennet Papers, Cambridge University Library; *The Times*, 5 March 1913, 7.

62 R. Pound, *The Strand Magazine, 1891–1950* (London, 1966), 12; H. G. Smith corr. with K. Scott, May 1913, MS 1453/175, SPRI.

63 *Outlook*, 8 September 1928, MS 1453/41, SPRI; G. N. Curzon to K. Scott, 17 April 1913, MS 841/1/1, SPRI.

64 See L. Beaumont correspondence with K. Scott, May–October 1913, MS 2, SPRI.

65 See, for example, L. Huxley note attached to R. J. Smith to A. Cherry-Garrard, 12 June 1913, MS 559/126/3, SPRI. Note also, Assistant to the Director of SPRI to Major Meade of Ealing Studios, 29 April 1947, section (g), MS 280/28/7, SPRI: 'Leonard Huxley, the Editor, was responsible for the footnotes and Appendix to the first volume of "Scott's Last Expedition" as published by Smith, Elder and Co. in 1913. Most of the surviving members of the Expedition who were available in England were consulted in connection with the compilation of these notes, but I think it is safe to assume that the bulk of them originated with Mr. A. Cherry Garrard'.

66 A. Cherry-Garrard diary, 3 March 1913, MS 559/11, SPRI.

67 S. Wheeler, *Terra Incognita: Travels in Antarctica* (London, 1996), 59. SPRI deny the accusation.

68 R. E. Priestley diary, 27 November 1912, MS 298/6/2, SPRI; W. M. Bruce diary, 1, no date [1913], MS 402/4, SPRI.

69 *Daily Mail*, 14 February 1913, 5. For Evans's comments see, among many, *Daily Express*, 17 February 1913, 1. Tryggve Gran quoted in P. King (ed.), *Scott's Last Journey* (London, 1999), 7.

70 L. Huxley, *The House of Smith Elder* (London, 1923), 243; *Daily Graphic*, 6 November 1913, 7; *Bookseller*, 14 November 1913, 1602.

71 *British Weekly*, 13 November 1913, 199, *Westminster Gazette*, 6 November 1913, 1; 'The Hero as Explorer', *Nation*, 8 November 1913, 260.

72 A. Cherry-Garrard diary, 26 January and 3 March 1913, MS 559/11, SPRI.

73 J. Kinsey to J. Gennings, 17 April 1913, MS 559/164, SPRI.

74 L. Beaumont to K. Scott, 15 July 1913, MS 2, SPRI; H. G. Ponting to F. Debenham, 7 January 1920, section(a), MS 280/28/7, SPRI.

75 J. S. Keltie to J. Charcot, 20 February 1913, R. F. Scott corr. block 1911–20, file (j) 'Memorial Fund corr.', RGS.

76 E. R. G. R. Evans to C. Oates, 13 April 1913, MS 1016/345, SPRI.

· CHAPTER FOUR ·

REMEMBERING THE DEAD

1 *Truth*, 26 February 1913, 495.

2 'The Majesty of Death', *Aberdeen Journal*, no date (probably 15 February 1913), MS 1453/40, SPRI; C. D. MacKellar to J. S. Keltie, 13 February 1913, R. F. Scott corr. block 1911–20, file (j) 'Memorial Fund corr.', RGS.

3 *Daily Telegraph*, 15 February 1913, 11.

4 E. T. Wilson to R. J. Smith, 14 February 1913, MS 559/147/1, SPRI. Also see 'W' to the Editor, *The Times*, 19 February 1913, 5.

5 *The Times*, 20 April 1874, 12.

6 *The Times*, 9 January 1874, 7.

7 G. N. Curzon, 'Address by the Right Hon. Earl Curzon of Kedleston', *GJ* 41 (1913), 212.

8 G. Scott to J. S. Keltie, 18 February 1913, R. F. Scott corr. block 1911–20, file (j) 'Memorial Fund corr.', RGS; *Guardian*, 21 February 1913, 231 and 258; *Bioscope*, 20 February 1913, 547.

9 *Daily Chronicle*, 15 February 1913, 7; 'In Memoriam', *The Times*, 15 February 1913, 9; T. B. Hennell, 'St. Paul's, February 14', *Daily Mirror*, 14 February 1913, 3.

10 *Guardian*, 21 February 1913, 259.

11 *Daily Mirror*, 15 February 1913, 4. *Westminster Gazette*, 14 February 1913, 8, also reported that the crowds outside the cathedral took up the anthem.

12 Cabinet letters 1913–14, MS Asquith 7, Department of Western Manuscripts, Bodleian Library, Oxford; J. S. Keltie to G. N. Curzon, 13 February 1913, R. F. Scott corr. block 1911–20, file (j) 'Curzon corr. re. disaster', RGS.

13 See, for example, *Daily Telegraph*, 15 February 1913, 7; 'In Memoriam', *Daily Express*, 15 February 1913, 4; Curzon, 'Address', 216.

14 'Presentation of Medals and Other Awards', *GJ* 42 (1913), 88–9; O. Wilson

to J. S. Keltie, 26 April 1913, R. F. Scott corr. block 1911–20, file (d) 'misc. corr. referring to the BAE', RGS.

15 *The Times*, 22 May 1913, 9–10; J. S. Keltie to C. K. Brooke, 19 May 1913, R. F. Scott corr. block 1911–20, file (j) 'Albert Hall Meeting', RGS; 'The British Antarctic Expedition – Reception at the Albert Hall', *GJ* 42 (1913), 28; F. Drake to J. S. Keltie, 6 June 1913, R. F. Scott corr. block 1911–20, file (d) Misc. corr. re. BAE, RGS.

16 *The Times*, 28 April 1913, 9.

17 'The Captain Scott Fund – Report of the Committee', July 1913, MS 1464/5, SPRI

18 H. Lawson to G. N. Curzon, 13 June 1913, MSS Eur F 112/53, Curzon Papers, India Office.

19 Handwritten sheet, no date [June–July 1913], MSS Eur F 112/53, Curzon Papers, India Office.

20 *Parliamentary Debates* (HL), 5th series, 14, 6 August 1913, col. 1628.

21 L. Earle telegram to F. Ponsonby, Royal Yacht, Cowes, no date, and F. Ponsonby telegram to L. Earle, no date, WORKS 20/121, PRO.

22 *Parliamentary Debates* (HL), 5th series, 14, 6 August 1913, cols. 1628–9.

23 See correspondence in *The Times*, 7 August 1913, 5; 9 August 1913, 5, 12 August 1913, 11; and 18 August 1913, 4.

24 W. Soulsby to G. N. Curzon, 3 November and 12 November 1913, MSS Eur F 112/53, Curzon Papers, India Office.

25 G. N. Curzon, 'Address to the Royal Geographical Society', *GJ* 42 (1913), 3; G. N. Curzon to K. Scott, 29 May 1913, MS 4, SPRI. Kathleen Scott also made no reference to the deposit of Scott's sledging journals with the RGS in a letter to Curzon written on the day of the medals ceremony, 26 May 1913, MSS Eur F 112/51, Curzon Papers, India Office.

26 G. N. Curzon to K. Scott, 19 October 1913, MS 4, SPRI; K. Scott to G. N. Curzon, 21 October 1913, R. F. Scott corr. block 1911–20, file (b) 'corr. with Lady Scott etc.', RGS.

27 G. N. Curzon to K. Scott, 24 October 1913, MS 4, SPRI.

28 G. N. Curzon to Lady Ellison-Macartney, 27 February 1913, MS 1464/23, SPRI; see correspondence in R. F. Scott corr. block 1911–20, file (b) 'corr. with Lady Scott etc.', RGS. Scott's sister Ettie had married the Unionist MP, William Ellison-Macartney in 1897.

29 Board of Trustees of the British Museum standing committee minutes, 10

January 1914, 3174, British Museum, London; F. Kenyon to K. Scott, no date (January 1914), MS 1453/123/10, SPRI. Kenyon brought the journals to the Museum on 18 December 1913.

30 '57th Annual Report of the Trustees of the National Portrait Gallery, 1913–14', 10–11, *National Portrait Gallery Annual Reports, 1900–1939* and Minutes of the Board of Trustees of the National Portrait Gallery, 12 February 1914, 9 (1913–17), 43, Heinz Archives, National Portrait Gallery, London.

31 *Builder*, 17 July 1914, 72. See also L. Earle to W. Soulsby, 9 July 1914, WORKS 20/121, PRO; *Builder*, 19 June 1914, 728. A reproduction of Babb's unsuccessful design was printed in the *Builder*, 9 March 1917, 164–5, while the model submitted by Derwent Wood is in the RGS's collection.

32 *Builder*, 9 March 1917, 164.

33 *The Times*, 11 July 1914, 6. This description was supplied to *The Times* by Sir William Soulsby. A. Hodge to A. Cherry-Garrard, 15 July 1914, MS 559/76/1, SPRI.

34 *Builder*, 15 August 1913, 163.

35 D. Freshfield to T. Brock, 21 August 1914; T. Brock to D. Freshfield, 31 August 1914; D. Freshfield to J. S. Keltie, 3 September 1914; T. Brock to D. Freshfield, 30 September 1914, R. F. Scott corr. block 1911–20, file (g) 're. Scott memorial fund', RGS.

36 *Builder*, 17 July 1914, 72.

37 See corr. in R. F. Scott corr. block 1911–20, file (b) 'corr. with Lady Scott etc.', RGS.

38 R. M. D. Hodge to W. Soulsby, 24 January 1918, WORKS 20/121, PRO. Roderick Hodge noted that his brother had completed: (1) scale drawings and full-size drawings for the granite pylon; (2) the four relief panels in plaster; (3) the portrait medallion and ornament on the pedestal in plaster; (4) the statue of Captain Scott; (5) a model for the revised design for the figure of 'Victory'. 'Before my brother died he expressed a wish that Mr. Doman and myself who have been his assistants during the progress of work, should be permitted to finish it from his design', overseen by a 'sculptor of eminence', such as Brock.

39 See correspondence in WORKS 20/121, PRO.

40 'Memorials to the Antarctic Heroes', *GJ* 44 (1914), 214–16.

41 A.M. Johnson, *Scott of the Antarctic and Cardiff* (revised edn., Cardiff, 1995).

42   G. Seaver, *Edward Wilson of the Antarctic: Naturalist and Friend* (London, 1933), 11–12; G. D. Robin to H. Scott, 5 April 1913, MS 1464/23, SPRI.

43   *Church Times*, 7 November 1913, 649.

44   E. Bowers to Lady Ellison-Macartney, 12 February 1914, MS 1464/23, SPRI; 'Memorial to Lieutenant Bowers', *GJ* 44 (1914), 320.

45   See uncatalogued memorials folder, 'L. E. G. Oates 92 (093.5)', SPRI; S. Limb and P. Cordingley, *Captain Oates: Soldier and Explorer* (revised edn., London, 1995), 211.

46   See correspondence in WORKS 20/127, PRO.

47   L. Earle to W. Graham Greene, 20 January 1914, WORKS 20/127, PRO.

48   L. Beaumont to K. Scott, 12 November 1914, MS 2, SPRI.

49   *Wide-World Magazine*, June 1913. See also *The Times*, 27 June 1913, 77; *Sphere*, 5 July 1913, 18–19.

50   K. Scott to E. R. G. R. Evans, 27 June 1913, MS 1453/153/1, SPRI.

51   This commemorative pattern had deep roots. In her study of monuments erected after the Napoleonic Wars, Alison Yarrington concluded that 'public awareness and appreciation of patriotic heroism was manifested on a local rather than a national level, provincial monuments of national heroes with strong local connections being more successful overall than large national monuments raised in London.' A. Yarrington, *The Commemoration of the Hero 1800–1864: Monuments to the British Victors of the Napoleonic Wars* (New York and London, 1988), 327.

· CHAPTER FIVE ·
'MARTYRS OF SCIENCE'

1   King George V to G. N. Curzon, 10 February 1913, Curzon Papers, MSS Eur F 112/51, India Office.

2   J. S. Keltie to G. N. Curzon, 11 February 1913, R. F. Scott. corr. block 1911–20, file (j) 'Curzon corr.', RGS.

3   *Daily Mail*, 15 February 1913, 3.

4   Leader, *Scotsman*, 15 February 1913, 8; 'The Antarctic Disaster', *The Times*, 11 February 1913, 9.

5   C. R. Markham, 'Robert Falcon Scott', *GJ* 41 (1913), 220; *Morning*

Post quoted in *Surrey Comet*, no date, MS 1453/40, SPRI; 'The British Antarctic Expedition', *Nature*, 13 February 1913, 650.

6   *Daily Mirror*, 12 February 1913, 10–11.

7   H. R. Mill to the Editor, *The Times*, 2 April 1912, 10.

8   'Captain Scott's Message', *The Times*, 12 February 1913, 7.

9   *British Weekly*, 20 February 1913, 609; 'Gallant Gentlemen', *Evening News*, 14 February 1913, 4.

10 F. Young, 'Is It Worth It?', *Saturday Review*, 15 February 1913, 202.

11 L. Darwin, 'Address to the Royal Geographical Society', *GJ* 38 (1911), 3.

12 G. N. Curzon, 'Address to the Royal Geographical Society', *GJ* 42 (1913), 1 and 4.

13 R. F. Scott corr. block 1911–20, file (h) 'condolences', RGS. The RGS received letters of condolence from the geographical societies of Leeds and Yorkshire, Liverpool, Manchester, Scotland, Tyneside, Adelaide, Algeria and North Africa, America, Anvers, Argentina, Australasia, Barcelona, Brussels, Chicago, Denmark, Geneva, Hungary, Le Mans, Lima, Lisbon, Madrid, Marseilles, Norway, Paris, Philadelphia, Rome, Russia, Sweden, and Vienna as well as the Dutch Geographical Society, the National Geographical Society (USA), and the Peary Arctic Club.

14 See, for example, R. Huntford, *Nansen: The Explorer as Hero* (London, 1997), 249, 362, and 379

15 Turkestan Section of Imperial Russian Geographical Society to RGS, 14 April 1913; Geographical Institute of Argentina to RGS, 13 February 1913; Geographical Society of Geneva to RGS, 13 February 1913; R. F. Scott corr. block 1911–20, file (h) 'condolences', RGS.

16 *Daily News and Leader*, 12 February 1913, 1; J. Charcot to J. S. Keltie, 22 March 1913, R. F. Scott corr. block 1911–20, file (e) 'Corr. with Dr. Charcot', RGS.

17 A street was named after Scott in Antwerp (*The Times*, 29 September 1913, 9), while monuments were erected on the Col du Lautaret (see R. F. Scott corr. block 1911–10, file (e) 'Corr. with Dr Charcot', RGS) and in Finse (see uncatalogued memorials folder, R. F. Scott 92 (093.5), SPRI).

18 'The British Antarctic Expedition – Reception at the Albert Hall', *GJ* 42 (1913), 10; 'The Annual Dinner', *GJ* 42 (1913), 97.

19 *The Times*, 2 February 1914, 7 and 10 February 1914, 7; *GJ* 43 (1914), 343.

20 Diploma issued by the Hungarian Geographical Society, 5 February 1914, R. F. Scott corr. block 1911–20, file (e) 'Corr. with Dr. Charcot', RGS.

21 *The Times*, 27 January 1914, 5 and 28 January 1914, 5; E. R. G. R. Evans to J. S. Keltie, 7 February 1914, R. F. Scott corr. block 1911–20, file (d) 'Misc. corr. referring to the BAE', RGS; J. Charcot to J. S. Keltie, 29 January 1914, R. F. Scott corr. block 1911–20, file (e) 'Corr. with Dr. Charcot', RGS; *Bioscope*, 29 January 1914, 484.

22 'To the South Pole. Captain Scott's Own Story, Told From His Journals', Part I, *Strand Magazine*, July 1913, 3.

23 'To the South Pole, etc.', Part II, *Strand Magazine*, August 1913, 137–8; G.R., 'In Memoriam. Edward Adrian Wilson – I', *Alpine Journal*, 27 (1913), 212.

24 C. R. Markham, 'Preface', *Scott's Last Expedition* (London, 1913), vol. i, p. vi.

25 Quoted in K. Lambert, *'Hell with a Capital H': An Epic Story of Antarctic Survival* (London, 2002), 133.

26 C. R. Markham *'Scott's Last Expedition'*, GJ 43 (1914), 18–19.

27 F. Debenham, 'The Geological History of South Victoria Land', *Scott's Last Expedition*, ii. 437.

28 'Scott's Last Expedition', *The Times*, 6 November 1913, 9.

29 H. Leach, 'The Heart of Things', *Chambers's Journal*, 7th ser., 4 (1913–14), 49.

30 Ibid. 674–5.

31 H. J. P. Arnold, *Photographer of the World: The Biography of Herbert Ponting* (London, 1969), 36.

32 H. G. Ponting, *The Great White South* (London, 1921), 1.

33 *Daily Mirror*, 12 February 1913, 4–5.

34 FAS exhibition sale book December 1912–July 1917, FAS.

35 *Daily Mirror*, 12 February 1913, 7.

36 H. G. Ponting to A. Cherry-Garrard, 17 December 1913, MS 559/102/2, SPRI.

37 M.B.H., 'Prefatory note', FAS Ponting exhibition catalogue, December 1913, FAS.

38 *Bioscope*, 26 March 1914, 1336; 14 May 1914, 689; 21 May 1914, 807, 819, and 865.

39 F. Whelan Boyle, 'Personal Reminiscences of Men who have Made Themselves Famous in Arctic or Antarctic Travel. Part II', *Boy's Own Annual*, 38 (1915–16), 168.

40 Copy of T. Roosevelt to H. G. Ponting, 16 June 1914, section (a), MS 280/28/7, SPRI.

41 *The Times*, 13 May 1914, 1; *Daily News and Leader* quoted in programmes for 'Ponting's Polar Pictures – With Captain Scott in the Antarctic', section (f) no.7, MS 280/28/7, SPRI; H. G. Ponting to A. Hinks (RGS secretary), 7 December 1917, MS 964/10/6, SPRI.

42 Programme for H. G. Ponting lecture, no date [1914], uncatalogued folder of ephemera on *Discovery & Terra Nova*, SPRI; Ponting, *Great White South*, 166.

43 H. G. Ponting to K. Scott, 10 February 1917, MS 15, SPRI. Although none of Ponting's scripts survives, the programme for 'With Scott in the Antarctic', section (f) no.4, MS 280/28/7, SPRI, includes a detailed synopsis.

44 Quoted in H. G. Ponting, 'Some Observations upon the Desirability of the Acquisition of the Moving-picture Record of the Scott South Pole Expedition being Taken in Hand by a Public Body', 17, no date [1917–19], section (a), MS 280/28/7, SPRI.

45 'The British Antarctic Expedition – Reception at the Albert Hall', *GJ* 42 (1913), 10.

46 M. B. H., 'Prefatory note', 5–6; programme for H. G. Ponting lecture, no date (1914), uncatalogued folder of ephemera on *Discovery and Terra Nova*, SPRI.

47 G. Sweven, *Riallaro: The Archipelago of Exiles* (London, 1901) and sequel *Limanora: The Island of Progress* (London, 1903). Sweven was a pseudonym for John Macmillan Brown. F. Lancaster Cordes, ' "Tekelili" or Hollow Earth Lives: A Bibliography of Antarctic Fiction', unpublished MA thesis, San Francisco State University (1991).

48 *Bioscope*, 29 January 1914, 400; R. Low, *The History of the British Film, vol. ii: 1906–14* (London, 1973 [1948]), 155.

49 G. Seaver, *Edward Wilson of the Antarctic: Naturalist and Friend* (London, 1933), 65, 69–70, 101.

50 Ibid. 151.

51 C.W., 'In Memoriam. Edward Adrian Wilson – II', *Alpine Journal*, 27 (1913), 213.

52 E. Davidson, 'Valedictory Address', *Alpine Journal*, 28 (1914), 11; Alpine Club Council minutes, addendum to minutes of 10 June 1913, 7 October 1913, 4 November 1913, 15 December 1913, 13 January 1914, Alpine Club, London.

53 *The Times*, 5 December 1913; *Evening Standard*, 10 December 1913; *Manchester Guardian*, 5 December 1913, Alpine Club press cuttings volume A15 (July 1913–April 1915), Alpine Club, London.

54 'Cui Bono?', *Sphere*, 24 May 1913, 188.

55 A. Cherry-Garrard, *The Worst Journey in the World* (2 vols., London, 1922), ii. 577: 'There are many reasons which send men to the Poles, and the Intellectual Force uses them all. But the desire for knowledge for its own sake is the one which really counts and there is no field for the collection of knowledge which at the present time can be compared to the Antarctic.'

56 *The Times*, 27 October 1913, 11, reported the ceremony at St Anne's Church, Eastbourne.

· CHAPTER SIX ·
'FOR THE HONOUR OF OUR COUNTRY'

1 R. Blair to RGS, 19 February 1913, R. F. Scott corr. block 1911–20, file (j) 'Memorial Fund corr.', RGS.

2 See, for example, J. M. MacKenzie, 'Empire and Metropolitan Cultures', in A. Porter (ed.), *The Oxford History of the British Empire, vol. iii: The Nineteenth Century* (Oxford, 1999), 270–93.

3 J. Harris, *Private Lives, Public Spirit: A Social History of Britain, 1870–1914* (Oxford, 1993), 247–8.

4 A.H.B., 'The Proposed Arctic Expeditions', *Cornhill Magazine*, 29 (1874), 364; 'The British National Antarctic Expedition', *GJ* 13 (1899), 425.

5 Quoted in R. Huntford, *Shackleton* (London, 1985), 298–9.

6 'Luncheon to British Antarctic Expedition, 1910', *GJ* 36 (1910), 21–2; Seymour quoted in R. Pound, *Scott of the Antarctic* (London, 1966), 185.

7 S. Low, 'Is Our Civilisation Dying?', *Fortnightly Review*, 1 April 1913, NS 93 (1913), 635 and 631. Low was sceptical of eugenicist scare-mongering.

8 The publication of similar statements in Scott's last letters to J. M. Barrie and Edgar Speyer in the first volume of *Scott's Last Expedition* reinforced the message.

9 'A Brave Man and an English Gentleman', *Daily Graphic*, 12 February 1913, 4; J. S. Keltie to C. Rabot, 28 February 1913, R. F. Scott corr. block 1911–20: file (h) condolences, RGS.

10 *Eton Chronicle*, 13 February 1913, 305; 23 October 1913, 442, 28 May 1914, 569–70. A second brass was placed in the chapel.

11 *Guardian*, 21 February 1913, 250; G. C. Gregor, *Swansea's Antarctic Explorer: Edgar Evans, 1876–1912* (Swansea, 1995), 75–6.

12 Lord Ellison to Lady Ellison-Macartney, 2 March 1913, MS 1464/23, SPRI.

13 *Evening News*, 12 February 1913, MS 1453/40, SPRI.

14 LCC education committee minutes, 12 February 1913, London Metropolitan Archives.

15 A. Machen, 'The Immortal Story of Captain Scott's Expedition–How Five Brave Englishmen Died', February 1913, uncatalogued binder of ephemera on *Discovery & Terra Nova*, SPRI.

16 See, among many, *Evening News*, 13 February 1913, 1 and *Daily Mail*, 14 February 1913, 5. Machen himself would achieve fame during the war with *The Bowmen*, a fictional account of ghostly British archers from the Battle of Agincourt rising up to fire on the Germans, which many readers believed was true.

17 *Daily Telegraph*, 17 February 1913, 12.

18 *Captain Scott's Message to England* (London, 1913). The anonymous preface by *Pars minima*, is probably a reference to Virgil, *Aeneid*, ii. 5: '*Quaeque ipse miserrima vidi | Et quorum pars magna fui*' [And the most miserable things which I myself saw and of which I was a major part], implying that the author played some small role in the organization of Scott's last expedition; possibly it was J. M. Barrie. *The Times*, 24 February 1913, 5; 'Books and Bookmen Supplement', *Jewish Chronicle*, 28 February 1913, p. iii. Proceeds were passed on to the Mansion House fund.

19 For example, 'The Man of the Hour: Lieutenant Shackleton', *Boy's Own Annual*, 32 (1909–10), 77; W. J. Gordon, ' "Southward Ho!" ', part III, *Boy's Own Annual*, 35 (1912–13), 695.

20 'More than Conquerors: The Immortal Story of Capt. Scott and his Comrades', *Young England*, January 1914, 164 and 163; the coloured plate was inside the *Boy's Own Paper*, 11 September 1914, see *Boy's Own Annual*, 36 (1913–14), 612.

21 *Evening News*, 14 February 1913, 3 and 17 February 1913, 1; *Scout*, 8 March 1913, 652.

22 'In Memory of Five Brave Englishmen', *Headquarters Gazette*, March 1913, 81.

23 R. Baden-Powell, 'Scout Yarns', *Scout*, 22 November 1913, 266.

24 *Ibid.*, 31 January 1914, 515.

25 *Maybury Herald* (1914), MS 1453/31, SPRI. Lord Mountbatten to R. Pound, 21 November 1962, extract quoted in photocopy of a page of an unidentified sale-catalogue relating to the auction of two autograph letters of Lord Mountbatten which was sent to SPRI, uncatalogued biographical folder, R. F. Scott UDC 92, SPRI.

26 ' "Well Done!" ', *Daily Mail*, 14 February 1913, 4; 'A Polar Epic', *Daily Chronicle*, 12 February 1913, 6; M. W. Steel, 'Heroes – on the Scott Tragedy', MS 1453/31, SPRI.

27 *Illustrated London News*, 15 February 1913, 196; *Observer*, 16 February 1913, 8.

28 *Scotsman*, 12 February 1913, 9, and leader, 25 February 1913, 6. *The Voyages of Captain Scott. Retold from 'The Voyage of the "Discovery" ' and 'Scott's Last Expedition' by Charles Turley* (London, 1914).

29 'Honour to the Brave', *Aberdeen Express*, no date [15 February 1913], MS 1453/40, SPRI.

30 *South Wales Daily News*, 12 August 1925, MS 1453/41, SPRI.

31 Unlabelled newspaper cutting, no date (June 1913), MS 1453/40, SPRI; A. M. Johnson, *Scott of the Antarctic and Cardiff* (revised edn., Cardiff, 1995), 56.

32 B. Harrison, *The Transformation of British Politics, 1860–1995* (Oxford, 1996), 85.

33 Johnson, *Scott and Cardiff*, 50 and unlabelled newspaper cutting, MS 1453/40, SPRI.

34 Anon. [J.E. Hodder Williams], *Like English Gentlemen* (London, 1913), 16.

35 M. Wharton, 'Captain Scott: Part 1', *Picture Postcard Monthly*, January 1992, 33.

36 'Luncheon to the British Antarctic Expedition, 1910', *GJ* 36 (1910), 22–3.

37 Thos. B. Trotter & Sons (Ship's Store Merchants, Cardiff and North Shields) to British Geographical Society 13 March 1912, R. F. Scott corr. block 1911–20, file (d) 'Misc. corr. re. BAE', RGS.

38 'Captain Scott's Message', *The Times*, 12 February 1913, 7; C.E.B., 'An Outpost of Empire', *Evening News*, 12 February 1913, 4; 'Very Gallant', *Daily Express*, 17 February 1913, 6.

39 *The Times*, 5 June 1913, 5; 'The Scott Antarctic Memorial Fund', Oamaru,

New Zealand, 20 March 1913, MS 1464/24, SPRI; unlabelled newspaper cutting and photograph, uncatalogued memorials folder, R. F. Scott 92 (093.5) SPRI; *Otago Daily Times*, 1 June 1914, uncatalogued binder of ephemera on *Discovery* and *Terra Nova* expeditions, SPRI.

40   I. Plotz & Co., to RGS, 4 August 1913; G. Curzon to J S. Keltie, 29 August 1913, Curzon corr. block 1911–20, RGS.

41   'Captain Scott's End', *Daily News and Leader*, 12 February 1913, 6.

42   H.G. Ponting, 'Some Observations upon the Desirability of the Acquisition of the Moving Picture Record of the Scott South Pole Expedition being Taken in Hand by a Public Body', no date [1917–19], 4, section (a), MS 280/28/7, SPRI.

43   N. Ferguson, *The Pity of War* (London, 1998), 15.

44   'Why Not Be Patriots?', *Review of Reviews*, March 1913, 253.

45   *Daily Mail*, 14 February 1913, 3.

46   *The Times*, 5 June 1913, 5.

47   *Daily Graphic*, 11 February 1913, 4; 'Tragedy of the South Pole', *Daily Telegraph*, 11 February 1913, 10; S. Limb and P. Cordingley, *Captain Oates: Soldier and Explorer* (revised edn. London, 1995), 164.

48   *The Times*, 20 March 1913, 4.

49   Teddy Evans quoted in *The Times*, 27 October 1913, 11.

50   F. Taylor, ' "No Surrender Oates" ', *Spectator*, 31 May 1913, 924.

51   Note, for example, *Daily Sketch*, 14, 18, 20, and 22 February 1913, and *Month*, March 1913, 302.

52   *Daily Mail*, 12 February 1913, 5; 'A Brave Man and An English Gentleman', *Daily Graphic*, 12 February 1913, 4.

53   Huntford, *Shackleton*, 360–2.

54   Limb and Cordingley, *Oates*, 169. By a stroke of historical good fortune, Oates's sister Violet secretly copied extracts from her brother's diary. On the fiftieth anniversary of the disaster, an 11-year-old schoolgirl, Sue Limb, was inspired to write to the expedition's elderly Australian geologist Frank Debenham. Debenham introduced her to Violet and, many years later, Limb would write the first biography of Oates to draw on the family papers, with Patrick Cordingley of the Inniskilling Dragoons. Their biography does not repeat Huntford's interpretation of Caroline Oates's behaviour.

55   N. W. Haig to C. Oates, 28 March 1914, MS 1016/366, SPRI.

56 *Observer*, 16 February 1913, 8.

57 *Illustrated London News*, 31 May 1913, 802.

58 F. H. Stafford, 'How to Enter the Merchant Service', *Captain*, January 1912, 323–7.

59 *The Times*, 17 January 1914, 6. Details of exhibits from *A Guide to the Exhibition Galleries of the British Museum* (London, 1910). While the display of Scott's journals in 1914 was reported in the press, the diaries were not included in the guide to the saloon until the 1920s.

60 I am grateful to Ms Undine Concannon, archivist at Madame Tussaud's, for this information.

61 S. Collini, *Public Moralists: Political Thought and Intellectual Life in Britain* (Oxford, 1991), 346.

62 *Herald of Peace and International Arbitration: The Organ of the Peace Society*, 2 June 1913, 43.

· CHAPTER SEVEN ·
'THESE WERE MEN'

1 *Daily Mirror*, 22 April 1912, 3.

2 D. Saunders, *Britain's Maritime Memorials and Mementoes* (Sparkford, 1996), identifies twenty-four *Titanic* memorials, predominantly erected due to local, familial, religious, or professional associations.

3 Gibbs quoted in R. Howells, *The Myth of the Titanic* (Basingstoke, 1999), 117; Reaves quoted in S. Biel, *Down with the Old Canoe: A Cultural History of the Titanic Disaster* (New York and London, 1996), 77.

4 Guggenheim, quoted in Biel, *Down with the Old Canoe*, 41; *Daily Mirror*, 20 April 1912, 4–5.

5 Biel, *Down with the Old Canoe*, 87.

6 Howells, *Myth of the Titanic*, 106.

7 'A *Titanic* Lesson', *Daily Telegraph*, 22 April 1912, in J. W. Foster (ed.), *Titanic* (London, 1999), 288; S. Kirkby, 'Be British'/ 'Tis a story that shall live forever', Zonophone 1050, National Sound Archive, London; 'The Polar Heroes', *Leicester Mail*, no date, MS 1453/40, SPRI.

8 *Daily Mirror*, 22 April 1912, 1

9 W.M., 'The Real Enemy', *Daily Mirror*, 18 April 1912, 6.

10 *Observer*, 16 February 1913, 8; *Cambridge Independent*, no date [February 1913], MS 1453/40, SPRI.

11 Quoted in Biel, *Down with the Old Canoe*, 109.

12 Howells, *Myth of the Titanic*, 67–8.

13 *Daily Mirror*, 19 April 1912, 1.

14 G. B. Shaw, 'The *Titanic*: Some Unmentioned Morals', *Daily News and Leader*, 14 May 1912, in Foster (ed.), *Titanic*, 214–15.

15 A. C. Doyle, 'The Whole Wonderful Epic', *Daily News and Leader*, 20 May 1912, and G. B. Shaw, 'Beating the Hysterics', *Daily News and Leader*, 22 May 1912, in Foster (ed.), *Titanic*, 217–23.

16 *Suffragette*, 18 April 1913, 458.

17 W. R. Inge diary, 25 November 1913, Old Library, Magdalene College, Cambridge.

18 *Vote*, 14 February 1913, 2.

19 *The Times*, 5 June 1913, 5; *Suffragette*, 13 June 1913, 584.

20 C. Pankhurst, 'Above the Law', *Suffragette*, 14 February 1913, 274.

21 'The Courage of Women', *Suffragette*, 21 February 1913, 286.

22 S. K. Kent, *Gender and Power in Britain*, 1640–1990 (London, 1999), 269; "Greater Love Hath No Man", *Votes for Women*, 13 June 1913, 540. Also note Pankhurst's praise of Joan of Arc, 'the militant women's ideal', *Suffragette*, 9 May 1913, 501.

23 'The Toll of the Antarctic', *Ulster Guardian*, no date [February 1913], 'The Toll of Science', *Irish Times*, no date [February 1913], MS 1453/40, SPRI.

24 'Martyrs of Progress', *Freeman's Journal*, 15 February 1913, 6. The idea of sacrifice featured prominently in the writing of Irish nationalists such as Patrick Pearse.

25 The number of working days lost to industrial disputes in 1912 was exceeded only in 1921 and 1926. A. H. Halsey (ed.), *British Social Trends since 1900* (revised edn., London, 1988), 194–6.

26 *Daily Herald*, 15 February 1913, 6; *Labour Leader*, 13 February 1913, 1; *Clarion*, 4 April 1913, 4.

27 *New Age*, 20 February 1913, 370–1.

28 *Clarion*, 14 March 1913, 6.

29 'Other Poles to be Reached', *Daily Herald*, 17 February 1913, 10.

30 *New Age*, 6 March 1913, 439.

31   *New Age*, 20 March 1913, 487.

32   *Copthorne School Chronicle*, May and October 1913.

33   *Henry V*, IV. iii. 60. See, among many, 'The Insatiate Pole', *Daily News and Leader*, 11 February 1913, 6; C. R. Markham, '*Adeste Fideles* I. Robert Falcon Scott', *Cornhill Magazine*, 34 (1913), 464.

34   A. Quiller-Couch, quoted in N. Vance, *The Sinews of the Spirit: The Ideal of Christian Manliness in Victorian Literature and Religious Thought* (Cambridge, 1985), 21; *Daily Mirror*, 12 February 1913, 4.

35   *Evening News*, 14 February 1913, 1; 'Tragedy of the South Pole', *Daily Telegraph*, 11 February 1913, 10.

36   H. W. Aubrey, 'The Snow Queen's Toll', no date [1913], uncatalogued folder of ephemera on *Discovery* and *Terra Nova* expeditions, SPRI.

37   *Daily Telegraph*, 17 February 1913, 12; *Eton Chronicle*, 20 February 1913, 310.

38   J. Bowker, *The Meanings of Death* (Cambridge, 1991), 99–100; *Jewish Chronicle*, 21 February 1913, 43.

39   J. Stirling-Hamilton to Lady Ellison-Macartney, 13 February 1913, and J. Pearson to Lady Ellison-Macartney, 18 February 1913, MS 1464/23, SPRI.

40   H. D. Rawnsley, 'In Honour of Captain Scott', *British Review*, April 1913, 81. Cf. the conclusion of E. L. A. Hentylet (Chaplain to the Bishop of London), 'March, 1912: February, 1913', MS 1464/23, SPRI: 'That loss of self is entry into life, | And kingliest crowns are twined about with thorn, | That victory still comes by sacrifice, | And death itself is nought – and love is all'.

41   Spurgeon, quoted in Vance, *Sinews of the Spirit*, 26; *Guardian*, 21 February 1913, 259.

42   R. F. Scott journal, 23 April 1911; A. Cherry-Garrard diary, 5 January 1913, MS 559/10, SPRI.

43   For example *Daily Express*, 11 February 1913, 4, and *Daily Mail*, 11 February 1913, 4.

44   Unlabelled newspaper cutting, 27 October 1913, uncatalogued memorials folder, L.E.G. Oates 92 (093.5), SPRI.

45   F. Stafford to Lady Ellison-Macartney, 12 February 1913, MS 1464/23, SPRI.

46   *The Times*, 30 March 1914, 5.

47   *The Voyages of Captain Scott. Retold from 'The Voyage of the "Discovery"' and 'Scott's Last Expedition' by Charles Turley* (London, 1914), 8 and 10.

48 *Scott's Last Expedition* (2 vols., London, 1913), i. 603–4.

49 G. Seaver, *Edward Wilson of the Antarctic: Naturalist and Friend* (London, 1933), 170.

50 R. Pound, *Scott of the Antarctic* (London, 1933), 250.

51 K. Scott to Mrs P. Dumas, 9 March 1913, MS 761/27, SPRI; 'An Awfully Big Adventure', *Daily Express*, 12 February 1913, 4.

52 J. Harris, *Private Lives, Public Spirit: A Social History of Britain, 1870–1914* (Oxford, 1993), 27.

53 'Heroism and a Social Problem', *Queen*, 22 February 1913, 318.

54 H. Leach, 'The Heart of Things', *Chambers's Journal*, 7th series, 4 (1913–1914), 49; *Punch*, 12 November 1913, 417; 'These Were Men', *Manchester Guardian*, 12 February 1913, 6.

55 E. R. G. R. Evans to C. Oates, 3 February 1913, MS 1016/344, SPRI; C. Borchgrevink to J. S. Keltie, 14 February 1913, R. F. Scott corr. block 1911–20, file (h) 'condolences', RGS.

56 Quoted in A. Greely (ed.), *Thrilling Experiences in Discovering the Poles* (New York, 1913), 33. I am grateful to Bill Bourland of the web-site www.framheim.com for publishing extracts from this obscure book on the web.

57 *The Times*, 6 November 1913, 9. See also *British Weekly*, 20 February 1913, 609. The phrase, widely circulated through *Foxe's Book of Martyrs*, can be traced to the early Anglican Hugh Latimer, who consoled Nicholas Ridley before they were burned at the stake for heresy in 1555: 'Be of good comfort, Brother Ridley, and play the man.'

58 'Killed in Action', Royal Naval College, Dartmouth, 16 February 1913, MS 1453/31, SPRI.

59 *Tablet*, 15 February 1913, 268.

60 *Bioscope*, 26 February 1914, 942.

61 *Month*, March 1913, 301–2.

62 *Eton Chronicle*, 28 May 1914, 570.

· CHAPTER EIGHT ·
'SO MANY HEROES'

1   B. MacArthur (ed.), *The Penguin Book of Twentieth-Century Speeches* (London, 1993), 31–6.

2   S. Wheeler, *Terra Incognita: Travels in Antarctica* (London, 1996), 54.

3   'The Fleet Memorial to Captain Scott', *GJ* 46 (1915), 436. The Cook Statue, by Thomas Brock, had been unveiled earlier in the year.

4   *Weekly Press*, 14 February 1917, uncatalogued memorials folder, R. F. Scott 92 (093.5), SPRI.

5   L. Earle to W. Soulsby, 24 February 1915, WORKS 20/82, PRO.

6   *The Times*, 6 May 1916, 5. Charles Carlton has argued that the Civil War claimed a higher percentage of casualties per head of the population, C. Carlton, *Going to the Wars: The Experience of the British Civil Wars, 1638–1651* (London, 1992). But in absolute terms the losses sustained during the First World War remain unparalleled in British history.

7   *Stratford Herald*, 1 October 1915. I am grateful to Colin Bishop for information about the Binton memorial.

8   The principal exceptions were George Simpson, who returned to India after the expedition and worked with the Indian Munitions Board during the war, and Thomas Griffith Taylor, who took up a post as Assistant Professor of Geography at Sydney University.

9   H. G. Ponting to F. Debenham, 10 January 1933, section (a), MS 280/28/7, SPRI; *Bioscope*, 21 September 1916, 1141; H. G. Ponting to K. Scott, 6 February 1917, MS 15, SPRI. The Gaumont Company had suspended distribution of the expedition films while Ponting lectured at the Philharmonic Hall, and pressured him to buy out the complete rights to his pictures, which he did for £5,100 in July 1914.

10   H. G. Ponting to K. Scott, 7 February [1917], MS 15, SPRI.

11   H. G. Ponting, 'Some Observations upon the Desirability of the Acquisition of the Moving-Picture Record of the Scott South Pole Expedition Being Taken in Hand by a Public Body', no date [1917–19], 22, section (a), MS 280/28/7, SPRI; H. G. Ponting, *The Great White South* (London, 1921), 297–8.

12   H. R. Mill, *The Record of the Royal Geographical Society, 1830–1930* (London, 1930), 168.

13   Quoted in H. Ludlam, *Captain Scott: The Full Story* (London 1965), 220.

14 A. Egerton Castle, 'The Precursor: A Memory of Robert Falcon Scott', *Treasury*, January 1916, 323, 324, and 328.

15 A. H. Pollen, 'The Spirit of the Nation', *Dublin Review*, 159 (1916), 47.

16 G. Seaver, *Edward Wilson: Nature-lover* (London, 1937), 35.

17 E. L. Atkinson, no date, section (a), 33–4, MS 280/28/1, SPRI.

18 G. Lansbury, *My Faith and Hope in View of the National Mission* (London, 1916), 5.

19 F. Whelan Boyle, 'Equipping a Polar Expedition', *Boy's Own Annual*, 38 (1915–16), 31.

20 For example, Ponting, *Great White South*, 297–8.

21 H. G. Ponting, correspondence with F. Debenham, section (a), MS 280/28/7, SPRI.

22 Three books by the crew of the *Terra Nova* had appeared before 1918: R. Priestley, *Antarctic Adventure: Scott's Northern Party* (London, 1914), G. Murray Levick, *Antarctic Penguins: A Study of their Social Habits* (London, 1914), and T. Griffith Taylor, *With Scott: The Silver Lining* (London, 1916). Priestley and Taylor told the story of the northern and western parties respectively, while Murray Levick offered an important new study of penguin life.

23 R. Pound to SPRI, no date [*c.*1960–3], uncatalogued biographical folder, E. R. G. R. Evans 92, SPRI.

24 S. Wheeler, *Cherry: A Life of Apsley Cherry-Garrard* (London, 2001), 211.

25 A. Cherry-Garrard, *The Worst Journey in the World* (2 vols., London, 1922), i. 202–3.

26 Reviews quoted in Wheeler, *Cherry*, 220 and 235.

27 Wheeler, *Cherry*, 221–2. Shaw attempted to smooth relations by sending Kathleen his own assessment of Scott (whom he had never met), which criticized the last-minute decision to take an additional man to the Pole, and the choice of Edgar Evans ahead of William Lashly; G. B. Shaw to K. Scott, 23 March 1923, IIIA E/1, Kennet Papers, Cambridge University Library.

28 J. Gordon Hayes, *Antarctica: A Treatise on the Southern Continent* (London, 1928), 293.

29 *Times Literary Supplement*, 2 January 1930, in C. A. Close scrapbook, vol. 3, AR120, RGS.

30 *The Times*, 10 December 1929, 24. Kathleen married Edward Hilton Young on 3 March 1922. He entered the House of Lords in 1935, taking the title Lord Kennet. I refer to her throughout as Kathleen Scott to avoid confusion.

31 S. Gwynn, *Captain Scott* (London, 1939 [1929]), 9 and 236.

32 *Observer*, 23 January 1930, MS 1453/41, SPRI; 'British Polar Exhibition (1930): Report & Statement of Accounts', Polar exhibitions (061.4), uncatalogued, SPRI; O. Wilson to Miss Drake, 9 July 1930, section (I), MS 280/28/7, SPRI.

33 O. Wilson to F. Debenham, 18 June 1934, section (I), MS 280/28/7, SPRI.

34 'The Discovery', 3-page typed note, no date [1938], 'Photographs' folder, *Discovery* box, Scout Association, London; *Cambridge Daily News*, 10 May 1937, MS 1453/41, SPRI.

35 H. Newbolt, *The Book of the Long Trail* (School Edition, London, 1923), pp. v–viii.

36 L. Young, *A Great Task of Happiness: The Life of Kathleen Scott* (London, 1995), 200–1; Lawrence quoted in Wheeler, *Cherry*, 233.

37 G. L. Mallory to G. Winthrop Young, 13 January 1914, G. Winthrop Young corr., B44, Alpine Club, London; P. and L. Gillman, *The Wildest Dream: Mallory, his Life and Conflicting Passions* (London, 2000), 240.

38 Quoted in D. Robertson, *George Mallory*, (London, 1999 [1969]), 251.

39 S. Leonard Bastin, 'Climbing Mount Everest', *Boy's Own Annual*, 44 (1921–2), 400.

40 The following account draws on A. Gregory, *The Silence of Memory: Armistice Day, 1919–1946* (Oxford and Providence, RI, 1994), 138–42.

41 *Radio Times*, 8 November 1935, 11.

42 G. Seaver, Foreword to the 1965 edition, A. Cherry-Garrard, *The Worst Journey in the World* (London, 1994), p. lxxii.

43 T. Bogacz, 'War Neurosis and Cultural Change in England, 1914–22: The Work of the War Office Committee of Enquiry into "Shell-Shock"', *Journal of Contemporary History*, 24 (1989), 227–56.

44 R. C. Sherriff, *Journey's End* (London, 1983 [1929]), II. i. 44.

45 Sherriff, *Journey's End*, II. ii. 57–8.

46 *Sunday Express*, 2 March 1930, MS 1453/41, SPRI. Kathleen also obstructed Gainsborough Pictures' plans for a film about Scott in 1938.

47 *Daily Express*, 17 February 1913, 2.

48 L. Darwin, 'Address to the RGS, 1910', *GJ* 36 (1910), 5.

49 Debenham confided to Oriana Wilson that 'A Scott Polar Research Department would be a fine and permanent memorial, but a Scott School of Geography would be better still. The Cavendish School of Experimental Physics is known and honoured all over the world, and one's natural wish is that the Scott School of Geography might become the same.' But he abandoned this proposal, fearing that a Scott School of Geography in Cambridge would not be considered an appropriate use for money raised by a *national* fund, as the department would be too strongly associated with a specific university. F. Debenham to 'Mrs. Bill' [O. Wilson], 26 October 1919, uncatalogued folder titled 'Early letters re. proposals for SPRI (1919–22)', SPRI.

50 F. Younghusband, 'Address at the Anniversary General Meeting, 30 May 1921', *GJ* 58 (1921), 2–6.

51 L. P. Kirwan, *A History of Polar Exploration* (London, 1962 [1959]), 316.

52 Frank Debenham was both the first Director of SPRI and the first Professor of Geography at Cambridge. Raymond Priestley enjoyed a successful career in Cambridge, Australia, and Birmingham, before becoming RGS President in 1961. George Simpson served as Director of the British Meteorological Office from 1920 to 1938. Thomas Griffith Taylor was an eminent Professor of Geography in Australia and North America. And Charles Wright worked on the scientific staff at the Admiralty, serving both as Director of Scientific Research (1934–46) and as the first head of the Royal Naval scientific service (1946–7).

53 W. Soulsby to F. Debenham, 23 July 1925, SPRI, uncatalogued folder titled 'Correspondence with Sir William Soulsby re Scott Memorial Fund (1919–26)', SPRI.

54 See papers in uncatalogued folders titled 'Inauguration of SPRI (May 22nd 1926)', and 'Inauguration of SPRI (May 22nd 1926) – Replies to Invitations', SPRI.

55 Young, *Great Task*, 213, 227, and 237.

56 A. Seward to H. Baker, 15 June 1933, F. Debenham to A. Seward, 20 April 1933, in uncatalogued folder titled 'Corr. with Sir Albert Seward re. new building (1931–34)', SPRI.

57 The first honours course in geography leading to a formal qualification came at Liverpool University (1917), and was followed by courses at the LSE (1918), Aberystwyth (1918), University College London (1919), Cam-

bridge (1919), Manchester (1923), Sheffield (1924), and Oxford (1933). See
D. R. Stoddart, *On Geography and its History* (Oxford, 1986), 41–58.

58   A. Scott Berg, *Lindbergh* (London, 1998), 151.

59   Quoted ibid. 149.

60   M. Cope to RGS, 1 December 1918, R. F. Scott corr. block 1911–20, file (b)
'corr. with Lady Scott etc.', RGS.

EPILOGUE

1   J. Giles and T. Middleton (eds.), *Writing Englishness, 1900–1950: An
Introductory Sourcebook on National Identity* (London and New York,
1995), 142.

2   K. J. Dodds, 'Screening Antarctica: Britain, the Falkland Islands
Dependencies Survey, and *Scott of the Antarctic* (1948)', *Polar Record*,
38 (2002), 1–10.

3   L. Moore, 'A Hero for our Time', *Observer*, 11 February 2001, 29.

4   S. Gwynn, *Captain Scott* (London, 1939 [1929]), 10.

5   F. Young, 'The Things that Matter', *Pall Mall Gazette*, 25 February 1914, 3.

6   G. Seaver, *Edward Wilson of the Antarctic: Naturalist and Friend* (London,
1933), 106. On the flyleaf of the sledging journal he began on 17 April 1911,
Scott wrote 'There is no part of the world that *can* not be reached by man.
When the "can be" is turned to "has been" the Geographical Society will
have altered its status'.

7   Vivian Fuchs achieved fame when he commanded one party during the
Commonwealth Trans-Antarctic expedition, meeting a second party led
by Edmund Hillary on 19 January 1958. Fuchs was a trained geologist, who
was elected to the Fellowship of the Royal Society and served as President
of both the BAAS and RGS. In 1958 the RGS awarded him its first special
gold medal since Robert Peary in 1910. After Fuchs, the RGS awarded
special gold medals to Francis Chichester 'for sailing single-handed round
the world' in 1968, and to Neil Armstrong in 1970. Wally Herbert led the
British Trans-Arctic Expedition from Alaska to Svalbard in 1968–9.

8   A. Chaikin, *A Man on the Moon: The Voyages of the Apollo Astronauts*
(London, 1998 [1994]), 34.

FURTHER READING

CAPTAIN SCOTT, POLAR EXPLORATION, AND HEROISM

P. van der Merwe *et al.* (eds.), *South: The Race to the Pole* (London, 2000), published to accompany a recent exhibition at the National Maritime Museum, offers an excellent introduction to the extensive and growing litera-ture on the heroic age of polar exploration. Of the many biographies of Captain Scott, R. Pound, *Scott of the Antarctic* (London, 1966) and E. Huxley *Scott of the Antarctic* (London, 1977) remain useful. For Bowers, Evans, Oates, and Wilson, see G. Seaver, *'Birdie' Bowers of the Antarctic* (London, 1938), G. C. Gregor, *Swansea's Antarctic Explorer: Edgar Evans, 1876–1912* (Swansea, 1995), S. Limb and P. Cordingley, *Captain Oates: Soldier and Explorer* (revised edn., London, 1995), and G. Seaver, *Edward Wilson of the Antarctic: Naturalist and Friend* (London, 1933). S. Wheeler, *Cherry: A Life of Apsley Cherry-Garrard* (London, 2001) offers an excellent account of one of the key narrators of the story of Scott of the Antarctic. Although his conclusions are open to question, Roland Huntford's three biographies – *Scott and Amundsen* (London, 1979), now published under the title *The Last Place on Earth*, *Shackleton* (London, 1985), and *Nansen: The Explorer as Hero* (London, 1997) – remain indispensable. For the revival of interest in Shackleton see, among many, C. Alexander, *The Endurance: Shackleton's Legendary Antarctic Exped-ition* (London, 1998) and S. Capparell and M. Morrell, *Shackleton's Way: Leadership Lessons from the Great Antarctic Explorer* (New York, 2000). S. J. Pyne, *The Ice: A Journey to Antarctica* (London, 1987) offers an unrivalled overview, surveying artistic, scientific, and geopolitical encounters with the Antarctic. For different approaches to the study of heroic icons, compare the anthropological perspective of J. Campbell, *The Hero with a Thousand Faces* (London, 1988 [1949]), with the historical perspective of G. Cubitt and A. Warren (eds.), *Heroic Reputations and Exemplary Lives* (Manchester, 2000). For recent echoes of Scott's last expedition see A. Michaels, *Fugitive Pieces* (London, 1997), A. Caesar, *The White* (Basingstoke, 2001), and D. Tartt, *The Secret History* (London, 2002).

· CHAPTER ONE ·
MEASURING THE WORLD

D. R. Stoddart, *On Geography and its History* (Oxford, 1986), D. N. Livingstone, *The Geographical Tradition: Episodes in the History of a Contested Enterprise* (Oxford, 1992), and F. Driver, *Geography Militant: Cultures of Exploration and Empire* (Oxford, 2001) have transformed our understanding of the relationship between geography, exploration, and empire since the 1980s. The three official histories of the RGS – C. R. Markham, *The Fifty Years' Work of the Royal Geographical Society* (London, 1881), H. R. Mill, *The Record of the Royal Geographical Society, 1830–1930* (London, 1930), and I. Cameron, *To the Farthest Ends of the Earth: The History of the Royal Geographical Society 1830–1980* (London, 1980) – remain essential sources for the history of exploration, Mill in particular. For debates about the cultural construction of maps, see D. Cosgrove (ed.), *Mappings* (London, 1999). F. Spufford, *I May be Some Time: Ice and the English Imagination* (London, 1996) and R. G. David, *The Arctic in the British Imagination, 1818–1914* (Manchester, 2000) examine the place of polar exploration in Victorian culture, including Sir John Franklin's heroic reputation, while B. Riffenburgh, *The Myth of the Explorer: The Press, Sensationalism, and Geographical Discovery* (Oxford, 1994) highlights the role of the press. F. Fleming's *Barrow's Boys* (London, 1998) and *Ninety Degrees North: The Quest for the North Pole* (London, 2001), and A. Savours, *The Search for the Northwest Passage* (London, 1999) offer accessible narratives of many pioneering expeditions.

R. Hyam, *Britain's Imperial Century, 1815–1914: A Study of Empire and Expansion* (3rd edn., Basingstoke, 2002) offers a good introduction to the history of the British empire. For a broader perspective, see N. Ferguson's provocative *Empire: How Britain Made the Modern World* (London, 2003). From the extensive literature on David Livingstone, see T. Jeal, *Livingstone* (revised edn., New Haven and London, 2001), J. M. MacKenzie (ed.), *David Livingstone and the Victorian Encounter with Africa* (London, 1996), and J. M. MacKenzie, 'David Livingstone: The Construction of the Myth', in G. Walker and T. Gallagher (eds.), *Sermons and Battle Hymns: Protestant Popular Culture in Modern Scotland* (Edinburgh, 1990). For the influence of empire on geography and exploration, see B. Hudson's seminal article, 'The New Geography and the New Imperialism, 1870–1918', *Antipode*, 9 (1977), 12–19, and two collections of essays: A. Godlewska and N. Smith (eds.), *Geography and Empire* (Oxford, 1994) and M. Bell, R. Butlin, and M. Heffernan (eds.), *Geog-*

raphy and Imperialism, 1820–1940 (Manchester, 1995). For the work of native surveyors, see D. Waller, *The Pundits: British Exploration of Tibet and Central Asia* (Lexington, Ky., 1990). M. H. Jones, 'The Royal Geographical Society and the Commemoration of Captain Scott's Last Antarctic Expedition', unpublished thesis, Cambridge University (2000), explores many of the themes addressed in this chapter in more detail.

· CHAPTER TWO ·
THE RACE TO THE SOUTH POLE

There is an urgent need for a new biography to replace A. H. Markham, *The Life of Sir Clements R. Markham* (London, 1917). A. Savours presents a new short account in R. Bridges and P. Hair (eds.), *Compassing the Vast Globe of the Earth: Studies in the History of the Hakluyt Society, 1846–1996* (London, 1996). For women's involvement in exploration, see L. Bloom, *Gender on Ice: American Ideologies of Polar Expeditions* (Minneapolis and London, 1993), A. Blunt, *Travel, Gender, and Imperialism: Mary Kingsley and West Africa* (London, 1994), and D. Middleton, *Victorian Lady Travellers* (London, 1965). For the opposition to women's involvement in public life, see B. Harrison, *Separate Spheres: The Opposition to Women's Suffrage in Britain* (London, 1978).

For the National Antarctic Expedition, 1901–4, see R. F. Scott, *The Voyage of the Discovery* (2 vols., London, 1905), T. H. Baughman, *Before the Heroes Came: Antarctica in the 1890s* (Lincoln, Nebr., and London, 1994), T. H. Baughman, *Pilgrims on the Ice: Robert Falcon Scott's First Antarctic Expedition* (Lincoln, Nebr., and London, 1999), and D. Yelverton, *Antarctica Unveiled: Scott's First Expedition and the Quest for the Unknown Continent* (Boulder, Colo., 2000). For a recent intervention in the ongoing dispute over the conquest of the North Pole, see R. M. Bryce, *Cook and Peary: The Polar Controversy, Resolved* (Mechanicsburg, Penn., 1997), which concludes that neither man reached the Pole. For the British Antarctic Expedition, 1910–13, see *Scott's Last Expedition*, arranged by L. Huxley (2 vols., London, 1913) and P. King (ed.), *Scott's Last Journey* (London, 1999). A. Cherry-Garrard, *The Worst Journey in the World* (2 vols., London, 1922) is the most perceptive of the many accounts by the crew of the *Terra Nova*, while H. G. Ponting, *The Great White South* (London, 1921) is beautifully illustrated with the author's photographs. D. Thomson, *Scott's Men* (London, 1977), illuminates many neglected aspects of the expedition, A. M. Johnson, *Scott of the Antarctic and Cardiff* (revised edn., Cardiff, 1995) presents a revealing local study, and K. Lambert, *'Hell with a Capital H': An Epic Story of Antarctic Survival* (London, 2002) retrieves the exploits of Victor Campbell's northern party from obscurity.

· CHAPTER THREE ·
DISASTER IN THE ANTARCTIC

For the development of the media before 1914 see, among many, O. Boyd-Barrett, *The International News Agencies* (London, 1980) and J. H. Wiener (ed.), *Papers for the Millions: The New Journalism in Britain, 1850s to 1914* (New York, 1988). For the history of the Mansion House memorial funds, see W. Soulsby, 'Mansion House Funds', *The Times* 'City of London' numbers, 8 and 9 November 1927. In order to calculate the modern purchasing power of historical currencies, visit http://www.eh.net. For a discussion of Anon. [J. E. Hodder Williams], *Like English Gentlemen* (London, 1913), see M. Voykovic, 'The Culture of Thriller Fiction in Britain, 1898–1945: Authors, Publishers and the First World War', unpublished Ph.D. thesis, University of New South Wales, Australia (1996). For recent re-assessments of the causes of the Antarctic disaster, see P. King (ed.), *Scott's Last Journey* (London, 1999) and S. Solomon, *The Coldest March: Scott's Fatal Antarctic Expedition* (New Haven and London, 2001). L. Bloom, *Gender on Ice: American Ideologies of Polar Expeditions* (Minneapolis and London, 1993) offers a cultural explanation, inspired by Roland Huntford. For an earlier interpretation see J. Gordon Hayes, *Antarctica: A Treatise on the Southern Continent* (London, 1928). For a microform edition of Scott's original sledging journals, see *The Diaries of Captain Robert Scott: A Record of the Second Antarctic Expedition, 1910–12* (6 vols., Tyler's Green, 1968).

· CHAPTER FOUR ·
REMEMBERING THE DEAD

J. Wolffe, *Great Deaths: Grieving, Religion, and Nationhood in Victorian and Edwardian Britain* (Oxford, 2000) presents a thorough survey of British commemorative practices. For an alternative approach, emphasizing contestation over consensus, see A. Ben-Amos, *Funerals, Politics, and Memory in Modern France, 1789–1996* (Oxford, 2000). D. Saunders, *Britain's Maritime Memorials and Mementoes* (Sparkford, 1996) provides a useful list of monuments, while S. Beattie, *The New Sculpture* (London and New Haven, 1983) offers an excellent guide to the development of artistic styles. For St Paul's cathedral, see W. M. Sinclair, *Memorials of St. Paul's Cathedral* (London, 1909) and S. Daniels, *Fields of Vision: Landscape Imagery and National Identity in England and the United States* (Cambridge, 1993), ch. 1. For royal ceremonial, see D. Cannadine, 'The Context, Performance and Meaning of Ritual: The British Monarchy and the "Invention of Tradition", *c.* 1820–1977', in E. J. Hobsbawm and T. Ranger (eds.), *The Invention of Tradition* (Cambridge, 1983), 101–64. For George Curzon, see D. Cannadine, *Aspects of Aristocracy: Grandeur and Decline in Modern Britain* (New Haven and London, 1994) and D. Gilmour, *Curzon* (London, 1994). R. B. Stephenson's 'Low-latitude Antarctic Gazetteer', publishes an extensive list of international Antarctic memorials on the World-Wide-Web accessed from http://www.antarctic-circle.org.

· CHAPTER FIVE ·
'MARTYRS OF SCIENCE'

J. Harris, *Private Lives, Public Spirit: A Social History of Britain, 1870–1914* (Oxford, 1993) offers a wealth of insights on a wide range of themes. M. J. Daunton and B. Rieger (eds.), *Meanings of Modernity: Britain from the Late-Victorian Era to World War II* (Oxford, 2001), S. Hynes, *The Edwardian Turn of Mind* (Princeton and London, 1968), and S. Kern, *The Culture of Time and Space, 1880–1918* (London, 1983) explore the tensions generated in British society before 1914. For scientific research in Antarctica, see G. E. Fogg and D. Smith, *The Explorations of Antarctica: The Last Unspoilt Continent* (London, 1990), G. E. Fogg, *A History of Antarctic Science* (Cambridge, 1992), and S. J. Pyne, *The Ice: A Journey to Antarctica* (London, 1987). For Herbert Ponting and Edwardian cinema, see H. J. P. Arnold, *Photographer of the World: The Biography of Herbert Ponting* (London, 1969), K. Brownlow, *The War, the West and the Wilderness* (London, 1979), L. Cruwys and B. Riffenburgh, *The Photographs of H. G. Ponting* (London, 1998), R. Low, *The History of the British Film, 1906–14* (London, 1948), and D. Lynch, 'Profile: Herbert G. Ponting', *Polar Record*, 26 (1990), 217–24. Ponting's feature film *Ninety Degrees South* (1933) is available on VHS and DVD. F. Lancaster Cordes, ' "Tekeli-li" or Hollow Earth Lives: A Bibliography of Antarctic Fiction', unpublished MA thesis, San Francisco State University (1991), exposes the influence of the polar regions on the literary imagination, with an updated version online accessed through http: www.antarctic-circle.org.

· CHAPTER SIX ·
'FOR THE HONOUR OF OUR COUNTRY'

There is now a rich literature on national identity in eighteenth-century Britain, inspired in part by L. Colley, *Britons: Forging the Nation, 1707–1837* (New Haven and London, 1992). Investigations of the period after 1850 are less well developed. Although patchy, the essays in R. Samuel (ed.), *Patriotism: The Making and Unmaking of British National Identity* (3 vols., London, 1989) are useful, while S. Collini, *English Pasts: Essays in Culture and History* (Oxford, 1999) contains many perceptive observations. For concerns about the nation's youth and the Boy Scout movement see T. Jeal, *Baden-Powell* (London, 1989) and J. A. Mangan and J. Walvin (eds.), *Manliness and Morality: Middle-class Masculinity in Britain and America, 1800–1940* (Manchester, 1987). For the relationship between England, Scotland, and Wales, see R. Colls and P. Dodd (eds.), *Englishness: Politics and Culture 1880–1920* (London, 1986), R. Colls, *The Identity of England* (Oxford, 2002), J. S. Ellis, 'Reconciling the Celt: British National Identity, Empire, and the 1911 Investiture of the Prince of Wales', *Journal of British Studies*, 37 (1998), 391–418, and J. M. MacKenzie, 'Empire and National Identities: The Case of Scotland', *Transactions of the Royal Historical Society*, 6th ser., 8 (1998), 215–31. For popular militarism, contrast N. Ferguson, *The Pity of War* (London, 1998), ch. 1, with M. Paris, *Warrior Nation: Images of War in British Popular Culture, 1850–2000* (London, 2000). From the extensive literature on popular imperialism, see J. M. Mac-Kenzie's *Propaganda and Empire: The Manipulation of British Public Opinion* (Manchester, 1984) and 'Heroic Myths of Empire', in J. M. MacKenzie (ed.), *Popular Imperialism and the Military: 1850–1950* (Manchester, 1992), 109–37. Also see C. Hall, *Cultures of Empire: A Reader. Colonisers in Britain and the Empire in the Nineteenth and Twentieth Centuries* (Manchester, 2000), D. A. Lorimer, 'Race, Science and Culture: Historical Continuities and Discontinuities, 1850–1914', in S. West (ed.), *The Victorians and Race* (Aldershot, 1996), 12–33, and J. Schneer, *London 1900: The Imperial Metropolis* (New Haven and London, 1999).

· CHAPTER SEVEN ·
'THESE WERE MEN'

S. Biel, *Down with the Old Canoe: A Cultural History of the Titanic Disaster* (New York and London, 1996), J. W. Foster (ed.), *Titanic* (London, 1999) and R. Howells *The Myth of the Titanic* (Basingstoke, 1999) explore the legacy of the *Titanic* disaster. For an introduction to the tensions generated by Irish nationalists, the campaign for women's suffrage, and the rise of organized labour, see P. F. Clarke, *Hope and Glory: Britain, 1900–1990* (London, 1996), J. Davis, *A History of Britain, 1885–1939* (Basingstoke, 1999), and S. K. Kent, *Gender and Power in Britain, 1640–1990* (London, 1999). For an important consideration of arguments about the 'separate spheres' occupied by men and women, see A. Vickery, 'Golden Age to Separate Spheres? A Review of the Categories and Chronology of English Women's History', *Historical Journal*, 36 (1993). For classical, chivalric, and religious influences on British culture before 1914, see M. Girouard, *The Return to Camelot: Chivalry and the English Gentleman* (New Haven and London, 1981), R. Jenkyns, *The Victorians and Ancient Greece* (Oxford, 1980), and N. Vance, *The Sinews of the Spirit: The Ideal of Christian Manliness in Victorian Literature and Religious Thought* (Cambridge, 1985). For masculinity and the idea of character, see S. Collini, *Public Moralists: Political Thought and Intellectual Life in Britain* (Oxford, 1991), G. Dawson, *Soldier Heroes: British Adventure, Empire, and the Imagining of Masculinities* (London, 1994), G. Mosse, *The Image of Man: The Creation of Modern Masculinity* (New York and Oxford, 1996), R. Phillips, *Mapping Men & Empire: A Geography of Adventure* (London, 1997), M. Roper and J. Tosh (eds.), *Manful Assertions: Masculinities in Britain since 1800* (London, 1991), and J. Tosh, *A Man's Place: Masculinity and the Middle-Class Home in Victorian England* (New Haven and London, 1999).

· CHAPTER EIGHT ·
'SO MANY HEROES'

For three different responses to Paul Fussell's seminal *The Great War and Modern Memory* (London, 1975), see B. Bond, *The Unquiet Western Front: Britain's Role in Literature and History* (Cambridge, 2002), S. Hynes, *A War Imagined: The First World War and English Culture* (London, 1990), and J. M. Winter, *Sites of Memory, Sites of Mourning: The Great War in European*

Cultural History (Cambridge, 1995). For shell shock, see P. Leese, *Shell Shock: Traumatic Neurosis and the British Soldiers of the First World War* (New York, 2002), and for R. C. Sherriff's *Journey's End*, see R. M. Bracco, *Merchants of Hope: British Middlebrow Writers and the First World War, 1919–1939* (Providence, RI and Oxford, 1992). For Lawrence of Arabia see Dawson, *Soldier Heroes*, and for the early Everest expeditions see P. Hansen, 'The Dancing Lamas of Everest: Cinema, Orientalism and Anglo-Tibetan Relations' in the 1920s', *American Historical Review*, 101 (1996), 712–47 and 'Debate: Tenzing's Two Wrist Watches: The Conquest of Everest and Late Imperial Culture in Britain, 1921–53', *Past & Present*, 157 (1997), 159–77. For the rise of aviation, see M. Paris, *From the Wright Brothers to 'Top Gun': Aviation, Nationalism and Popular Cinema* (Manchester, 1995). For an intriguing interpretation of Lindbergh's significance, see M. Eksteins, *Rites of Spring: The Great War and the Birth of the Modern Age* (London, 1990). For the history of the Scott Polar Research Institute, see F. Debenham, 'The Captain Scott Polar Research Institute', *GJ* 68 (1926), 43–9 and 'Retrospect: the Scott Polar Research Institute, 1920–45', *Polar Record*, 4 (1945), 222–35.

EPILOGUE

K. Dodds, *Pink Ice: Britain and the South Atlantic Empire* (New York and London, 2002) charts Britain's involvement in the Antarctic after Scott. Also see P. Beck, *The International Politics of Antarctica* (London, 1986). C. Barnett, *The Collapse of British Power* (London, 1972) and M. J. Wiener, *English Culture and the Decline of the Industrial Spirit, 1850–1980* (Cambridge, 1981) offer two classic accounts of British decline. For a robust refutation of Wiener's thesis, see W. D. Rubinstein, *Capitalism, Culture, and Decline in Britain, 1750–1990* (London, 1993), while for an overview of the debate see P. Mandler, 'How Modern Is It?', *Journal of British Studies*, 42 (2003). From the extensive literature on space exploration, I enjoyed A. Chaikin, *A Man on the Moon: The Voyages of the Apollo Astronauts* (London, 1998 [1994]), while T. Wolfe's classic *The Right Stuff* (London, 1979) investigates the character of the first atsronauts. S. Wheeler, *Terra Incognita: Travels in Antarctica* (London, 1996) skilfully weaves the stories of the polar pioneers, with observations on life in Antarctica in the 1990s.

INDEX

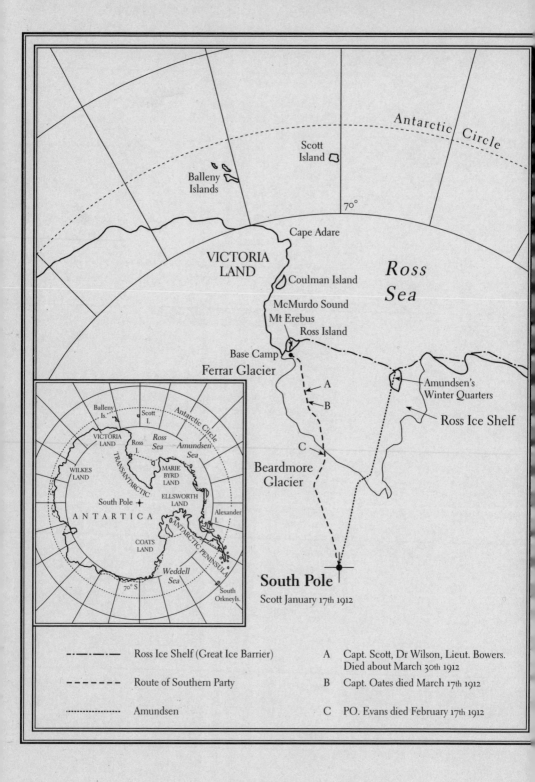

Antarctic Circle

Scott
Island

Balleny
Islands

70°

Cape Adare

VICTORIA
LAND

Coulman Island

*Ross
Sea*

McMurdo Sound
Mt Erebus
Ross Island

Base Camp
Ferrar Glacier

A

B

Amundsen's
Winter Quarters

Ross Ice Shelf

C

Beardmore
Glacier

South Pole

Scott January 17th 1912

Inset map:

Balleny
Is.

Scott
I.

Antarctic Circle

VICTORIA
LAND

Ross
I.

*Ross
Sea*

*Amundsen
Sea*

WILKES
LAND

TRANSANTARCTIC

MARIE
BYRD
LAND

South Pole +

ELLSWORTH
LAND

ANTARTICA

Alexander
I.

ANTARCTIC PENINSULA

COATS
LAND

*Weddell
Sea*

70° S

South
Orkney Is.

–·–·–·– Ross Ice Shelf (Great Ice Barrier)

– – – – – Route of Southern Party

················· Amundsen

A   Capt. Scott, Dr Wilson, Lieut. Bowers.
    Died about March 30th 1912

B   Capt. Oates died March 17th 1912

C   PO. Evans died February 17th 1912